Hebrews
James &
Jude

Rousas John Rushdoony

**ROSS
HOUSE
BOOKS**

Vallecito, California

Library of Congress Catalog Card Number: 00-090841
ISBN:1-879998-20-3

Printed in the United States of America

The publication of this book was made possible
by the generous contributions
of the following individuals or organizations.

Don & Jeannie Alexander
Michael & Marian Bowman
James & Judith Bruner
Stephen & Janet Coakley
Kenneth W. Cope
Jon & Patricia Davidson
Dr. Anne Davis
David & Joan Dobert
Justin & Melanie Dock
Colonel & Miriam Doner
Hal & Sharon Dunn
John & Joan Dyer
Dale Dykema
David & Maurietta Estler
Harry & Marcella Fagan
Jack Faris
Fieldstead & Co.
Robert & Marisa Frank
Michael & Mary Ann Frodella
Craig & Leslie George
Cathy Harnish
Dr. & Mrs. Herbert Hopper
Emmanuel Horton
Kenneth & Cindy Ii
Earl & Dorothea Keener
John B. King
John & Karen La Fear

Marguerite A. Lane
Dr. & Mrs. J.H. Lawson
Gary Livingston
Steve & Belle Merritt
Norman Milbank
Charles & Alfreda Moore
Dr. Heriberto Ortega
Chris & Anne Passerello
Howard & Margaret Phillips
Gavin & Rachel Quill
Eldon P. Rosenthal
April Emily Rushdoony
Virginia Schlueter
Anthony Schwartz
Ford & Andrea Schwartz
Martin & Darlene Selbrede
Phil & Petiflor Spielman
Eileen Stanley
Scot Sullivan
Don & Betty Thompson
Ellen Van Buskirk
Magnus Verbrugge
Mary & Stephen Walker II
Jerri & Howard Walter Jr.
Jeff & Jennifer White
Roy S. Wright
Jeff & Cynthia Zylstra

With special thanks to Eldon P. Rosenthal
in memory of his wife, Peggy J. Rosenthal.

To Mark Rousas Rushdoony,
who in his childhood and youth
was always a source of joy; now in my old age
he is a daily joy and help in his care of Dorothy and myself,
doing all that a godly son should do and more,
along with Darlene, his wife.

In addition to his care of me morning and night,
his gratifying leadership of Chalcedon gives me rest.

Other books by
Rousas John Rushdoony

The Institutes of Biblical Law, Vol. I
The Institutes of Biblical Law, Vol. II, Law & Society
The Institutes of Biblical Law, Vol. III, The Intent of the Law
Systematic Theology (2 volumes)
The Gospel of John
The Biblical Philosophy of History
Thy Kingdom Come
Foundations of Social Order
The "Atheism" of the Early Church
The Messianic Character of American Education
The Philosophy of the Christian Curriculum
Christianity and the State
Salvation and Godly Rule
Romans & Galatians
God's Plan for Victory
Politics of Guilt and Pity
Roots of Reconstruction
The One and the Many
Revolt Against Maturity
By What Standard?
Law & Liberty

For a complete listing of available books
by Rousas John Rushdoony and other
Christian reconstructionists, contact:

ROSS HOUSE BOOKS
PO Box 67
Vallecito, CA 95251

Table of Contents

Introduction 1

HEBREWS

1. The Mandate
   (Hebrews 1:1-4). 5

2. The King and His Servants
   (Hebrews 1:4-14). 11

3. The Mediator
   (Hebrews 2:1-8). 15

4. Atonement and Society
   (Hebrews 2:9-18). 19

5. The Center
   (Hebrews 3:1-19). 23

6. The Meaning of Rest
   (Hebrews 4:1-5). 27

7. Faith and Obedience
   (Hebrews 4:6-16). 31

8. Atonement and the Kingdom
   (Hebrews 5:1-5). 35

9. The High Priest
   (Hebrews 5:1-5). 39

10. Babies vs. Mature Men
    (Hebrews 5:6-14). 43

11. Moving Towards Maturity
    (Hebrews 6:1-8). 47

12. God's Promise and Our Hope
    (Hebrews 6:9-20). 51

13. Accreditation
    (Hebrews 7:1-6). 55

14. Melchizedek
    (Hebrews 7:7-14). 59

15. No Priest, No King
    (Hebrews 7:15-28). 63

16. Priority
   (Hebrews 8:1-5). 67

17. The Atonement
   (Hebrews 8:6-13). 71

18. The True Sanctuary
   (Hebrews 9:1-12). 75

19. Rite versus Reality
   (Hebrews: 9-13-17) 79

20. Atonement and Action
   (Hebrews: 9:18-28) 83

21. "To Do Thy Will, O God"
   (Hebrews: 10:1-10) 87

22. Remission of Sins and Freedom
   (Hebrews: 10:11-18) 91

23. The Call to Service
   (Hebrews 10:19-25). 95

24. Apostasy
   (Hebrews 10:26-39). 99

25. Faith
   (Hebrews 11:1-3). 103

26. Faith: From Abel to Noah
   (Hebrews 11:4-7). 107

27. Abraham, The Man of Faith
   (Hebrews 11:8-19) 111

28. "By Faith Moses"
   (Hebrews 11:20-29). 115

29. Faith Triumphant
   (Hebrews 11:30-40). 119

30. Sons or Bastards?
   (Hebrews 12:1-11). 123

31. Esau
   (Hebrews 12:12-17). 127

32. The Warning
   (Hebrews 12:18-29). 131

33. The Conclusion
   (Hebrews 13:1-25). 135

JAMES

Introduction 141

1. James, the Servant
   (James 1:1) 143

2. Faith and Wisdom
   (James 1:2-7) 147

3. The Double Minded
   (James 1:8-18) 151

4. "Pure Religion and Undefiled"
   (James 1:19-27) 155

5. "Respect of Persons"
   (James 2:1-13) 159

6. Faith and Works
   (James 2:14-26) 163

7. The Tongues of Leaders
   (James 3:1-5) 167

8. The Tongue and Self-Revelation
   (James 3:6-12) 171

9. Two Kinds of Wisdom
   (James 3:13-18) 175

10. Problems and Growth
    (James 4:1-6) 179

11. The Holy War
    (James 4:7-10) 183

12. Law and Time
    (James 4:11-17) 187

13. Judgment on the Rich
    (James 5:1-6) 191

14. Judgment
    (James 5:7-9) 195

15. Unction
    (James 5:11-20) 199

JUDE

1. The Enemy
   (Jude 1-4). 205
2. Examples of Apostasy
   (Jude 5-7). 209
3. Righteous Judgment
   (Jude 8-16). 213
4. The Battle
   (Jude 17-25). 217

SCRIPTURE INDEX. 221
INDEX. 231

Introduction

There is a resounding call in Hebrews 13:13 which we cannot forget without going astray: "Let us go forth therefore unto him without the camp, bearing his reproach." This is a summons to break with Judaism, i.e., the reigning, commanding culture of the Hebrews, and to serve Christ the Redeemer-King fully and faithfully, without compromise. In our time, it calls for a break, not only with the prevailing culture of humanistic statism and its messianic claims and pretensions, but also with a wayward church that has made itself the handmaiden to Christ's enemies.

The epistle of James is a restatement in part of the Sermon on the Mount that insists on an uncompromising faith that governs us and our world, and Jude similarly recalls us to Jesus Christ's apostolic commission, "Remember ye the words which have been spoken before by the apostles of our Lord Jesus Christ" (v. 17). Jude's letter is usually classified as an apocalyptic tract, but we cannot forget that all the Bible speaks of a division between fallen and redeemed humanity, between the saved and the lost, of the necessity for a new creation beginning with us, and of the inescapable triumph of the Kingdom of God.

History is a great over-turning until the Savior-King "whose right it is" triumphs and prevails (Ezek. 21:27). This Priest-King shall reign (Zech. 6; Ps. 110) over all creation.

We cannot remain "within the camp" and yet become part of the victory, and yet today the call seems to be to join the camp, to become a part of the world's establishment rather than members of the new creation and the people of the Great King (1 Tim. 6:15f.).

These studies in Hebrews, James, and Jude were written from April, 1996 to May, 1997.

Rousas John Rushdoony
Vallecito, California

HEBREWS

Chapter One
The Mandate
(*Hebrews 1:1-4*)

1. God, who at sundry times and in divers manner spake in time past unto the fathers by the prophets,
2. Hath in these last days spoken unto us by his son, whom he hath appointed heir of all things by whom also he made the worlds;
3. Who being the brightness of his glory, and the express image of his person, and upholding all things by the word of his power, when he had by himself purged our sins, sat down on the right hand of the Majesty on high;
4. Being made so much better than the angels, as he hath by inheritance obtained a more excellent name than they.
(Hebrews 1:1-4)

It has been said of Hebrews that it is, *first*, "the least known of all the New Testament epistles." *Second*, it requires a knowledge of the five books of Moses, and this may impede knowledge of Hebrews for many. *Third*, the classical view of this epistle is that it was written to a congregation, and implicitly for others like it, which was in danger of returning to the synagogue and Temple worship (Heb. 2:1; 3:12; 5:13-14, etc.).[1]

There is also the unending controversy about its authorship. More than a few of the greatest champions of the faith, including John Calvin, denied Paul's authorship. Badcock rightly spoke of a plural authorship, stating:

> Except for the single conventional phrase, "And what shall I more say? for the time will fail me..." (xi. 32), the whole is written in the plural number until we come to the personal messages of the last chapter; so, though it is convenient to speak of the "author," it would be more correct in regard to the main bulk of the epistle to speak of the "authors."[2]

There was a crisis in the life of one church specifically which was also a concern elsewhere. For Paul alone to have addressed this would weaken its force among those of Jewish origin; the letter was a summary statement by an apostolic fellowship, and, like the decision of the Council of Jerusalem (Acts 15), was thereby given added authority in the churches. The last chapter seems to convey the personal comments and greetings of Paul. Joseph A. McAuliffe has called my attention to the personal note in Hebrews 10:34 that echoes Paul.

---

[1] Everett F. Harrison, editor, *The Wycliff Bible Commentary* (Chicago, Illinois: Moody Press, 1962), 896f.
[2] F. J. Badcock, *The Pauline Epistles and the Epistle to the Hebrews in their Historical Setting* (London, England: Society for Promoting Christian Knowledge, 1937), 183.

Hebrews is emphatic in declaring the absolute and sole sufficiency of Jesus Christ, and this again echoes the Pauline letters. In line with this is a fact which the Australian scholar, Noel Weeks, called attention to:

> ...the stress of Hebrews is that the "age to come" has already come with the coming of the Lord. The future age is not set over against the New Testament age. The "future age" begins with the New Testament age. However, from the stand-point of Israel in the wilderness that age was definitely in the future.[3]

Today we see Christians longing for the rapture, or for the millennium, and forgetting that the cross and the resurrection are our victory, and we now have a task of applying that victory to every area of life and thought. Hebrews 1:2 speaks of "these last days" because we are in *history's last era, the application of Christ's victory.* Hebrews 11 tells us of the Old Testament saints who fought but did not receive the promise, *Jesus Christ,* in their lifetime (11:39f). We are now in the last and great shaking of the things which are, whereby the things which cannot be shaken may alone remain (12:26f). We *have* received a kingdom, the new world order, "which cannot be removed." Therefore, we must with grace "serve God acceptably with reverence and godly fear" (12:28).

Those who were planning to defect back to the synagogue are reminded that "our God is a consuming fire" (12:29). They are told of the pilgrimage of the Old Testament saints and their problems, sins, and griefs.

This was written while the Temple was still standing in all its splendor, and the churches were small groups meeting in homes. The writer in 13:23f is free in Italy, and Timothy was just freed. This indicates a date before the Jewish-Roman war and the destruction of the Temple in A.D. 70.[4]

The victory of "these last few days" is cited repeatedly in the psalms, the prophets, and the New Testament. Some of these views are important as reminders to us that ours is this great victory (1 John 5:4):

> And there was given him dominion, and glory, and a kingdom, that all people, nations, and languages should serve him: his dominion is an everlasting dominion, which shall not pass away, and his kingdom that which shall not be destroyed (Daniel 7:14).

> All things are delivered unto me of my Father: and no man knoweth the Son, but the Father; neither knoweth any man the Father, save the Son, and he to whomsoever the Son will reveal him (Matt. 11:27).

> And Jesus came and spake unto them, saying, All power is given unto me in heaven and in earth (Matt. 28:18).

[3.] Noel Weeks, "Admonition and Error in Hebrews," *The Westminster Theological Journal,* vol. 39, no. 1, 78f.
[4.] W. J. Conybeare and J. S. Howson, *The Life and Letters of Saint Paul* (Hartford, Connecticut, 1913 reprint) 848, 855.

He shall be great, and shall be called the Son of the Highest: and the Lord God shall give unto him the throne of his father David (Luke 1:32).

The Father loveth the Son, and hath given all things into his hand (John 3:35).

For to this end Christ both died, and rose, and revived, that he might be Lord of the dead and living (Romans 14:9).

For he hath put all things under his feet. But when he saith all things are put under him, it is manifest that he is excepted, which did put all things under him (1 Cor. 15:27).

That in the dispensation of the fullness of times he might gather together in one all things in Christ, both which are in heaven, and which are on earth; even in him (Eph. 1:10).

9. Wherefore God also hath highly exalted him, and given him a name which is above every name:
10. That at the name of Jesus every knee should bow, of things in heaven, and things in earth, and things under the earth;
11. And that every tongue should confess that Jesus Christ is Lord, to the glory of God the Father (Phil. 2:9-11).

Martin J. Wyngarden, in *The Future of the Kingdom in Prophecy and Fulfillment* (1955), gave us a detailed account of the realization of prophetic declarations in Jesus Christ. Calvin called attention to this stress on fulfillment by his arrangement of vv. 1-2 thus:

> God spake formerly by the prophets...now by the Son: Then to the Fathers...but now to us: Then at various times...now as at the end of the times.[5]

In other words, there is a finality here. The implication, as Hebrews develops its argument, is clear. If Israel had simply remained on the Arabian side of the Red Sea, there would have been no Promised Land. Similarly, if we as Christians do not move on in terms of our salvation by Jesus Christ to occupy all things in His Name, we will remain in our own wilderness and without the fullness of victory. The age to come is ours now if we act in His Name and power. It clearly will not be struggle free, but neither will it be victory free. *Hebrews is a summons to victory.* To miss this fact is to fail to understand Hebrews. Discouragement is real, but victory is certain. Hebrews 12:12 commands as a result, "Wherefore lift up the hands which hang down, and the feeble knees." These are words to exhausted and discouraged pilgrims. A much sharper word would apply to those who refuse to march and want instead to be raptured out of the battle.

---

[5] John Calvin: *Commentaries on the Epistle to the Hebrews* (Grand Rapids, Michigan: Eerdmans, 1949 reprint), 31.

What these verses which introduce Hebrews to us say, is that the key to life and history is the incarnation of Jesus Christ. At the same time, the actual number of times that either the name *Jesus* or the title *Christ* is used is not many, although the meaning of Jesus Christ and His person and work is the central subject of Hebrews. Because Jesus Christ cannot be comprehended simply in the person of one who walked about Palestine, He is not so much referred to, as presupposed, as the center of all things. Previously, God had spoken by or rather *in the prophets*, "*in the prophets themselves* as the vessels of divine inspiration."[6] Now, in Jesus Christ, we have God the Son revealed. The worlds were created by the triune God, which means that God the Son not only made all things but is also the designated "heir of all things" (v. 2). The focus is not on the person of Jesus of Nazareth, but on who He was, God the Son, the Maker, Sustainer, and Lord over all things. The implication is clear: leave Christ and you leave life.

In v. 3, we are told five things about the incarnate Son: *first*, He is "the brightness of God's glory." The word *brightness* is better rendered by some as *effulgence*. He is the expression or open manifestation of God's glory. We are told that the *person* of Jesus Christ was the focus of more than met the eye. *Second*, Jesus was the express image of God's person, i.e., the substantial nature of God, the reality of God's Being. *Third*, Jesus Christ upholds all things by the word of His power. He sustains all things, and all things move in terms of His decree. *All things* means all things in creation. The world was called into being by the Triune God, and, moment by moment, it is totally sustained by God the Son, the heir of all things. *Fourth*, Jesus Christ by Himself purged us of all our sins. He is our Redeemer: He made atonement for us. *Fifth*, Jesus is now at the right hand of God, seated, or, in session, because He is our ruler and our judge as well as our mediator.[7]

Verse 4 connects us to the next passage by its reference to angels. Jesus Christ, who before His incarnation was God the Son, "so much better than the angels," has by His redemptive work now gained "a more excellent name than they" (v. 4). The angels are servants of the Most High, but Jesus Christ surpassed all angels (and certainly all men) in His work as God's Servant. His was the greatest possible service.

God's right hand, the place of intercession and of judgment, will be the place of Jesus Christ until all things are subdued unto Him (1 Cor. 15:27f.). He will continue as King when His work as intercessor and judge is ended.

---

[6] M. R. Vincent, *Word Studies in the New Testament*, vol. II (MacDill AFB, Florida: MacDonald Publishing Company, n.d), 1091.

[7] *Ibid.*, 1093f.

Verse 2 tells us that Jesus Christ is the "appointed heir of all things." Paul in Romans 8:17 tells us that we are "joint-heirs with Christ; if so be that we suffer without him, that we may be also glorified together." Hebrews is a summons to make "the age to come" Christ's Kingdom in all its fullness. We are not handed a ticket to easy living with our salvation but a summons to disciple all nations for Christ (Matt. 28:18-20). Our goal is God's great sabbath.

In vv. 1-2, we are told that God has spoken: we do have a revelation, and this revelation has its finality and perfect expression in Jesus Christ. Leon Morris rendered the phrase in v. 3 as "the exact representation of his (God's) being," and the Revised Standard Version reads "the very stamp of his nature."[8]

Barclay pointed out that the Jews of our Lord's day "divided all time into two ages — the present age and the age to come." The Day of the Lord would divide the two ages. As against this, Hebrews sees that new age as having dawned with Jesus Christ.[9] Thus, from the beginning, Hebrews declares unequivocally that Christ's work is done, and we must now conquer our Canaan in His Name and power. Hebrews is a mandate for action. Much of this is set forth in typology, by references to Old Testament history, but there is also much direct admonition.

[8.] Leon Morris, *Hebrews* (Grand Rapids, Michigan: Zondervan, 1983), 19.
[9.] William Barclay, *The Letter to the Hebrews* (Philadelphia, Pennsylvania: The Westminster Press, 1957), 2.

Chapter Two
The King and His Servants
(*Hebrews 1:4-14*)

4. Being made so much better than the angels, as he hath by inheritance obtained a more excellent name than they.
5. For unto which of the angels said he at any time, Thou art my son, this day have I begotten thee? And again, I will be to him a Father, and he shall be to me a Son?
6. And again, when he bringeth in the firstbegotten into the world, he said, And let all the angels of God worship him.
7. And of the angels he saith, Who maketh his angels spirits, and his ministers a flame of fire.
8. But unto the Son he saith, Thy throne, O God, is for ever and ever: a sceptre of righteousness is the sceptre of thy kingdom.
9. Thou hast loved righteousness, and hated iniquity; therefore God, even thy God, hath anointed thee with the oil of gladness above thy fellows.
10. And, Thou, Lord, in the beginning hast laid the foundation of the earth; and the heavens are the works of thine hands:
11. They shall perish; but thou remainest; and they all shall wax old as a garment;
12. And as a vesture shalt thou fold them up, and they shall be changed: but thou art the same, and thy years shall not fail.
13. But to which of the angels said he at any time, Sit on my right hand, until I make thine enemies thy footstool?
14. Are they not all ministering spirits, sent forth to minister for them who shall be heirs of salvation? (Hebrews 1:4-14)

We have in these verses a clear critique of angel worship, and yet it has been said that the Jews never worshipped angels. This is true, but angels appeared in apocryphal writings, and, apparently, in popular thinking. Paganism gave evidence of no small attention paid to a variety of spirits and powers analogous to angels. Jewish gnosticism was rife with such things. Formal worship may have been lacking, but the importance of such powers in popular thinking was real.

In these latter years of the twentieth century, we have a considerable interest in angels, and a few books on angels have appeared. In one such work, there is no mention of God. A humanistic era is ready to believe in angels because they can give help when needed *without* requiring worship. Angels are thus creatures who can give man some of the benefits of God without God's commanding power. The angels *help*: they do not *command*, and they are therefore more popular than God with fallen man.

Some years ago, I knew briefly a pastor who had an amazing knowledge of the history of thinking about angels. At the same time, his knowledge of the Bible and doctrine was very weak. In time, his adulteries came to light, making clear to me why he preferred angels to God, and curious bits of knowledge to God's law.

The purpose of Hebrews is to eliminate any trivial interests that interfere with the sole mediatorship and supremacy of God the Son. The Bible makes clear throughout that the Son is preeminent and is very God of very God. He is far greater than the angels and the prophets, and He is the Creator of both. As Westcott pointed out, we are told of the superiority of Jesus because He is, *first*, God the Son (vv. 5-6); *second*, He is "heir of all things" (vv. 7-9), and, *third*, He is the "creator of the world" (vv. 10-12).[1] Clogg summarized the theme and message in these words:

> The theme is the finality of the revelation in Jesus the Son of God. God had never left Himself without witness, but in the last days He has revealed Himself in One Who is the Son. The Son is superior to angels, not in spite of but because of His incarnation and death (ii. 9-10). He is greater than Moses, a servant in the house (iii. 5- 6). Since it was the purpose of His coming to bring many sons to glory, it was fitting that He should be in all things like unto His brethren (ii. 17-18).[2]

In v. 5, we have a statement from Psalm 2:7, "Thou art my Son, this day have I begotten thee." In Luke 3:22, we have a similar statement from heaven on Jesus' baptism. But this refers to Christ's enthronement, not to an adoptionist view of His person, because in v. 6 Jesus is called God's firstbegotten, and all angels are commanded to worship Him, which echoes Psalm 97:7.

No angel has been appointed "the heir of all things" (v. 2), but God the Son, in His incarnation, comes as that heir to redeem His inheritance.

The angels are God's servants, powerful ones, like wind and fire (v. 7), but they have no independent power. Their reason for being is to do God's will, and they therefore do not issue a law or bring judgment to any man on their own. When they exercise force comparable to wind and fire, it is because God has so ordained it, not they.

Conversely, the Son is king over all creation, over heaven and earth. His throne is an eternal one, and His sceptre is unto righteousness or justice, so that all His works result in absolute justice (v. 8).

God the Son in His incarnation manifested His love of justice and His hatred of *iniquity* (*anomian*) or *lawlessness*. 1 John 3:4 defines sin as *anomian*, *lawlessness*. We are thus told that Jesus *hated lawlessness*, the hostility to God and His law. God celebrates Christ's love of justice and

---

[1] Brooke Foss Westcott, *The Epistle to the Hebrews* (Grand Rapids, Michigan: Eerdmans, 1952), 18f. Originally published in 1889.
[2] Frank Bertram Clogg, *An Introduction to the New Testament* (New York, N.Y.: Charles Scribner's Sons, 1937), 139.

His hatred of lawlessness by anointing Him with "the oil of gladness" above all others. His is the greatest victory and the greatest reward.

In v. 10-12, Psalm 102:26-28 is cited, words that tell us that while creation grows old and perishes, God remains King forever. These words are applied to God the Son.

God the Father has never said to any angel, "Sit on my right hand, until I make thine enemies thy footstool" (v. 13). This citation is from Psalm 110:1. Because Jesus, God incarnate, underwent the judgment upon us for our sakes, God the Father subdues all His enemies under His feet. Their destruction and submission will be total.

Angels cannot be given worship. They are ministering spirits sent to serve God's elect, those "who shall be the heirs of salvation" (v. 14). Thus, to give special attention, let alone worship, to angels is to detract from the worship, honor, and glory due to God. No angel has died for our sins, nor ever acted independently on our behalf. To give to angels the glory and honor due to God the Son is to denigrate the King and to thank a servant.

Calvin called attention to the fact that,

> It was a common notion among the Jews, that the Law was given by angels; they attentively considered the honourable things spoken of them everywhere in Scripture; and as the world is strangely inclined to superstition, they obscured the glory of God by extolling angels too much.[3]

Buchanan stressed the fact that angels are temporal while the Son is eternal. The Greek word for "angels" means "messengers." Angels of God "never were given administrative power. They were responsible for carrying out orders, not for giving them."[4] The church and Christians are given ministerial (but not legislative) powers, so that our status is above that of angels. To exalt angels is a hypocritical demeaning of ourselves.

The royal sceptre of authority, legislative power, and judgment is given to God the Son in His incarnation and His session at the right hand of God. The entire focus of this text is on God's Kingdom, and the Son on its throne. The goal is not the salvation of God's people, but the Kingdom of God, which is far more than heaven. When in chapter 4 the great sabbath rest is discussed, it is compared to the conquest of Canaan, to the fulfillment of a pilgrimage to the great City of God (Heb. 11:10). Abraham, we are told, looked for a city with eternal foundations, "whose builder and maker is God." It is the new creation of God's perfect justice. If God's authority

---

[3.] John Calvin, *Commentaries on the Epistle to the Hebrews* (Grand Rapids, Michigan: Eerdmans, 1949 reprint), 40.

[4.] George Wesley Buchanan, *To the Hebrews* (Garden City, New York: Doubleday, 1972), 19.

granted to the Son is the sceptre of justice, we cannot belong to that Kingdom and realm if we despise His justice.

Jesus Christ was crucified as the "King of the Jews," as a potential threat to Caesar. This made the Christians a suspect group. Now we have, however carefully worded as a theological statement, the affirmation that Jesus Christ reigns from an eternal throne with the sceptre of justice. Very shortly, after the fall of Jerusalem, Christians would become a persecuted group, more so than Acts tells us they were preceding that fall. For Jesus Christ to reign with "the sceptre of justice" (v. 8) meant clearly that apart from Him and His law, there is no justice. Clearly, if Jesus Christ possesses the sceptre of justice, none ruling apart from Him can ever provide justice. Justice or righteousness is the expression of His being, not the expression of fallen man nor of man-made civil governments. For Rome, *another* law meant *another* ruler. Hence the persecution of Christians. Christians were counseled to obey their rulers (Rom. 13:1ff.), not because their claims were acceptable, but because regeneration, not revolution, was the starting point of Christ's Kingdom.

Clearly, the presupposition of Hebrews is a radical one, and the men who wrote it knew the meaning of their statement. Ruthven's comment is especially relevant:

> Before it became the state religion, the profession of Christianity was treasonable under Roman law because the Christian refused to acknowledge the state gods and the emperor's dignity as high priest of the state religion; and this, of course, entailed refusal to participate in those public ceremonies, such as sacrificing to the emperor's genius, which Roman citizens were obliged to perform. Thus Christians were liable to fall into the crime of *perdullio* whether or not they were Roman citizens, and to be treated as public enemies.[5]

It is difficult to understand the New Testament apart from this fact. We are to affirm, not Caesar's law, but God's law.

---

[5]. Malise Ruthven, *Torture, The Grand Conspiracy* (London, England: Weidenfeld and Nicolson, 1978), 34.

Chapter Three

The Mediator
(*Hebrews 2:1-8*)

1. Therefore we ought to give the more earnest heed to the things which we have heard, lest at any time we should let them slip.
2. For if the word spoken by angels was steadfast, and every transgression and disobedience received a just recompense of reward;
3. How shall we escape, if we neglect so great salvation; which at the first began to be spoken by the Lord, and was confirmed unto us by them that heard Him;
4. God also bearing witness, both with signs and wonders, and with divers miracles, and gifts of the Holy Ghost, according to his own will?
5. For unto the angels hath he not put in subjection the world to come, whereof we speak.
6. But one in a certain place testifieth, saying, What is man, that thou are mindful of him? or the son of man, that thou visitest him?
7. Thou madest him a little lower than the angels; thou crownest him with glory and honour, and didst set him over the works of thy hands:
8. Thou hast put all things in subjection under his feet. For in that he put all in subjection under him, he left nothing that is not put under him. But now we see not yet all things put under him. (Hebrews 2:1-8)

A mediator in the modern world is a *neutral* person who arbitrates between two sides in terms of a given law, or a contract between them. His neutrality is necessary because he does not mediate his own law nor his own cause: he is an outsider. This is not the case here. God's mediator, the God-man Jesus the Christ, is the great Law-giver and Judge. He mediates the law He has given, and He is not neutral concerning man's sins and transgressions.

This is important to remember in reading Hebrews. Gnostic, semi-gnostic, and apocalyptic ideas were current in the Jewish world of thought. Angels and emanations in such thinking were neither absolute judges nor law-givers, and the result was *at best* a diffused responsibility and culpability for men. Such thinking was elitist: it appealed to man's pride to be the possessor of a secret knowledge.

But with Jesus Christ as mediator, man was face to face with the Judge whose law was transgressed and broken. The answer then was not *gnosis*, not knowledge, but repentance for sin, restitution, and pardon from the Throne of Glory. We face a mediator with total power, not a neutral stance without much force.

It is dangerous therefore to neglect the Son, the Mediator. We must earnestly heed His every word "lest at any time we should *let them slip*," or, "*run out as leaking vessels*" (v. 1). Because the Gospel comes from the highest

15

possible source, the Throne of the Triune God, we are under the most urgent necessity to hear and obey.

The angels of God had a hand in the revelation of God's law; it was not their law but God's. According to Acts 7:53 and Galatians 3:19, the angels had a part in the revelation of the law to Moses. That law was *steadfast, proved sure*, founded on and expressive of God's holiness, so that Jesus Christ said of it, "Till heaven and earth pass, one jot or one tittle shall in no wise pass from the law" (Matt. 5:18). God's justice *required* the punishment of "every transgression and disobedience" (Heb. 2:2).

Given this fact, "how shall we escape, if we neglect so great salvation" which was declared by the Lord and confirmed to the church by those around Jesus Christ? (v. 3).

This witness by Jesus Christ and the apostolic company was confirmed by signs, wonders, and miracles, and also by gifts of the Holy Spirit "according to his own will" (v. 3). The will of the Holy Spirit is stressed: He is fully a Person of the Godhead. His will is His own, and yet it is in total unity with the will of the Father and the Son.

"The world to come," which means the triumph of the new creation in time and in eternity, is not in the control of the angels. It is not "in subjection" to them, so that any exaltation of angels is an exaltation of servants over their lord (v. 5). The signs, wonders, and miracles, as well as the gifts of the Spirit, did not confirm the power of angels but the lordship and mediation of Jesus Christ.

Jesus is the Son of Man (v. 6), the Messiah. It is He who suffers, making atonement for our sins (v. 9). The angels underwent no such passion, nor did they surrender any heavenly status, as did God the Son in becoming our Redeemer and Mediator.

Man is the recipient of God's grace and salvation because man is the creature called into being by God's creative word to exercise dominion and to subdue under God the creation He had made (Gen. 1:26-28). The two key points in this cosmic battle are man the creature and God the Son in His incarnation. Hebrews here cites Psalm 8, a messianic psalm. It looks to the certain triumph of the Messiah and His people. It allows man no place for self-pity, but speaks rather of his calling to dominion in the new man and last Adam, Jesus Christ. According to the psalm, *and Hebrews as well*, man's triumph in Christ is inevitable: it is predestined by God. The world is not to be under angels but under man. All things are to be placed in subjection to man in Christ. Man's calling at creation and again in Christ, our last Adam, is to rule over all the works of God's hands (v. 7). "Thou hast put all things in subjection under him" (v. 8). As M. R. Vincent commented:

The writer's object is to show that the *salvation*, the new order of things inaugurated by Christ, is in the pursuance of the original purpose of creation, to wit, that universal dominion was to pertain to man, and not to angels. The great salvation means lordship of the world to be. This purpose is carried out in Christ, who, in becoming man, became temporarily subject to the earthly dispensation of which angels were the universal administrators. This was in order that he might acquire universal lordship as man. Being now exalted above angels, he does away with the angelic administration, and, in the world to come, will carry humanity with him to the position of universal lordship. This thought is developed by means of Ps. 8.[1]

Since man's calling is universal lordship in Christ, it is Christ he needs and not angels. To worship angels is to demean himself. The King of all creation is Jesus Christ, the Lord *of* all believers and the Lord *over* all things. Citing Clogg again, in Hebrews "The theme is the finality of the revelation in Jesus the Son of God."[2] To turn aside from Jesus Christ and towards angels is like throwing away gold in favor of copper. Our Mediator has total power, and in Him we are heirs of all things. Should we forsake wealth for poverty?

Psalm 8 is used by Paul in 1 Corinthians 15:24-28, in a sense like that in Hebrews 2:6ff. In Corinthians, we are told that *all things* will be put under Christ's feet before the end, and then death itself shall be destroyed. This means that the power of sin on earth is replaced by the power of Jesus Christ, and then the fullness of God's new creation and eternal life replace the fallen world order.

This is the purpose of Hebrews, to bring the church to an awareness and knowledge of its purpose and goal in Christ. It is far more than the salvation of our souls, important as that is; the purpose of our salvation is to recall us to the creation mandate. We are not saved for "flowery beds of ease," but for God's holy purpose, a new creation wherein justice reigns. It does not have us as its focus but rather the Kingdom of God and His righteousness, or justice (Matt. 6:33).

And Jesus Christ is our only mediator with God, not Judaism, not the church, and not angels. To seek anything less is dangerous, and an abandonment of our Savior.

[1.] M. R. Vincent, *Word Studies in the New Testament*, vol. II (MacDill AFB, Florida: MacDonald Publishing Company, n.d.), 1099.

[2.] F. Bertram Clogg, *An Introduction to the New Testament* (New York, New York: Charles Scribner's Sons, 1937), 139.

Chapter Four

Atonement and Society
(*Hebrews 2:9-18*)

9. But we see Jesus, who was made a little lower than the angels for suffering of death, crowned with glory and honour; that he by the grace of God should taste death for every man.

10. For it became him, for whom are all things, and by whom are all things, in bringing many sons unto glory, to make the captain of their salvation perfect through sufferings.

11. For both he that sanctifieth and they who are sanctified are all of one: for which cause he is not ashamed to call them brethren,

12. Saying, I will declare thy name unto my brethren, in the midst of the church will I sing praise unto thee.

13. And again, I will put my trust in him. And again, Behold I and the children which God hath given me.

14. Forasmuch then as the children are partakers of flesh and blood, he also himself likewise took part of the same; that through death he might destroy him that had the power of death, that is, the devil;

15. And deliver them who through fear of death were all their lifetime subject to bondage.

16. For verily he took not on him the nature of angels; but he took on him the seed of Abraham.

17. Wherefore in all things it behoved him to be made like unto his brethren, that he might be a merciful and faithful high priest in things pertaining to God, to make reconciliation for the sins of the people.

18. For in that he himself hath suffered being tempted, he is able to succour them that are tempted. (Hebrews 2:9-18)

Paul, in 1 Corinthians 1:18-31, calls attention to the fact that, to the Jews, Christ crucified was a stumblingblock, and, to the Greeks, foolishness. For neither group was the atonement other than an ugly and offensive thing because it was attained by crucifixion. God had made man to be the one to exercise dominion under Him over the earth, and man had fallen. Man the sinner is incapable of Godly dominion, and yet this is his calling. As Franz Delitzsch observed, "Man in his present natural state is evidently not lord of the universe; his destiny to rule over it is not yet fulfilled. But in Jesus it is fulfilled already."[1] The work of Jesus Christ is to restore man to this calling, to enable man to exercise dominion and to subdue the earth under God (Gen. 1:26-28). Man's dominion task must be preceded by the atonement and the regeneration of man. One of the basic aspects of the atonement is the restoration of man to his original task and calling. To separate the atonement from the dominion mandate is to give a man-centered meaning to the atonement, to reduce its meaning to man's personal

---

[1] Franz Delitzsch, *Commentary on the Epistle to the Hebrews*, vol. I (Grand Rapids, Michigan: Eerdmans, 1952 reprint), 107.

peace as God's goal. Because dominion belongs to man and not to angels, the purpose of the atonement is to remake man for his calling and duty.

In terms of this, at the right time, God sent His Son to become "a little lower than the angels for the suffering of death, crowned with glory and honour; that he by the grace of God should taste death for every man" (v. 9). Christ's subordination to the angels was in His submission to the death penalty for man. The ministry of angels is never of so radical a scope. Jesus Christ "tastes death" for us. The expression to "taste death" appears in Matthew 16:28, Mark 9:1, Luke 9:27, and John 8:52; it means the total experience of death in all its horror and isolation.

Verse 10 tells us that this was necessary because our Savior had to be made "perfect through sufferings." "To make perfect" means literally "to carry to the goal or consummation." It does not imply moral imperfection, but rather means that Jesus Christ experienced to the full man's experience of suffering and death.[2] He is "crowned with glory and honor" because He has tasted death for every man, not as one deserving it, but as our vicarious substitute. He is the "captain" or leader of our salvation (v. 10).

By His incarnation, Jesus Christ, God the Son, becomes man, our brother. All things were made by Him (John 1:3), and all things exist because of Him. But here we are told that God the Father made all things and causes all things to exist for the Redeemer as the Lord over all the redeemed. This "captain" or leader is made "perfect through sufferings" (v. 10). Jesus Christ was made all the more perfect or mature a brother to His new humanity by the sufferings He experienced on their behalf.

"Sanctification is the path to glorification."[3] The Sanctifier and the sanctified are alike the new humanity, with Jesus Christ as the last Adam (1 Cor. 15:43ff., Heb. 2:11).

In v. 12, the reference is to Psalm 22:22; the Messiah is there shown speaking to us, His brethren. The word "church" is the Greek *ekklesias*, which has as its meaning the governing council of a community. The church thus has the duty of making its community a Godly one, to be God's government in its sphere, furthering the work of the Kingdom. This the early church did by its evangelism, education, charity, courts of arbitration (1 Cor. 6:1ff.), and more.

Verse 13 is a quotation from Isaiah 8:17 freely rendered. The Messiah's praise of God (v. 12) will be put to His trust in God. This, given the sufferings He faced, was not easy to do. However, the Messiah includes us in that trust. Earlier, we are referred to as His brothers, here as His children.

---

[2] M. R. Vincent, *Word Studies in the New Testament*, vol. II (Mac Dill AFB, Florida, reprint), 1102.
[3] *Ibid.*, 1102.

Christ, because we are flesh and blood, became the same as we are, and mortal, so that through death He might "destroy him that had the power of death, that is, the devil" (v. 14). Because the devil introduced sin, he brought in death, so that *his power is the negation of life.* The devil is not lord over death but the one who introduced it, like a plague bearer. He does not inflict death but rather carries it, and all who follow him contract it.

God the Son comes to deliver those who have been in bondage to death (because sin was brought into the world by the tempter, Gen. 3:5). The fear of death was pronounced in antiquity, and no less so over the centuries (v. 15). Modern anti-Christian bravado tries to pretend otherwise, but not very effectively.

What God the Son did was not to become an angel, one who serves God but without the exposure to sin and death. Instead He became a man, in the line of Abraham (v. 16).

His incarnation was thus, from His birth on, very real. He was in all things like His fellow men so that He could be "a merciful and faithful high priest in all things pertaining to God, to make reconciliation for the sins of the people" (v. 17). The reality of the incarnation made possible the reality of the atonement. In every area of His work as our high priest, His incarnation made Him our effectual brother. He is our true intercessor, because He knows our wants and needs as well as our sins and shortcomings. Where our brothers after the flesh cannot know us, He knows us. Unlike purely human high priests, who have been exalted and remote persons, Jesus Christ is closer to us than we are to ourselves, and He is both "merciful and faithful."

Because Jesus Christ was tempted, He is able to aid and rescue those of His brethren who are tempted (v. 18). His sufferings were His trial and temptation.

The nature of society as given to us in Hebrews is totally in line with the whole of Scripture. Basic to community is atonement. All societies outside of Christ, whatever foundation they may seek to have or profess to have, are founded on sin. No social order established on sin can experience anything other than death. It is without atonement, without grace, and without a valid hope. If society has as its foundation Christ's atonement, and God's law as its way of sanctification, then it has a future under God because it is in the realm of life, not death.

Hebrews thus tells us that without Christ's atonement, there is no true society or community. It strikes at a purely personal "gospel" which sees salvation as simply the salvation of the individual's soul. Christ's atonement is cosmic in its scope.

Chapter Five

The Center
(Hebrews 3:1-19)

1. Wherefore, holy brethren, partakers of the heavenly calling, consider the Apostle and High Priest of our profession, Christ Jesus;
2. Who was faithful to him that appointed him, as also Moses was faithful in all his house.
3. For this man was counted worthy of more glory than Moses, inasmuch as he who hath builded the house hath more honour than the house.
4. For every house is builded by some man; but he that built all things is God.
5. And Moses verily was faithful in all his house, as a servant, for a testimony of those things which were spoken after;
6. But Christ as son over his own house; whose house are we, if we hold fast the confidence and the rejoicing of the hope firm unto the end.
7. Wherefore (as the Holy Ghost saith, To day if he will hear his voice,
8. Harden not your hearts, as in the provocation, in the day of temptation in the wilderness:
9. When your fathers tempted me, proved me, and saw my works forty years.
10. Wherefore I was grieved with that generation, and said, They do alway err in their heart; and they have not known my ways.
11. So I sware in my wrath, They shall not enter into my rest.)
12. Take heed, brethren, lest there be in any of you an evil heart of unbelief, in departing from the living God.
13. But exhort one another daily, while it is called To day; lest any of you be hardened through the deceitfulness of sin.
14. For we are made partakers of Christ, if we hold the beginning of our confidence stedfast unto the end;
15. While it is said, To day if ye will hear his voice, harden not your hearts, as in the provocation.
16. For some, when they had heard, did provoke: howbeit not all that came out of Egypt by Moses.
17. But with whom was he grieved forty years? was it not with them that had sinned, whose carcasses fell in the wilderness?
18. And to whom sware he that they should not enter into his rest, but to them that believed not?
19. So we see that they could not enter in because of unbelief. (Hebrews 3:1-19)

Calvin very briefly summarized this chapter in these words: "We are always to make progress even unto death; for our whole life is as it were a race."[1] Too often believers see conversion as the goal. While our conversion is a finished act insofar as salvation is concerned, sanctification is a life-long

---

[1.] John Calvin, *Commentaries on the Epistle to the Hebrews* (Grand Rapids, Michigan: Eerdmans, 1949 reprint), 82.

23

work. The whole law-word of God must be applied to ourselves and our areas of responsibility. The Christian life is one of obligations.

Because Moses was to the Hebrews the great person in their perspective, Moses is compared to Jesus Christ. Moses belonged to the house as one of the elect community, whereas Christ is the builder thereof. Moses was a servant in the house or kingdom, but, from all eternity, Jesus Christ is its builder and Lord.[2]

As Pink noted, "There are two great basic truths which run through Scripture, and are enforced on every page, that God is sovereign, and that man is a responsible creature."[3] To return to Moses, the creature and servant, after knowing the Lord and Creator, Jesus Christ, was thus a fearful sin. Hence Hebrews warns, "Consider the Apostle and High Priest of our profession, Jesus Christ" (v. 1). As high priest, Jesus Christ is the builder of the new house or Temple; moreover, He is the builder of all things because He is a member of the Godhead (v. 4). Moses was God's faithful servant in all God's household (Num. 12:7); to be faithful like Moses means to be faithful to Jesus Christ. "Our first foundation" (v. 14) means, "Literally, *the beginning of our foundation.*" It means "*that whereon any things else stands, or is supported,*" with the implication of *substance.*[4]

Verses 7-11 are a grim warning. The Holy Spirit Himself gave warning to old Israel not to harden their hearts against God. Because of their rebellion against obedience to God, the generation of the Exodus perished in the wilderness. God Himself condemned them to failure. They saw God's works, His miracles, for forty years, and they disgusted God because of their rebellious doubt and unbelief.[5] They could not enter into Canaan because of their unbelief. As Lenski observed, "When grace is exhausted, judgment descends."[6]

In v. 1, we have the only instance in the New Testament where Jesus Christ is called God's *Apostle.* An apostle was an agent or an ambassador. Within the limits of his assignment, an apostle had the authority of the one who sent him. He was legally empowered to act for the one who sent him, having the power of attorney.[7] Jesus is thus the Son of God (1:2), greater than all angels (1:5ff.), the Apostle of God, and our great High Priest (3:1).

---

[2] E. F. Scott, "Hebrews," in Arthur S. Peake, with A. J. Grieve, editors, *A Commentary on the Bible* (London, England: T. C. and E. C. Jack, 1920), 891.

[3] Arthur W. Pink, *An Exposition of Hebrews* (Grand Rapids, Michigan: Baker Book House, 1968), 176.

[4] W. J. Conybeare and J. S. Howson, *The Life and Epistles of Saint Paul* (Hartford, Connecticut: S. S. Scranton, 1913 edition), 859f.n.

[5] R. C. H. Lenski, *The Interpretation of the Epistle to the Hebrews and of the Epistle of James* (Columbus, Ohio: Wartburg Press, 1946), 114.

[6] *Ibid.,* 124.

[7] George Wesley Buchanan, *To the Hebrews* (Garden City, New York: Doubleday, 1972), 55.

At the same time, true believers are called "holy brethren" (3:1) and "partakers of the heavenly calling." This does not mean here that all individuals in the church are holy but that their *calling* is to be holy. Doubt separated us from God and Christ, whereas faith draws us close to Him (vv. 7-19). It is not faith that saves us but Jesus Christ; what faith does is to enable us to know His salvation. We become "partakers" or sharers in Christ's victory over sin and death if we are "stedfast to the end." The church is reminded that those who left Egypt with Moses did not necessarily enter into the Promised Land (vv. 15-19). Their unbelief caused them to die in the wilderness. What led them to follow Moses was their desire to escape from slavery and death. This was not enough: they had a calling to serve and obey God, but they chose rather to demand that God save and obey them. The issue was and still is, Who is the Lord? Whose will must be obeyed? God is not at man's command, nor at man's beck and call. The chief end of God is not to glorify man and obey him forever, but very much the reverse. Hebrews is emphatic, here and elsewhere, that a man-centered faith is implicitly hostile to the God of Scripture. To be "hardened through the deceitfulness of sin" (v. 13) means to make ourselves and our wishes the focus of God's work, and this is a form of blasphemy, albeit a common one.

The failure of Israel, so strongly stressed in this text, was an insistent demand that God serve Israel, and we now have a like requirement by many in the church that God serve them. Special prayer services are commonplace to call God to our aid, but rare in seeking to ascertain how we can better serve the Lord.

The word *consider* in v. 1 is a summons to change from a man-centered faith to a God-centered one. Israel was self-centered, i.e., it focused on itself as the goal of God's work rather than on His atonement. The church is even more self-centered now, in that the individual sees himself as the focus, not God and His Kingdom. But our Lord tells us, "Seek ye first the kingdom of God, and his righteousness" (Matt. 6:33) or justice. We are called to be the instruments of God, not His commanders. The faithfulness of Moses is commended to the Hebrews. In fact, in v. 5 Moses is highly praised as a faithful house-servant, and he is implicitly held up as an example of Godliness and holiness. If we see ourselves as the *goal* of God's work in Christ rather than as His *instruments*, how can we enter into Christ's rest when we warp the meaning of His work? The center of our faith is not ourselves but Christ and His Kingdom. Our salvation therefore is not the *end* of Christ's work but its starting-point in our restoration into His household and calling. Calvin was right: our whole life must be our endeavor to fulfill His calling. Christ is the foundation, not we ourselves.

Chapter Six

The Meaning of Rest
(Hebrews 4:1-5)

1. Let us therefore fear, lest, a promise being left us of entering into his rest, any of you should seem to come short of it.
2. For unto us was the gospel preached, as well as unto them: but the word preached did not profit them, not being mixed with faith in them that heard it.
3. For we which have believed do enter into rest, as he said, As I have sworn in my wrath, if they shall enter into my rest: although the works were finished from the foundation of the world.
4. For he spake in a certain place of the seventh day on this wise, And God did rest the seventh day from all his works.
5. And in this place again, If they shall enter into my rest.
(Hebrews 4:1-5)

To understand this chapter and all of Hebrews, it is necessary to know what is meant by the word *rest*. It is an error to assume that rest means an absence of work. To read Hebrews in this sense is to give *rest* a man-centered meaning. In Hebrews 4:10, it is clear that this *rest* is God's *rest*. This is seen by some as meaning *heaven*. But in Genesis 2:2, we see that it means God *resting* from His work of creation, from making heaven and earth in six days. In the modern sense of cessation from hard work, the word is meaningless. God does not grow weary, nor does He require rest in that sense. The *rest* of creation (Gen. 2:2) refers to a completion, to a task accomplished, so that it is a celebration and a victory.

We miss the meaning of the *Sabbath* if we fail to understand it in this sense. It celebrates Christ's accomplished work of atonement and the destruction of the power of sin and death. In this sense, rest refers to salvation and victory. In Isaiah 57:20-21, we are told:

20. But the wicked are like the troubled sea, when it cannot rest, whose waters cast up mire and dirt.
21. There is no peace, saith my God, to the wicked.

The *rest* spoken of in Hebrews is the antithesis of this: it is a moral and a theological fact. This *rest* is broken by the fall, by sin and death, and it cannot be entered into apart from Jesus Christ. The rest we gain in Jesus Christ is the rest of God after creating a world that was very good (Gen. 1:31). By our regeneration through Jesus Christ, we are now reestablished in our dominion mandate (Gen. 1:26-28), and we are commissioned to enter into God's rest by doing His will, and by bringing every area of life and thought into captivity to Jesus Christ and placing all things under the government of God's law-word.

The rest of God was offered to man when he was called to his task in Eden, and, after the fall, it was this rest that awaited God's chosen people for their obedience.

The Hebrews are told that their forefathers did not enter into that rest because of unbelief and disobedience. Will they turn back from Christ and also perish?

This *rest* is ordained and prepared for the people whom God had called in Christ. Those to whom it was proclaimed by Moses did not gain it because of their unbelief (v. 1-2). Like the Israelites in the wilderness, the young Christian community had an opportunity to move into the Promised Land or perish in the wilderness. Hence the warning begins, "Let us fear therefore..." (v. 1). The story of the Exodus was the most familiar part of Hebrew history. Were the Hebrews in the church now going to repeat the sin of their forefathers?

It is the seriousness of this crisis that governs Hebrews and accounts for its collective authorship. It is a solemn warning and an explanation of the seriousness of any turning backward. They should be afraid of repeating an ancient sin. *They* are on trial, not God. The apostolic company, like Moses, is summoning them back from the brink of judgment and death.

The promise of the Exodus remains, even though that generation perished because of unbelief. God does not change, and His promise remains. God's rest, like all His being and work, is perfect, and He summons His people into that rest. Jesus Christ has now opened that rest to His people, and He calls them to enter into His rest by fulfilling the creation mandate. The word of promise did not profit the Exodus generation because they lacked true faith (v. 2). The concern of the Exodus people was man-centered: what could God do for them? No matter how many the miracles and gifts of God were, they demanded still more. God had in their eyes a duty to answer man's prayers and petitions on demand. If God did not meet their demands, the Hebrews of the Exodus generation were actually ready to threaten a return to Egypt (Num. 11:20; 14:1-4), although God felt no fear at their threat!

These arrogant unbelievers could not enter into God's rest (v. 3f), but, if we are faithful, we can. God *works* always, as our Lord tells us in John 5:17, so that His *rest* refers to the triumph of His creative purpose.

The Hebrews to whom this general letter was addressed were in a position to understand its warning. Certainly the promised *rest* had not been attained in Israel's history. Despite brief periods of peace and prosperity, their history was marked mainly by apostasies and invasions. They were currently under Roman rule, and many feared that an outbreak of war was near. The promised rest had not come.

To them now was "the word preached" (v. 2), or, literally, "the word of hearing." It means that, even as the Exodus generation heard the word, so too this generation; so they are without excuse. One cannot condemn the men who left Egypt without condemning oneself. There is the same ingratitude and obtuseness to reality.

The Sabbath rest of God is not something handed to a people for their readiness to give merely verbal assent to God. It recalls us to God's triumphant rest after creating all things. We have a task to do under God, and we have the revelation of His justice, His law, whereby we can overcome the powers of sin and injustice and make this world the Kingdom of God. God's threat in v. 5 is from Psalm 95:7-11:

> 7. ...Today if ye will hear his voice,
> 8. Harden not your heart, as in the provocation, and as in the day of temptation in the wilderness:
> 9. When your fathers tempted me, proved me, and saw my work.
> 10. Forty years long was I grieved with this generation, and said, It is a people that do err in their heart, and they have not known my ways:
> 11. Unto whom I sware in my wrath that they should not enter into my rest.

God was not content with verbal professions of faith where the Exodus generation was concerned, and He has not changed since then. His *rest* was a triumphant one. Our *rest* with Him requires that the sin and death brought into this world by Adam's fall should be overcome by the people of the last Adam, Jesus Christ. If we neglect our calling to exercise dominion through Jesus Christ and by means of God's law-word, we too shall perish in the wilderness.

In Hebrews 10:36-39, we are told that we must do the will of God to receive the promise. To obey God in this way is called living by faith, so that faith and law are not seen as separate but as one. God, we are told, has no pleasure in those who draw back from this calling.

Chapter Seven
Faith and Obedience
(*Hebrews 4:6-16*)

6. Seeing therefore it remaineth that some must enter therein, and they to whom it was first preached entered not in because of unbelief:
7. Again, he limiteth a certain day, saying in David, To day if ye will hear his voice, harden not your hearts.
8. For if Jesus had given them to rest, then would he not afterward have spoken of another day.
9. There remaineth therefore a rest to the people of God.
10. For he that is entered into his rest, he also hath ceased from his own works, as God did from his.
11. Let us labour therefore to enter into that rest, lest any man fall after the same example of unbelief.
12. For the word of God is quick, and powerful, and sharper than any two-edged sword, piercing even to the dividing asunder of soul and spirit, and of the joints and marrow, and is a discerner of the thoughts and intents of the heart.
13. Neither is there any creature that is not manifest in his sight: but all things are naked and opened unto the eyes of him with whom we have to do.
14. Seeing then that we have a great high priest, that is passed into the heavens, Jesus the Son of God, let us hold fast our profession.
15. For we have not an high priest which cannot be touched with the feeling of our infirmities; but was in all points tempted like as we are, yet without sin.
16. Let us therefore come boldly unto the throne of grace, that we may obtain mercy, and find grace to help in time of need. (Hebrews 4:6-16)

In v. 9, we have a pivotal statement concerning *rest*. The reading of v. 9, "There remaineth therefore a rest to the people of God," can be better read with *rest* meaning "a keeping of the sabbath," a *sabbatismos*. Vincent said of this,

> *Remaineth*, since in the days of neither Moses, Joshua, or David was the rest appropriated. He passes over the fact that the rest had not been entered into at any later period of Israel's history. Man's portion in the divine rest inaugurated at creation had never been really appropriated: but *it still remaineth*. This statement is justified by the new word for *rest* which enters at this point, *sabbatismos*. ...*Sabbatismos*...signifies a *keeping Sabbath*. The *Sabbath* rest points back to God's original rest, and marks the ideal rest — the rest of perfect adjustment of all things to God, such as ensued upon the completion of his creative work, when he pronounced all things good. This falls in with the ground-thought of the Epistle, the restoration of all this to God's archetype. The sin and unbelief of Israel were incompatible with that rest. It must remain unappropriated until harmony with God is restored. The Sabbath-rest is the consummation of the new creation in Christ,

through whose priestly mediation reconciliation with God will come to pass.[1]

This Sabbath-rest means the fullness of victory. Life is good, but in a fallen world we do not experience the full richness of it, and we are pointed to the future in Christ. An unbeliever once commented in my hearing about his dissatisfaction with his life, saying, "Some day I hope to *live*, really to *live*." This is a longing common to many.

Our Lord, in Mark 2:27, says, "The sabbath was made for man, and not man for the sabbath," but He does not thereby make the sabbath man-centered. God's rest (Gen. 2:2) refers not only to the completion of His glorious work of creation, but also to the fact of His eternal perfection in all His being and works. There is in Him the perfect coincidence of work and rest. The sabbath each week, and God's eternal sabbath, were made for man to find therein his completion in working God's will and finding His perfect peace and rest in Him.

Verse 10 tells us that whoever has entered into God's rest has "ceased from his own works, as God did from his." *Rest* is compared to a land, like Canaan, to be occupied (3:17-19). Joshua's conquest gave no rest to the people because Canaan was no more than the starting-point of their conquest. They had the duty of bringing themselves and every area of life and thought into submission to God by his law-word. This was not a matter of works but of the application of faith.

We are summoned in v. 10 to cease from our own works and to do God's work in terms of God's law-word (John 5:17). God rested from His work (Gen. 2:2). We are to rest from our works in His work in order to find rest in Him whereby we can in peace and strength do His work.

God's sabbath rest is the "condition of faith."[2] The phrase, "lest any man fall after the same example of *unbelief*," should read, "the same example of *disobedience*"; the word in Greek is *apeitheias*, which can be translated as either *unbelief* or *disobedience*. The church has separated *faith* and *obedience*, *unbelief* and *disobedience*, but their meaning in Scripture is the same. The separation of faith and obedience had deadly consequences for the church and had led to antinomianism and impotence. Joshua (Jesus) could not lead Israel into God's rest, although he led them into Canaan, because they were more interested in their advantages than in God's rest (v. 8).

In v. 12, we are told that the word of God is like a two-edged or two-mouthed sword, cutting or piercing to the heart of our being to expose all falsity. It is a "living word" because God is the living word whose being governs all His works and words. It penetrates our total being with its

---

[1.] M. R. Vincent, *Word Studies in the New Testament*, vol. II (MacDill AFB, Florida: MacDonald Publishing Company, n.d.), 1112.
[2.] *Ibid.*, 1113.

cutting and healing power. Thus, the reading of God's word is unlike any other book because it has a personal power unlike all others.

According to Robert W. Ross, five assertions are made concerning the word of God: *first*, it is *living*; *second*, it is the word of power, or creative energy; *third*, it *severs*, it cuts through all things; *fourth*, it judges our innermost thoughts; and, *fifth*, God deals directly with us by means of His word.[3]

To say that the word of God lives or is living is alien to man's thinking because we separate life from words, writing, or books. However, in John 6:63, our Lord declares that the Holy Spirit and His works are alike "life." "It is the spirit that quickeneth: the flesh profiteth nothing: the words that I speak unto you, they are spirit, and they are life" (John 6:63). Attempts to reduce the Bible to literature have failed: it has a disturbing element that does not permit such a reduction.

Immediately after this statement about the word of God, we are told that all our being has a total visibility to God Himself, and "all things are naked and opened unto the eyes of him with whom we have to do" (v. 13). The written word is thus essentially tied to God. Nothing escapes the eyes of God, for there is nothing too small nor too great for Him. By closing the Bible, we do not escape from God.

In vv. 14-16, we have an introduction to the next section of Hebrews, from 5:1-10:18, which tells us of our great High Priest. We have in 5:11-6:20 what appears to be a digression but is not.

According to Buchanan, in v. 11, as elsewhere, "The author took frequent opportunities to exhort his readers to hold fast to their confidence, keep all the laws, and be careful not to go astray."[4] Buchanan sees "the entire document (1:1-12:29)" as "based on Ps. 110."[5] This means that it is an exhortation to victory.

In vv. 14-16, Jesus Christ is called both our great High Priest and the Son of God. As Son of God, He is our God-given King and Law-giver. As High Priest, He is the mediator between God and man.

There are many kinds of mediators with differing tasks. A mother mediates the father's will to the children. A church mediates God's word and will to the people, and so on. Jesus Christ's mediatorship is unique because He represents God to us, and us to God, and He is totally authoritative in His mediation, and unique. He alone effects remission of sins by atonement, and He alone is our sufficient Savior. He is one of us, very man of very man, "yet without sin" (v. 16), and He is also God the

---

[3.] Robert W. Ross, "Hebrews," in Charles F. Pfaffer, Everett F. Harrison, editors, *The Wycliffe Bible Commentary* (Chicago, Illinois: Moody Press, 1962), 913f.
[4.] George Wesley Buchanan, *To the Hebrews* (Garden City, New York: Doubleday, 1972), 74.
[5.] *Ibid.*, 79.

Son, the second person of the Trinity. He is thus total power with total understanding, more in communion with us than any other person can be. He is "touched with the feeling of our infirmities" (v. 15), so that we can be more open with Him than any other man. We can make confession and petition to Him as to no other man.

Previously, we were told that Jesus is greater than the Levitical priesthood (4:14-13:3); He is greater than all the prophets (1:1-3), than all angels (1:4-2:18), and greater than Moses (3:10-4:13). As A. T. Robertson summed it up:

> "Let us keep on holding fast." This keynote runs all through the Epistle, the exhortation to the Jewish Christians to hold on to the confession (3:1) of Christ already made. Before making the five points of Christ's superior priestly work (better priest than Aaron, 5:1-7:28; under a better covenant, 8:1-13; in a better sanctuary, 9:1-12; offering a better sacrifice, 9:13-10:18; based on better promises, 10:19-12:30), the author gives a double exhortation (4:14-16) like that in 2:1-4 to hold fast to the high priest (v. 14f.) and to make use of him (16).[6]

Faith and obedience are one in Jesus Christ. They are the key to *rest*. To rest in Jesus Christ, we must believe and obey.

---

6. Archibald Thomas Robertson, *Word Pictures in the New Testament*, vol. V (Grand Rapids, Michigan: Baker Book House, 1932), 365.

Chapter Eight
Atonement and the Kingdom
(*Hebrews 5:1-5*)

1. For every high priest taken from among men is ordained for men in things pertaining to God, that he may offer both gifts and sacrifices for sins:
2. Who can have compassion on the ignorant, and on them that are out of the way; for that he himself also is compassed with infirmity.
3. And by reason hereof he ought, as for the people, so also for himself, to offer for sins.
4. And no man taketh this honour unto himself, but he that is called of God, as was Aaron.
5. So also Christ glorified not to himself to be made an high priest; but he that said unto him, Thou art my Son, to day have I begotten thee.
(Hebrews 5:1-5)

Our text here is concerned with the work of the high priest. The basic task of the high priest in the law in the Old Testament was atonement. This was an essential task, because without atonement there is no peace with God. Because man is a fallen creature, a sinner, he is under the death penalty. Nothing he can do can nullify that judgment because he is a tainted creature, with tainted motives, and capable of no good thing. He needed a priest, a high or great priest, to be his mediator before God.

The death penalty requires the termination of life. The sacrificial system provided substitutes for the sinner in the form of clean and unblemished animals. These typified the sacrifice to come, One like His brethren, yet without sin.

Atonement cannot be costless. When David bought the threshing floor of Araunah the Jebusite to build there an altar, Araunah offered it freely to David, but David refused it as a gift and insisted on a purchase, saying, "Nay; but I will surely buy it of thee at a price: neither will I offer burnt offerings unto the LORD my God of that which doth cost me nothing" (2 Sam. 24:24). Atonement requires a price, and because the true and final high priest, Jesus Christ, would make the atonement for the sins of His people, it could not be costless: it would require His life. The Hebrews had to realize that, with Christ's atonement, there no longer existed any approach to God other than Jesus Christ, God's High Priest.

No high priest of Aaron was called to die for his people's sins. This Jesus Christ came to do. In v. 5, we see that when Jesus was baptized, a voice from heaven had declared, "This is my beloved Son, in whom I am well pleased" (Matt. 3:17). This is a citation from Psalm 2:7 (cf. Luke 9:35). The voice from heaven, according to Hebrews, declared Him to be God's High Priest, the high priest pleasing to Him.

In v. 1, the purpose of the office of high priest is declared to be to make sacrifice for sin. The two essential requirements here cited are, *first*, He is taken from among men, but, *second*, He is appointed by God. The office is not of man's creation. The view of Jewish believers was that Jesus was the Messiah, and, whatever new meaning had to be given to this calling, it was the essential one. Hebrews insists that it is the high priesthood of Jesus that is basic. Before the royal calling can be realized, the priestly function must prevail. Jesus Christ can be no man's King if He is not his priest, and, if He is man's High Priest, it must follow that He is also his King and Lawgiver.

In v. 2, we are told that, because He is chosen from among men and is truly incarnate, He can have compassion on those who sin ignorantly and on those with infirmity. Because He is also very God of very God, He is able to be patient with us where other men would find our sins and shortcomings repulsive.

In v. 3, we are reminded that all purely human high priests had to offer sacrifices for themselves and for their people. Up to this point, the Hebrew believer would have trouble seeing Jesus as a valid high priest because He was not of the order of Aaron. Hebrews lays the foundation for reminding one and all that God does have another priestly order. In v. 4, we are prepared for this when we are reminded that the office was not of man's creation but of God's ordination.

Like Aaron, Jesus Christ had a divine calling and ordination. It was not self-glorification on His part but submission to the Father. The use of Psalm 2:7 makes it clear that God's calling was ordained from of old and was an aspect of His sovereign purpose.

There is an aspect to this that men today miss, because the fully recognized Biblical pattern separates the offices of king and high priest. God's judgment on such a confusion appears in the case of Uzziah, who, when gaining power by usurping the priestly office, was smitten with leprosy and died a leper (2 Chron. 26:16-23).

The separation of powers on the human level is a Biblical doctrine. The Hebrew believers would find it difficult to see Jesus Christ as both King and High Priest. The limitation on men, however, does not apply to Jesus Christ: He is both King and High Priest.

The union of the two offices in Jesus Christ means that He as High Priest makes atonement for us, and He also regenerates us, to make us new creatures of His new human race as our second or last Adam. As our King, He then commissions us to disciple all nations (Matt. 28:18-20). This discipling is not their conversion alone. To believe so is to have a man-centered gospel and to make man's salvation the whole of the purpose of God. Our Lord plainly says that we are to seek *first* or above all the Kingdom of God and His righteousness or justice (Matt. 6:33).

In Hebrews, the purpose of the apostolic fellowship was to correct limited views of the Gospel. We cannot understand Hebrews except in terms of a broader purpose in Christ's coming than "saving souls," however necessary that is. An army called together for no other purpose than to express joy at being so called is a mockery and a futility.

The goal is God's sabbath rest. Jesus Christ is God's lawful High Priest because He is God's lawful King. What cannot be done lawfully by man, the union of the two callings, is God's ordination for Jesus Christ. We receive atonement and regeneration to serve our King, not to retreat into a waiting for the end amidst pious gushings.

Man's fall led to the prevalence sin and death as the governing facts in a man's life and history. The purpose of the atonement is to undo the fall, to empower man with grace and life to do God's will, and to make this world into God's Kingdom. Deny this fact and you deny God's purpose in the atonement.

Chapter Nine

The High Priest
(Hebrews 5:1-5)

1. For every high priest taken from among men is ordained for men in things pertaining to God, that he may offer both gifts and sacrifices for sins:
2. Who can have compassion on the ignorant, and on them that are out of the way; for that he himself also is compassed with infirmity.
3. And by reason hereof he ought, as for the people, so also for himself, to offer for sins.
4. And no man taketh this honour unto himself, but he that is called of God, as was Aaron.
5. So also Christ glorified not to himself to be made an high priest; but he that said unto him, Thou art my Son, to day have I begotten thee. (Hebrews 5:1-5)

Verse 1 begins by telling us that, *first*, a high priest is *taken from among men* as their representative in approaching God. He is *taken*, denoting a passive action on his part, because he is neither self-appointed, nor, if a true high priest or priest, appointed by men. *Second*, since the priestly calling is to approach God on behalf of men, the high priest must be acceptable to God. This at once presents a major problem. The high priest is needed to approach God because men are sinners under sentence of death. All human priests are by nature fallen men and in the same class as those whom they represent. Aaron's conduct in the creation of the golden calf and the fertility worship that followed, without reference to any other incident, is enough to indicate that Aaron was a sinful man, himself in need of an intercessor. Thus, any totally human high priest was himself in need of an intercessor. *Third*, it was the duty of the high priest to offer "both gifts and sacrifices for sins" (v. 1). How could a sinful man offer gifts and sacrifices for sin that would be acceptable to God? Only because the high priest was a type of the true high priest to come was this possible. He acted, not in his own right or in terms of his credentials, but in terms of the true high priest whom he represented. He was a "stand-in" until the destined high priest arrived and made the ordained sacrifice. Both the high priests before Jesus Christ and their sacrifices were *types*: they represented the reality to come, and their efficacy rested on Him. The ritual of the high priest was strictly prescribed because he was not independent in his work.

Hebrews thus far discusses the priesthood as Israel knew it, of the line of Aaron. Jesus Christ as the true high priest was still an alien idea. We are logically led to the conclusion that the only valid high priest can be Jesus Christ, and all before Him were only types and "stand-ins" for Him.

The high priest must "offer" (v. 1) or, literally, "bring toward" the altar and God only that which is acceptable to God. But there are two aspects to this acceptability: *first*, the offering; and, *second*, the offerer. In the long history of Israel, if we grant that the offerings were commonly acceptable, the priestly offerers were often not so. Delitzsch's note on this is very good:

> The high priest's three confessions — the first for himself and his own family, the second for the priesthood in general, and the third for all Israel — ...The first, for himself and family, ran thus: *O for Jehovah's sake* (or, *O Jehovah*, according to another reading) *do thou explicate the misdeeds, the crimes, and the sins wherewith I have done evil, and have sinned before Thee, I and my house, as it is written in the law of Moses Thy servant: "On that day shall he make an atonement to cleanse you; from all your sins shall ye be clean before Jehovah"* (Lev. 16:30). Only as one who had been himself atoned could the high priest make atonement for others, in accordance with the received principle, "An innocent man must come and make an atonement for the guilty; but the guilty may not come and make atonement for the innocent."[1]

In v. 2, we are told that a true high priest is marked by compassion for the ignorant, for those who sin ignorantly. The fall blinds man to his own sins in many areas, so that the light of God's law is needed to make the ignorant aware of their sins. False pastors will not proclaim God's law, so that many people are unaware of their own waywardness. The high priest, being a man, is himself "compassed with infirmity," or, weakness. This was a description of high priests as Israel had known them: they were compassed with weakness. The contrast between these high priests and Jesus Christ is cited in 7:28.

Sins of presumption are not covered by the high priest's atonement, but rather sins of ignorance and weakness.

The high priests after the order of Aaron made atonement for themselves, and for the people (v. 3). On the day of atonement, the high priest made atonement for his sins and those of his family by offering a calf, and then he atoned for the sins of Israel (Lev. 9:7-17; 16:6-19). The words "by reason hereof," mean that because of his weakness and sinfulness, the high priest must make atonement for his own sins. He cannot make atonement for others if his own sins are unatoned for.

In v. 4, we are told that no man can presume to have the honor of becoming a high priest but only those called by God, as was Aaron. The high priest must be a man, but he must be called by God. No man can presume to fill the office except one called by God. The phrase, "as was Aaron," is important: Aaron's sin did not nullify his office as high priest. His calling was from God, and Moses, as God's servant, rebuked Aaron for his sin, but it was not Moses' prerogative to replace Aaron.

---

[1] Franz Delitzsch, *Commentary on the Epistle to the Hebrews*, vol. 1 (Grand Rapids, Michigan: Eerdmans, 1952 reprint), 232n.

Jesus Christ, although God incarnate, did not glorify Himself by claiming the high priestly status. Rather, God exalted Him to that office, declaring at Jesus' baptism, "Thou art my Son, today have I begotten thee" (v. 5; Matt. 3:17; Luke 9:35). This is a citation from Psalm 2:7, where the reference is clearly to the Son's royal status. Here it refers to His high priestly calling. The difference is important. The royal calling of Jesus Christ was apparent from His birth. His kingdom, however, could not exist apart from the atonement. The realm of the first Adam is one of sin and death. The second Adam's new human race is one of justice or righteousness and life (1 Cor. 15:45ff.). There can be no such messianic kingdom while sin and death reign. As a result, the very proclamation of Psalm 2:7, of Christ the cosmic King, requires atonement for that royal realm to exist and flourish. Without the atonement, there is no kingdom.

All this points ahead to a logical conclusion: the priesthood of Aaron is no longer needed. It was only a "stand-in" for the true High Priest who has now come. A return to the Temple and its priesthood is apostasy; it can be compared to old Israel's talk about a return to Egypt. Israel had been called to enter into the Promised Land, but it refused to do so at God's bidding. Its later attempt to conquer Canaan on its own was doomed by God.

In the church today, vast segments are content to sit in the wilderness and indulge in pious gush. They resent talk about the duty to exercise dominion in Christ's name, labelling it "unspiritual." They have equated spirituality with irrelevance. Those outside the fold sin against God; those who see themselves as within the fold sin in Christ's name. They add blasphemy to sin.

Chapter Ten
Babies vs. Mature Men
(*Hebrews 5:6-14*)

6. As he saith also in another place, Thou art a priest for ever after the order of Melchizedek.
7. Who in the days of his flesh, when he had offered up prayers and supplications with strong crying and tears unto him that was able to save him from death, and was heard in that he feared;
8. Though he were a Son, yet learned he obedience by the things which he suffered;
9. And being made perfect, he became the author of eternal salvation unto all them that obey him;
10. Called of God an high priest after the order of Melchizedek.
11. Of whom we have many things to say, and hard to be uttered, seeing ye are dull of hearing.
12. For when for the time ye ought to be teachers, ye have need that one teach you again which be the first principles of the oracles of God; and are become such as have need of milk, and not of strong meat.
13. For every one that useth milk is unskillful in the word of righteousness: for he is a babe.
14. But strong meat belongeth to them that are of full age, even those who by reason of use have their senses exercised to discern both good and evil. (Hebrews 5:6-14)

Hebrews here uses a verse from Psalm 110:4 which must have startled the readers. God declares to His Messiah, "Thou art a priest for ever after the order of Melchizedek." In modern Hebrew commentary, this verse is rendered as, "You shall be a priest forever, in accord with Melchizedek's word," and it is held to refer to Abraham.[1] In terms of this, Abraham's works suffice to atone for Jews to the end of time. Normally, a high priest's efficacy ended with death. Hebrews tells the Jewish followers that it is Jesus Christ who is the true high priest, a living high priest in heaven.

In vv. 7-8, we are told that God the Son was prepared for His high priestly calling by His agonized prayers and sufferings as our sin bearer. Although He was the Son of God, "yet learned he obedience by the things which he suffered" (v. 7). He was spared none of the griefs of humanity but was required to experience them all; to learn obedience through suffering (v. 8). As Delitzsch noted, "Had He not experienced the terrors of death Himself, He would not have been...*like* us, nor what is needed that our high priest should be."[2] Christ's life was a training for His eternal priesthood. It was a preparation for the cross, but also for His present place as our

---

[1] Rabbi Avrohom Chaim Feuer, *Tehillim (Psalms)*, vol. 4 (Brooklyn, New York: Mesorah Publications, 1982).
[2] Franz Delitzsch: *Commentary on the Epistle to the Hebrews*, vol. 1 (Grand Rapids, Michigan: Eerdmans, 1952 reprint), 250.

mediator. He knows our frailty and our needs, and the reality of our sufferings.

He is "the author of eternal salvation unto all them that *obey* him" (v. 9). As M.R. Vincent rightly observed, "If the *captain* of salvation must learn obedience, so must his followers."[3] Paul in 2 Thessalonians speaks of the day of God's wrath as one of "taking vengeance on them that know not God, and that obey not the gospel of our Lord Jesus Christ (2 Thess. 1:8). Faith does not displace obedience but rather requires it. There is no virtue in disobedience.

It was God the Father who called Jesus Christ to be a "high priest after the order of Melchizedek" (v. 10). Much more can be said on this, Hebrews states, but it is hard to do so, "seeing ye are dull of hearing" (v. 11). Verses 11-14 are a sharp rebuke to the people addressed by this letter. They see themselves as wise and mature believers, unlike the Gentile congregations, but their pride has made them dull-witted. This was, in a way, an insulting statement, because the moral and religious superiority of the Jews to the Gentiles was a very substantial one. This, however, created their problem: they were therefore less willing to learn. This made highly intelligent people dull-witted.

In v. 12, the Hebrews are told, you should be the teachers of others, but instead you need to relearn the first principles of God's word. If, for example, they saw Abraham as the great high priest after the order of Melchizedek, they would not see the meaning of Psalm 110, whereas a Gentile with no preconceived ideas about the psalm could be taught its relevance to Christ. Their preconceptions make the Hebrew believers unfit for strong meat; like babies, they can only take milk.

Any person who was theologically a baby would be unskilled at interpreting God's word (v. 13). This was a very sharp rebuke to a people who saw themselves as superior to the Gentile believers. From all that we know, the Gentile believers were often deficient in many ways, so that it is easy to say that Hebrews is rather unfair. But what we have here is the word of God, and we must accept it because we now face a like situation. The European peoples have an advanced *knowledge* of God's word, but not an advanced *understanding*. Many peoples on the mission fields are a maze of strange beliefs, but they also have a simple trust in God now lost among the historically Christian peoples.

In. v. 14, we are told the reason for the harsh judgment on the Jewish believers. They are told that maturity comes with a willingness to grow and to learn. They must cultivate maturity. Maturity does not mean an end to growing, but, with respect to spiritual and intellectual discernment, the

---

[3] M.R. Vincent, *Word Studies in the New Testament*, vol. 2 (MacDill AFB, Florida: MacDonald Publishing Co., n.d.), 118.

ability to learn and to discern. It means as aptitude for grasping implications and meanings and acting on them.

In recent generations, we have had many "no growth" doctrines which have seen sanctification as completed at the time of regeneration, others affirming spiritual "perfection," and so on and on. Such beliefs tell us why the churches have become impotent.

The Hebrew believers were ready to return to the synagogue. Others were ready to separate themselves from the rest of the church, and some did. However, at the end of the first century, the overwhelming majority of Christians were Jews. For centuries, many Christian leaders, well into the medieval era, were from Jewish families. Obviously, Hebrews was effective in its declared purpose.

Hebrews is needed today to accomplish the purpose of recalling European and American believers to their task of dominion and victory. Even among professing evangelicals, there is little evidence of a calling to triumph in Christ.

The maturity of the Hebrew believers then, and the evangelicals now, was a self-styled one. They were babies, not mature men, and where children rule, disaster follows.

Chapter Eleven

Moving Towards Maturity
(*Hebrews 6:1-8*)

1. Therefore leaving the principles of the doctrine of Christ, let us go on unto perfection; not laying again the foundation of repentance from dead works, and of faith toward God,
2. Of the doctrine of the baptisms, and of laying on of hands, and of resurrection of the dead, and of eternal judgment.
3. And this will we do, if God permit.
4. For it is impossible for those who were once enlightened, and have tasted of the heavenly gift, and were made partakers of the Holy Ghost,
5. And have tasted the good word of God, and the powers of the world to come,
6. If they shall fall away, to renew them again unto repentance; seeing they crucify to themselves the Son of God afresh, and put him to an open shame.
7. For the earth which drinketh in the rain that cometh oft upon it, and bringeth forth herbs meet for them by whom it is dressed, receiveth blessing from God:
8. But that which beareth thorns and briers is rejected, and is nigh unto cursing; whose end is to be burned. (Hebrews 6:1-8)

The understanding of these verses depends in part on Matthew 13:1-9, where our Lord speaks of the word as seed cast upon the ground. Seed sown by the wayside is quickly eaten by birds. Seed cast upon stony ground without much earth springs up while the ground is wet and then is killed when sunshine and hot weather arrive. The seed sown among thorns is soon choked out. Only seed cast into good ground bears fruit. In Hebrews 6:7-8, the reference to our Lord's parable is very clear.

The selection of the parable is very important. For those Hebrews in the church who were thinking of a return to the synagogue, their decision was to be, they felt, an intellectual and religious evaluation of the issues. But the apostolic fellowship here makes it clear that their thinking may be evidence of moral failure in the making. They are not the judges; God is, and they are close to a severe judgment.

Bishop B.F. Westcott titled these eight verses, "The duty of Christian progress: the perils of relapse." This is exactly so. Hebrews warns the church against seeing salvation as a stagnant fact. It is not a deposit we receive which is then our permanent possession, inalienable and inseparable from us. There is a *semblance* of truth to such a view, but it is a distortion and a lie. Salvation is rather victory over sin and death, and the granting of new life, a life to be lived in and for Christ. Life means growth, not stagnation.

47

As a result, in vv. 1-2, we are urged to move ahead to "perfection," or maturity. Just as blind men are worthless soldiers, so too are church peoples who need endlessly to be taught the doctrine of Christ, of repentance from dead works and of faith toward God, of baptisms, about the laying on of hands, of the resurrection of the dead, and of eternal judgment. All this describes much of the teaching and preaching of many churches, and many more go no further than John 3:16. They thereby turn great matters into baby food. The requirement of seeking first God's Kingdom and His righteousness or justice (Matt. 6:33) is bypassed. The gospel is reduced to man's salvation rather than God's Kingdom.

But the apostolic fellowship insists: "Let us go on unto perfection" (v. 1), or, literally, as M. R. Vincent gives it, "Let us be borne on to completeness."[1] Where most are concerned, if they are not adults, if they are not mature, it is willful and evil on their part. It is sad and sickening that many churchmen who are outstanding men in their vocations delight in being childish in their "faith."

The foundational aspects of Christianity cited in vv. 1-2 do not exhaust what we must know. The stress here is that much, much more is required of us. There is no virtue in remaining a babe in Christ, only a sad idiocy.

In vv. 4-6, the people are warned that there is no second chance for them if they reject this very real Jesus, High Priest, Messiah-King, and Prophet. It is not for them to judge Him, for He shall judge, and is judging them. They may see themselves as believers in Jesus, but they have become a part of the crucifying mob if they will not have Him on His terms. In *The Apostlic Constitutions* (6.16.2) such heretics are denounced.

They who are in the church have been, *first*, "enlightened": they are ones to whom the truth was proclaimed; *second*, they also have "tasted of the heavenly gift," the gift of new life through Christ who came from heaven; *third*, they have been made "partakers of the Holy Ghost" because they have been in the church where the Spirit works; *fourth*, they "have tasted the good word of God," so that the truth has been made known unto them; and *fifth*, they have tasted "the powers of the world to come," i.e., "the world of men under the new order which is to enter with the fulfillment of Christ's work."[2]

For men to depart from Christ after all this, is to manifest their reprobate character. They have put Christ to open shame, in effect they have re-crucified Him, and they are too hardened ever to be renewed by repentance. Too often, people raise the question here, does this verse (v. 6) negate the doctrine of eternal security? Eternal security is not even in mind

---

[1] M.R. Vincent, *Word Studies in the New Testament*, vol. 2 (MacDill AFB, Florida: MacDonald Publishing Co., reprint), 1120.
[2] *Ibid.*, 1122.

here. The purpose of the text is to tell readers and hearers how to identify the reprobate. Are they themselves reprobate? We are to question ourselves if we are straying, not the text!

Verses 7 and 8 echo the parable of the sower and the seed of Matthew 13:1-9. In fact, they go further. These people may not even be good seed in bad ground, but the thorns and briars which are wrongly in the sower's field. Their "end is to be burned" (v. 8). Those who sit in judgment over Jesus shall be judged.

These verses were used much later by Tertullian and others to deny reentrance into the church to Christians who in fear turned from the faith to avoid a death sentence during the Roman persecutions. This was not valid, however. *Fear* was responsible for such apostasies. Hebrews speaks rather of a self-conscious and unforced decision to depart from Christ. With such, the governing factor is not weakness but a deliberate rejection of Christ's total claim on all their being. The apostolic company, headed by Paul, did not try to coax anyone back into the church but to warn one and all of their danger.

The word *baptisms* is in the plural in v. 2. It refers not only to what we call *baptism*, but also to all forms of ritual purification. Holiness before God requires as a routine matter our physical and spiritual purity.

Moving towards maturity is a religious necessity. In the twentieth century, we see a general satisfaction with the childish kind of Christian commitment. As a result, we have seen the faith recede and its power diminish. An army of blind men will perhaps most easily damage itself.

Chapter Twelve

God's Promise and Our Hope
(Hebrews 6:9-20)

9. But, beloved, we are persuaded better things of you, and things that accompany salvation, though we thus speak.
10. For God is not unrighteous to forget your work and labour of love, which ye have shewed toward his name, in that ye have ministered to the saints, and do minister.
11. And we desire that every one of you do shew the same diligence to the full assurance of hope unto the end:
12. That ye be not slothful, but followers of them who through faith and patience inherit the promises.
13. For when God made promise to Abraham, because he could swear by no greater, he sware by himself,
14. Saying, Surely blessing I will bless thee, and multiplying I will multiply thee.
15. And so, after he patiently endured, he obtained the promise.
16. For men verily swear by the greater: and an oath for confirmation is to them an end of all strife.
17. Wherein God, willing more abundantly to shew unto the heirs of promise the immutability of his counsel, confirmed it by an oath:
18. That by two immutable things, in which it was impossible for God to lie, we might have a strong consolation, who have fled for refuge to lay hold upon the hope set before us:
19. Which hope we have as an anchor of the soul, both sure and steadfast, and which entereth into that within the veil;
20. Whither the forerunner is for us entered, even Jesus, made an high priest for ever after the order of Melchizedek. (Hebrews 6:9-20)

The problem among the Hebrew believers is now apparent. *First*, Jesus was to them their Messiah; this hope may have become dimmed by the turn of events since the ascension. When would He establish His Kingdom? *Second*, the Hebrews still believed that they had a valid high priest in Jerusalem. He was near, and the ascended Jesus remote. When Paul returned to Jerusalem, the leaders of the church there urged Paul to go with others to the Temple for purification (Acts 21:23-26). The Temple ceremonies and sacrifices obviously still had validity for them. Only the destruction of the Temple in the Jewish-Roman War, A.D. 66-70, ended that relationship. Before the fall of Jerusalem, Rome itself did not see Christianity as another religion but simply as a dissident group within Judaism. Hebrews gives us the theological reasons which *required* a clear-cut *separation*. At the same time, Hebrews enables us to understand the *continuity* with Israel's faith.

Hebrews thus gives us blunt statements requiring separation while commending continuity. We see this in vv. 9-10. The Hebrews are in line with the Mosaic law in their ministry to need, and in their readiness to help their Christian brethren in particular. Calvin spoke very strongly of the importance of charity in commenting on these two verses, saying, in part,

> ...for he intimates that God holds himself indebted to us for whatever good we do to our neighbours, according to that saying, "What ye have done to one of the least of these, ye have done unto me" (Matt. 25:40); and there is also another, "He that giveth to the poor lendeth to the Lord" (Prov. 19).[1]

The Bible, from beginning to end, has much to say about charity as revelatory of true faith. Here the apostolic fellowship commends the Hebrew believers as faithful to their Lord because of their care for the brethren. This does not mean that charity acquires merit, but rather that it manifests our faith and our trust that God's requirements are best for us and for all men.

Notice that this assurance comes from the pastoral group: "*we* are persuaded," "*we* thus speak" (v. 9), "*we* desire" (v. 1), and so on. It is a company of men who so speak.

It is their desire that all the Hebrew believers show this "same diligence" that so many already manifest, and that they persevere "unto the end" (v. 11). This is to be done in "the full assurance of hope," or, faith. They are urged to "be not slothful," but to follow those who through patience and faith "inherit the promises" (v. 12). More literally, this reads "are inheriting" even here and now.

Then Hebrews turns to God's promise or oath to Abraham. Oaths are made before God. For God, who cannot lie, to make an oath, is a remarkable fact. As W. F. Moulton wrote on v. 17:

> *Confirmed it by an oath* — Literally, *mediated with an oath.* When a man confirms a promise or declaration to another by solemn appeal to God, between the two God is Mediator. Condescending to man's weakness, that the certainty may be "more abundant," God thus confirms His word, at once the Promiser and the Mediator, God the Promiser (if we may so speak) makes appeal to God the Hearer and Witness of the oath. We cannot doubt, as we read the whole passage, that there is a special reason for the emphasis thus laid on God's *oath* to Abraham. The writer dwells on the confirmation of the divine word of promise, not merely because it is the first recorded in sacred history, but because he has in thought the declaration of Ps. cx. 4. To this as yet he makes no reference; though he has quoted from the verse repeatedly, it has been without mention of the divine oath: but throughout the section before us he is preparing the way for his later argument in chapter 7 verse 21.[2]

[1.] John Calvin, *Commentaries on the Epistle to the Hebrews* (Grand Rapids, Michigan: Eerdmans, 1949), 144.

[2.] W. F. Moulton, "Hebrews," in Charles John Ellicott: *Commentary on the Whole Bible*, vol. 8 (Grand Rapids, Michigan: Zondervan, n.d., reprint), 305.

An oath now has little meaning, but then, and throughout most of history, it has meant the end of all doubt and argument because it invited the judgment of God if broken. For God to swear an oath to Abraham meant that God on His own placed His being on the line in support of His promise. God promised to bless Abraham, and Abraham, assured of the fulfillment of the promise, lived in full confidence that God would keep His word.

Verse 15 tells us that Abraham, having received the promise, *received* the promised gift as a fact and therefore endured many trials, for God's promise by oath was to Abraham the same as the thing promised, God having said, "Surely blessing I will bless thee, and multiplying I will multiply thee" (v. 14). Man's promises offer a hope that something will be done; God's promises give the full assurance of actual possession of the thing promised, even if there is a time lapse in between.

In all things among men, an oath settles the matter, according to v. 16; the oath ends all controversy or strife. How much more so does not God's oath totally settle the matter?

Verse 18 refers to "two immutable things," God's promise and His oath. Through God, Who cannot lie, we are given strong encouragement and have found a refuge, altar, or sanctuary in Jesus Christ. We can therefore hold fast to the hope set before us.

This hope (v. 19) is "an anchor of the soul," and a "sure and steadfast" one. "The veil" refers to the veil of the Temple, separating the Most Holy Place from the Holy Place. By faith we enter into the inner shrine, and we are a part of the fulfilled promise here and now. By faith men of old were citizens of the City of God.

Of course, our "forerunner," Jesus Christ, has already entered into the heavenly Holy of Holies and there represents us. He is there our great High Priest "for ever after the order of Melchizedek" (v. 20). Having Him, we have no need of an earthly high priest now, because the reality has replaced the type or "stand-in."

Although the use here of the *anchor* as a symbol is new, not appearing in the Old Testament, according to Westcott, Clement of Alexandria mentioned it (*Paed* 3:59) as a device on Christian rings, and, like *ichthus*, commonly used.[3]

The word *hope* in v. 18 is *elpidos*, its stem *elpis*. It means expectation, hope. According to E. Hoffmann, "In the NT the words (for hope) never indicate a vague or a fearful anticipation, but always the expectation of something good." The paganization of language has led us to reduce terms, juridical and non-juridical, to an emotional meaning, whereas often in the

---

[3.] B. F. Westcott: *The Epistle to the Hebrews* (Grand Rapids, Michigan: Eerdmans, 1952), 163. Originally published in 1892.

Bible their meaning is legal. We have here an *oath*, a legal fact, and the oath is our ground for *hope* or expectation. We are therefore not involved in an emotional wish but in a legally guaranteed fact. As Hoffmann also noted, "In many passages *elpis* denotes not the personal attitude but the objective benefit of salvation toward which hope is directed (thus Gal. 5:5; Col. 1:5; Tit. 2:13). The fulfillment is eschatological."[4] While we know this *hope* subjectively, it is never itself simply a subjective thing. *Elpis*, hope, and *agape*, love, are "essentially related" in the New Testament.[5]

The God of hope is in the God of the future because He totally governs and ordains it. This hope rests on Christ's kingship and high priestly status, and our standing in that hope is God's ordination and our apprehension by faith.

If we make faith essentially subjective, then we also make our hope in Christ subjective and therefore problematic. We can summarize the matter thus. *First*, Jesus Christ, our last Adam (1 Cor. 15:47ff), cannot be our King if He is not our High Priest who makes atonement for us and then regenerates us to be His new humanity, His new human race. This is God's doing, not ours. *Second*, because He is, with the Father and the Spirit, our predestinator (John 15:16), our future does not depend upon us but upon Him. We can therefore with Abraham regard our hope as the promise of the God who cannot lie. It is thus our certain and assured hope. *Third*, as our High Priest, Jesus Christ is even now actively working to bring His Kingdom into total power in and around us. *Fourth*, that Kingdom requires much effort on our part, beginning with the simple requirement of Christian charity (vv. 9-11). *Fifth*, we are not here on earth to get what we want but to do what God ordains, and we must not be "slothful" but devoted to those "who through faith and patience inherit the promises" (v. 12).

We have a calling that transcends ourselves.

4. E. Hoffmann, "Hope," in Colin Brown, general editor: *The New International Dictionary of New Testament Theology*, vol. 2 (Grand Rapids: Michigan: Zondervan, 1976), 241.
5. *Ibid.*, vol. 2, 243.

Chapter Thirteen

Accreditation
(Hebrews 7:1-6)

1. For this Melchizedek, king of Salem, priest of the most high God, who met Abraham returning from the slaughter of the kings, and blessed him;
2. To whom also Abraham gave a tenth part of all; first being by interpretation King of righteousness, and after that also King of Salem, which is, King of peace;
3. Without father, without mother, without descent, having neither beginning of days, nor end of life; but made like unto the Son of God; abideth a priest continually.
4. Now consider how great this man was, unto whom even the patriarch Abraham gave the tenth of the spoils.
5. And verily they that are the sons of Levi, who receive the office of the priesthood, have a commandment to take tithes of the people according to the law, that is, of their brethren, though they come out of the loins of Abraham:
6. But he whose descent is not counted from them received tithes of Abraham, and blessed him that had the promises. (Hebrews 7:1-6)

Hebrews very early insists on declaring Jesus Christ to be our great and eternal high priest, and this statement at once raised questions in the minds of all Hebrews within the church. What were Jesus' credentials for that office? We can understand their mindset if we think in terms of our own times. Anyone claiming to be a valid healer, or a valid scholar, will at once be asked to produce his credentials and his membership in certain organizations. It is unrealistic to assume that people were then less suspicious about any unusual claims. The office of high priest was most powerful in Judea, and for any man to declare himself the valid officeholder without the mandatory credentials was normally unthinkable. For Jesus to be declared high priest required thus the joint statement of an apostolic fellowship.

First, the fellowship reminds the Hebrews that Melchizedek was such a high priest, and also at the same time King of Salem, later known as Jerusalem. *Second*, Abraham was blessed by this Melchizedek, which means that Melchizedek was the greater man before God than was Abraham (v. 7). *Third*, this high priest Melchizedek was the King of righteousness, or justice, and King of peace (v. 2). *Fourth*, we are told that Melchizedek was "without father, without mother, without descent, having neither beginning of days, nor end of life; but made like unto the Son of God; abideth a priest continually" (v. 3). In more modern speech, this could be rendered thus: Melchizedek lacked any genealogical or hereditary right to his office. Neither on his father's nor his mother's side did Melchizedek inherit his office. Neither did it begin at a particular time, nor did it end with his death. He was forever a priest.

Now, the expression, "without father, without mother, without descent," was not necessarily a complimentary one. A man converting to Judaism was for centuries, according to the rabbis, a man without a father because he had no prior heritage in Jerusalem.[1]

Now the Hebrew reader faced a strange contradiction. To have no inherited right to the office made a man ineligible, or at least a questionable claimant. However, there was the strange witness of Genesis 14:18-24 and Psalm 110, both of which greatly exalted Melchizedek. Various odd interpretations were used to get around Melchizedek. He was supposedly Shem under another name, but God set aside this priesthood with Aaron's.[2] Now to link Jesus to Melchizedek was a startling and major interpretation, one looking forward rather than backward.

The incontestable fact was that Abraham had paid a "tenth of the spoils" to Melchizedek (v. 4). This meant that Abraham recognized Melchizedek's priesthood as a valid one, coming from the covenant God. In Abraham's person, the Levitical priesthood acknowledged the priority of Melchizedek and his office (vv. 5-6).

Melchizedek received tithes, and he gave a blessing. He was thus superior to Abraham and to the Levitical priesthood.

In these few verses, Hebrews undermines the Jewish view of the high priest using the words of the Old Testament. Moreover, the perspective was shifted from the past to the present and future.

Implicit also was another very important consideration. How old the view is of Melchizedek as Shem, we cannot say. Many interpretations of Judaism were subjected to revision to blunt the force of the early church's use of the Hebrew Scriptures. If the plain text stands, Melchizedek was a priest-king of Salem totally outside the Hebrew heritage. Had he been a relative, had he been Shem, major attention would have been called to that fact. Melchizedek as a *foreigner*, an alien, and a Canaanite is a remarkable fact, and it points to the universality of the faith. The covenant God does not limit Himself to one people. In Amos 9:7, God tells Israel that to Him they are no different than the Ethiopians, whom, if He chose, He could bring forward as His chosen people.

Men are concerned with humanistic forms of accreditation, and, within reason, these sometimes have their place, but this does not give God's imprimatur. The old high priesthood was now forever dead. With Christ's

---

[1.] Franz Delitzsch, *Commentary on the Epistle to the Hebrews.* vol. 1 (Grand Rapids, Michigan: Eerdmans, 1952 reprint), 332.

[2.] Rabbi Avrohom Chaim Feuer, *Tehillim, (Psalms)*, vol. 4 (Brooklyn, New York: Mesorah Publications, 1982), 1343.

crucifixion, there was no longer a possibility of atonement by the blood of animals. The old priesthood of Aaron at its best was never the King of justice nor of peace. Its function ended with Christ's atonement.

The new high priest, Jesus Christ, gives access to heaven, to the throne of grace, because He sits and reigns there. His accreditation is that, as the eternal Son of God, He is the source of all authority and power. He is the great Prophet, the Son of God, and the King over all creation. The totality of His work and office included the priesthood. Jesus Christ cannot be understood as other than Priest, King, and Prophet.

As for accreditation, He is the source of all validity and authority. His royal and prophetic offices required that He be also our High Priest. His central work for our redemption, atonement, required that He be our high priest as well.

It is important to note that Melchizedek was King of righteousness or justice, and therefore King of peace. Without justice, there can be no true peace.

Chapter Fourteen
Melchizedek
(Hebrews 7:7-14)

7. And without all contradiction the less is blessed of the better.
8. And here men that die receive tithes; but there he receiveth them, of whom it is witnessed that he liveth.
9. And as I may so say, Levi also, who receiveth tithes, payed tithes in Abraham.
10. For he was yet in the loins of his father, when Melchizedek met him.
11. If therefore perfection were by the Levitical priesthood, (for under it the people received the law,) what further need was there that another priest should rise after the order of Melchizedek, and not be called after the order of Aaron?
12. For the priesthood being changed, there is made of necessity a change also of the law.
13. For he of whom these things are spoken pertaineth to another tribe, of which no man gave attendance at the altar.
14. For it is evident that our Lord sprang out of Juda; of which tribe Moses spake nothing concerning priesthood. (Hebrews 7:7-14)

Precedence is now cited by Hebrews as establishing the superiority of the order of Melchizedek. The blessing of Abraham by Melchizedek (Gen. 14:19) made it clear that Melchizedek was greater than Abraham. This is the essential point of these verses. "And without all contradiction the less is blessed of the better" (v. 7). This is why Melchizedek is a problem for rabbinical commentators.

Then v. 8, to make the matter even clearer, says, "And here men that die receive tithes; but there he receiveth them of whom it is witnessed that he liveth." The men who die who receive tithes are those of the Levitical order. But, in Genesis 14, the priest who received them did not depend on ancestry, nor was his priesthood voided by his death. The priesthood of Melchizedek neither depended on birth nor was it ended by death. It was from God, and therefore the human limitations were not imposed on it. The priesthood, in other words, was God's endowment on Melchizedek's *person*, not on his *lineage*. This raises questions that man cannot answer, but Psalm 110:4 is emphatic that the Messiah is a priest after the order of Melchizedek, a God-ordained priesthood radically different from the Levitical line.

In vv. 9-10, we are told that Levi, yet unborn, paid tithes to Melchizedek in the person of his great grandfather Abraham. This clearly establishes the priority of Melchizedek, and it tells us why his person must somehow be absorbed into that of Abraham to preserve the priority of the Levitical priesthood. The Bible is clear about Melchizedek, and Abraham without

hesitation acknowledges him as his high priest. Clearly, priority is not
Levitical.

All this complicated matters for the Hebrews who looked to Jerusalem
and its high priest. The Messiah plainly had all nations in mind, as the Great
Commission (Matt 28:18-20) makes clear. Now the priesthood is taken
from old Israel and given to Jesus Christ in the name of Melchizedek. One
of the problems in the early church, dealt with at the Council of Jerusalem
(Acts 15), was the place of the Gentiles in the church. Was it necessary for
them to become Jews as a first step towards becoming Christians? The
answer was no, and this troubled many. Now Hebrews negates the
Levitical priesthood and declares it to be dead.

There was thus a radically changed situation, and yet a continuity was
asserted, but with a displacement and a replacement. "Perfection," or a full
maturity, was not possible through the Levitical priesthood because its rites
of atonement were typical, not actual. True and effectual atonement
required a different sacrifice *and* a different priesthood. This required a new
high priest, one after the order of Melchizedek rather than of Aaron (v. 11).
This meant a change in the law. Since the reference is to the priesthood and
to the sacrifice, the change in the law has to do with the same. Antinomians
make this change general, and they see it as abolishing the law, which is
absurd. Theft, murder, adultery, and all the law, were as much law after the
crucifixion as before. When Christ died on the cross, the veil of the Temple
"was rent in twain from the top to the bottom" (Matt. 27:51), signifying the
end of the validity of Aaron's priesthood and the old sacrificial system. God
Himself had desecrated it by this act.

What follows in vv. 12-14 makes this very clear. Because God changed
the priesthood, "there is made of necessity a change also in the law" (v. 12).
This is very specific: the new high priest requires a different law because
His is a greater and a totally efficacious sacrifice. There is no reference here,
for example, to any change in the law of weights and measures (Deut.
25:13-16). To make large claims about the law as a whole being set aside is
to rewrite the Bible by false exegesis.

In v. 12, we are told that the priesthood is "being changed," or, better,
"*transferred* to another order."[1] This transfer to another priesthood was in
order to secure efficacious atonement, and to create a people capable of
obeying God's law. The atonement clears the redeemed from the law as a
death penalty against us, as a handwriting of ordinances that condemn us,
into obedience to the law as the way of life for the Godly. Men can be free
from the law as a death penalty, or they can be free from the law to do as
they please.

---

[1] M. R. Vincent, *Word Studies in the New Testament*, vol. 2 (MacDill AFB, Florida:
MacDonald Publishing Company, reprint), 1128.

Jesus Christ was not of the tribe of Levi but of Judah, and he was thus alien to the old priesthood, which, in fact, was responsible for His sentence of death (v. 13). Jesus Christ was a member of the tribe of Judah, which had nothing to do with the priesthood (v. 14).

The Levitical priesthood is clearly set aside. Those who cling to it will become part of an obsolete order.

Hebrews cites the precedents which validate Christ's priesthood, but it also negates the older form of the priesthood. The priesthood of Aaron was centuries old, and yet it was also a temporary one. Man cannot dictate the course of God's work; he must follow God's word which alone gives authoritative directions.

Psalm 110 tells us that the Messiah-King is also the world conqueror, and the priest forever for His people, a priest after the order of Melchizedek. Melchizedek preceded Aaron so that God provides the precedent, and He tells us of it in advance of Christ's coming.

Chapter Fifteen

No Priest, No King
(*Hebrews 7:15-28*)

15. And it is yet far more evident: for that after the similitude of Melchizedek there ariseth another priest,
16. Who is made, not after the law of a carnal commandment, but after the power of an endless life.
17. For he testifieth, Thou art a priest for ever after the order of Melchizedek.
18. For there is verily a disannulling of the commandment going before for the weakness and unprofitableness thereof.
19. For the law made nothing perfect, but the bringing in of a better hope did; by the which we draw nigh unto God.
20. And inasmuch as not without an oath he was made priest:
21. (For those priests were made without an oath; but this with an oath by him that said unto him, The Lord sware and will not repent, Thou art a priest for ever after the order of Melchizedek:)
22. By so much was Jesus made a surety of a better testament.
23. And they truly were many priests, because they were not suffered to continue by reason of death:
24. But this man, because he continueth ever, hath an unchangeable priesthood.
25. Wherefore he is able also to save them to the uttermost that come unto God by him, seeing he ever liveth to make intercession for them.
26. For such an high priest became us, who is holy, harmless, undefiled, separate from sinners, and made higher than the heavens;
27. Who needeth not daily, as those high priests, to offer up sacrifice, first for his own sins, and then for the people's: for this he did once, when he offered up himself.
28. For the law maketh men high priests which have infirmity; but the word of the oath, which was since the law, maketh the Son, who is consecrated for evermore. (Hebrews 7:15-28)

This text begins by asserting (v. 15) that another priest "after the similitude of Melchizedek" has of necessity arisen or been given. The Levitical priesthood was provisional because its sacrifices were types of what was to come. They set forth atonement but not the atoner.

The old priesthood, v. 16 tells us, was made "after the law of a carnal commandment," meaning that the law for the Levitical priesthood had reference to the body: there were physical and genealogical qualifications, and the requirement of ceremonial purity. But Jesus Christ, who is Life, does not need to meet such requirements because He is Himself the standard. He is "a priest for ever after the order of Melchizedek" (v. 17). His priesthood is not from man and has no beginning or ending, nor any limitations on its efficacy.

Verse 18 tells us, "For there is verily a disannulling of the commandment going before for the weakness and unprofitableness thereof." In v. 19 we are told, "the law made nothing perfect," but now "a better hope" enables us to "draw nigh unto God." *The law* here refers to the law of the Levitical priesthood. It does violence to the text to refer *the law* to the whole of the law of God. What is under discussion is the law of priesthood and sacrifice, *and no more*. The old laws of the priesthood are now obsolete because the great High Priest has come, and His order is from heaven. The old law of the priesthood and of sacrifices "made nothing perfect" (v. 19) because only Jesus Christ could make an efficacious atonement for us. We now have "a better hope" and a sure one, and we are brought near to God by Jesus Christ, our great High Priest.

In vv. 20-22, we are told that more than a proper genealogy stands behind the priesthood of Jesus Christ: we have God's oath. Psalm 110:4 is again referred to; this new priesthood is not bound by any human qualifications, nor is it at all under man's government and control. Jesus Christ is not our high priest by a "carnal commandment" (v. 16), literally, a commandment of flesh, one limited to human and historical factors. The Levitical priesthood was ordained by God as an historical fact. The priesthood after the order of Melchizedek was directly given by God without reference to human precedents, controls, and rules. This means that Jesus was made the surety or pledge of a better testament (v. 22). Because the renewal of the covenant is now made by the great Prophet of God, the Messiah-King, and God's great High Priest, it is the superior covenant.

Until now, there have been many priests, and high priests as well, in the history of the covenant people, but, in every case, their priesthood ended with death (v. 23). This means that all of them assumed the priesthood *for a time only*, whereas Jesus Christ is forever High Priest. Jesus Christ, who lives forever, "hath an unchangeable priesthood" (v. 24). A man can be a soldier for a few or for many years, but he is not born a soldier nor is he one forever. The priesthood of Jesus Christ is not a temporary aspect of His history but forever an essential part of His being.

Verse 25 tells us, "Wherefore he is able also to save them to the uttermost that come unto God by him, seeing he ever liveth to make intercession for them." Verses 25-28 give us a magnificent hymn, as it were, to Christ our High Priest. According to M. R. Vincent, "The idea is not intercession, but intervention."[1] This means that Christ, in His infinite wisdom, is totally active on our behalf. Having shed His blood for us, it is nothing for Him now to care for us. There are no limits on His power and activity for us: they are "to the uttermost" for those who "come unto God by Him." The

---

[1] M. R. Vincent, *Word Studies in the New Testament*, vol. 2 (MacDill AFB, Florida: MacDonald Publishing Company, n.d.), 1131.

concluding clause is more than man would dare to say: "seeing that he ever liveth to make intercession for them." This does not mean a man-centered concern for us but a Kingdom-centered one for the people of His service.

Our High Priest is "holy, harmless (or, *guileless*), undefiled, separate from sinners, and made higher than the heavens" (v. 26). He is far greater than our conceiving can grasp, for He is God the Son.

Verse 27 says of Jesus Christ that He "needeth not daily, as those high priests, to offer up sacrifice, first for his own sins, and then for the people's: for this he did once, when he offered up himself." His was the great and only true sacrifice, and it ended the sacrificial system. However, as Acts 6:7 tells us, *many* priests became Christians, and obedient ones. In time, however, some felt the need to perpetuate the sacrificial system in some fashion, and this led to the idea of an unbloody sacrifice and ultimately to the Mass.

"For the law maketh men high priest which have infirmity: but the word of the oath, which was since the law, maketh the Son, who is consecrated for evermore" (v. 28). The Levitical priesthood relied on infirm and limited men, but the oath (Ps. 110:4) consecrates the Son as eternal high priest. The oath of Psalm 110:4 came after the giving of the Mosaic law and its laws for the priesthood.

The implications are now clear. Hebrews began by declaring what none reading the letter would question, namely, that Jesus Christ is God the Son, by whom the worlds were made (Heb. 1:2). Psalm 102:25 is cited in Hebrews 1:10 to declare Jesus Christ the Creator King. Now Hebrews goes on to declare, in effect, No priest, no king. If Jesus Christ is not your High Priest, He cannot be your King. If He is not your King of righteousness or justice, He cannot be your King of Peace. To go back to the Temple and its high priest is to abandon their God and King.

Hebrews is an uncompromising manifesto. If offered no compromises to the Hebrew church members. Its message was, "Choose ye this day whom ye shall serve."

Chapter Sixteen
Priority
(*Hebrews 8:1-5*)

1. Now of the things which we have spoken this is the sum: We have such an high priest, who is set on the right hand of the throne of the Majesty in the heavens;
2. A minister of the sanctuary, and of the true tabernacle, which the Lord pitched, and not man.
3. For every high priest is ordained to offer gifts and sacrifices: wherefore it is of necessity that this man have somewhat also to offer.
4. For if he were on earth, he should not be a priest, seeing that there are priests that offer gifts according to the law:
5. Who serve unto the example and shadow of heavenly things, as Moses was admonished of God when he was about to make the tabernacle: for, See, saith he, that thou make all things according to the pattern shewed to thee in the mount. (Hebrews 8:1-5)

A logical question must have occurred to the Hebrew reader of this epistle. Jesus was of the line of David according to His ostensible father's ancestry. Because Joseph received Jesus as his son, Jesus had legal title to Joseph's prerogatives. He was thus the son of David. But what about His priestly heritage? Would it not have been possible for God somehow to make Jesus a legal heir of Aaron, or acceptable candidate for the office of high priest? God could have done this, but He did not. Why not?

In v. 1, we are told that the sum of the things thus far said tells us that "we have such an high priest, who is set on the right hand of the throne of the Majesty in the heavens." He sits there as King and Priest. Neither Judea nor Israel was a Hebrew kingdom in our Lord's day: Judea was ruled by Galilee by an Edomite (or, Idumean) king and Israel as such did not exist. But there was a Hebrew high priest, one controlled by Rome but still of the line of Aaron. As King, Jesus Christ owed loyalty only to God, and as high priest, He was God's appointed high priest, not Judea's, or Rome's.

Moreover, as God's High Priest, He was, v. 2 tells us, "A minister of the sanctuary, and of the true tabernacle, which the Lord pitched, not man." Jesus Christ is the minister of God's sanctuary, or holy place, of the true tabernacle, not the one built in Moses' day, but the heavenly one built by God. This true sanctuary is in some sense the model for the one built under the direction of Moses. The implication is a clear one: the tabernacle and Temples built by man are inferior to, and also very much subordinate to, the heavenly sanctuary. Why should God's eternal High Priest be at all under the authority and jurisdiction of the Levitical priesthood? The priesthood of Aaron was circumscribed, and it was always under the controls of man. Not so the priesthood of Melchizedek.

Verse 3 tells us, "For every high priest is ordained to offer gifts and sacrifices; wherefore it is of necessity that this man have somewhat also to offer." It was required of a high priest that he offer gifts and sacrifices to God. In this he represented the people and made peace with God on their behalf. This meant that he had to have something to offer. Christ as high priest must have gifts and sacrifices to offer, and a place to offer them, namely, the heavenly sanctuary. This, we are told, is a matter "of necessity." Since Christ's sacrifice is the *necessary* one, and all the Levitical sacrifices are simply types of His atoning sacrifice, the absolute necessity of His offering is stressed. It transcends the typical offerings of the Temple, and it is therefore separated from the Temple and its priesthood. We cannot limit God's efficacious activity then to the Temple, any more than we can limit it now to the church. We miss the point of Hebrews if we fail to see that the Hebrew believers wanted to confine God to Levitical channels, even as the church since has often tried to limit God to the church. But God can be neither controlled nor limited.

In v. 4 we are told, "For if he were on earth, he should not be a priest, seeing that there are priests that offer gifts according to the law." Not being a Levite, Jesus could not be a Levitical priest. The Levitical priests offered gifts to God "according to the law," the law of sacrifices. Christ's sacrifice of Himself as the Lamb of God would not have been legal! Because He was God's High Priest according to another order, Jesus Christ was not limited to Levitical functions. Moreover, His priestly function was beyond the man-made sanctuary's nature and function. It had an eternal frame of reference, and it was therefore a sacrifice in terms of the heavenly sanctuary.

The Levitical priesthood is simply a "stand-in" for the heavenly one. These Aaronic priests "serve unto the example and shadow of heavenly things, as Moses was admonished of God when he was about to make the tabernacle: for, See, saith he, that thou make all things according to the pattern shewed to thee in the mount" (v. 5). The tabernacle which God ordered built was after a pattern given by God at Sinai. This tabernacle or sanctuary was patterned after the God-given plan which echoed a heavenly sanctuary. The construction had to be strictly in terms of the God-given plan, which meant reflection of the heavenly one.

The obvious conclusion is that the heavenly sanctuary is far superior. Then, logically, it follows that the high priest of that heavenly sanctuary is far, far superior to any of the Roman puppet high priests presiding in Jerusalem. This eternal high priest, Jesus Christ, "is set on the right hand of the throne of the Majesty in the heavens" (v. 1). He is God the Son, God the incarnate, our eternal high priest. And they prefer the sorry high priests in Jerusalem?

But, of course, men do; they prefer rascals to honest men because as sinners they understand them better. Too often corrupt pastors are preferred to Godly ones because they are less threatening.

In Exodus 25:40, Moses is commanded strictly to build the tabernacle after the pattern revealed to him on Mount Sinai. This clearly meant that priority belongs to the heavenly sanctuary.

But the essence of original sin is that man seeks to be his own god and his own source of law, morality, and determination (Gen. 3:5). This sin crops up in all his activities, including those in church and state. He seeks to give priority in determination to himself and to this world over God and His word.

Thus, whether the issue is the high priesthood, or the authority of church rules and regulations, man wants no revealed pattern, God's word, to take priority over man's words and patterns.

It has become routine in church trials to refuse any hearing, on appeal, on the *justice* of the appeal. The only question allowed is *procedural*. Were the proper legal forms followed in the judgment? Justice is no longer legal!

Chapter Seventeen

The Atonement
(*Hebrews 8:6-13*)

6. But now hath he obtained a more excellent ministry, by how much also he is the mediator of a better covenant, which was established upon better promises.
7. For if that first covenant had been faultless, then should no place have been sought for the second.
8. For finding fault with them, he saith, Behold the days come, saith the Lord, when I will make a new covenant with the house of Israel and with the house of Judah:
9. Not according to the covenant that I made with their fathers in the day when I took them by the hand to lead them out of the land of Egypt; because they continued not in my covenant, and I regarded them not, saith the Lord.
10. For this is the covenant that I will make with the house of Israel after those days, saith the Lord; I will put my laws into their mind, and write them in their hearts: and I will be to them a God, and they shall be to me a people:
11. And they shall not teach every man his neighbour, and every man his brother, saying, Know the Lord: for all shall know me, from the least to the greatest.
12. For I will be merciful to their unrighteousness, and their sins and their iniquities will I remember no more.
13. In that he saith, A new covenant, he hath made the first old. Now that which decayeth and waxeth old is ready to vanish away. (Hebrews 8:6-13)

In v. 6, the premises are bold and clearly startling ones for devout Hebrews: Jesus Christ, the mediator, represents "a more excellent ministry," a "better covenant," and one "established upon better promises." Clearly, the covenant made by Moses was in some sense imperfect because it was not the final one. The proof for this statement is then cited, Jeremiah 31:31-34, which plainly states that a better covenant will in due time be made. But what changed? God's law does not change, nor did God suddenly annul the law given by Moses. The change was that the mediator was now God the Son, Jesus Christ, not Moses, and the atonement made by Him was not a typical one but the sacrifice of Himself.

Hebrews at times uses the word *covenant*, and at other times *testament*. The reason for this is that familiarity with the word *covenant* had come in time to obscure its unilateral nature: it was totally the work of God, given to man, whose only part in it was to receive it. Even man's reception of the covenant was by the grace of God. The use of the word *testament* strengthened this fact. The Greek word means *will*, as in "last will and testament." According to F. S. Ranken, in a Greek will "the contradictions of inheritance were, indeed, in the first place at the sole discretion of the

71

testator, but it was publicly and solemnly executed, and there upon at once became absolute, irrevocable, and unalterable."[1] The use of the word *testament* thus gave a finality to the covenant: the covenant made of old, fully set forth through Moses, now had its finality through the great Mediator, Jesus Christ, whose atoning death ratifies and validates the ancient covenant. The true mediator has come: He has made the sacrifice, Himself, and the covenant now has its final form.

In the making of a covenant, in addition to the two parties involved, there must be a law, and there must be the shedding of blood. The law had already been given by God from heaven to Moses. Now, the sacrifice, the Lamb of God (John 1:36), had come from heaven to make atonement for the sins of His people, the new human race born again in Him.

Hebrews then cites Jeremiah 31:31-34:

> 31. Behold, the days come, saith the LORD, that I will make a new covenant with the house of Israel, and with the house of Judah:
> 32. Not according to the covenant that I made with their fathers in the day that I took them by the hand to bring them out of the land of Egypt; which my covenant they brake, although I was an husband unto them, saith the LORD:
> 33. But this shall be the covenant that I will make with the house of Israel; After those days, saith the LORD, I will put my law in their inward parts, and write it in their hearts; and will be their God, and they shall be my people.
> 34. And they shall teach no more every man his neighbour, and every man his brother, saying, Know the LORD: for they shall all know me, from the least of them, unto the greatest of them, saith the LORD: for I will forgive their iniquity, and I will remember their sin no more.

In v. 8, God is spoken of as "finding fault with them," i.e., Israel. The covenant was good, but Israel was not. Therefore, a new covenant must be made, new in that another people will replace Israel. The twelve apostles replaced the twelve patriarchs, the sons of Jacob or Israel, to indicate that, while there was continuity, new peoples would be grafted into Abraham's stock (John 15:1-6; Rom. 11:15-24). God's covenant is the same one He made with the patriarchs, but new in that another people now replaces most of Israel. There is, however, a marked difference, v. 9 tells us, between the covenant made by Moses and that made by Jesus Christ. With the covenant at Sinai, God demonstrated in very remarkable and miraculous ways His redeeming power towards Israel, but they were rebellious and faithless.

With this new covenant, God now writes His covenant and the covenant law in the hearts of His people (v. 10). God gives the law to their *minds* and writes it on their *hearts*. It is now not only God's law, but also the very

---

[1] F. S. Ranken, "Testament," in James Hastings, editor, *A Dictionary of Christ and the Gospels*, vol. 2 (Edinburgh, Scotland: T. & T. Clark, 1908), 717.

personal law of His people. The law was then engraved on tablets of stone, now in the life and flesh of His people. Paul speaks of this in 2 Corinthians 3:7-18. The Holy Spirit indwells Christ's new human race in a way surpassing His presence in the Old Testament era.

Because God's law now indwells His people, He is fully their God, and they are His new human race (1 Cor. 15:45ff.).

When the fullness of this change triumphs, then, in the words of Isaiah 11:9, "They shall not hurt nor destroy in all my holy mountain: for the earth shall be full of the knowledge of the LORD, as the waters cover the sea." In that time of victory, all men shall know the LORD, "from the least of them to the greatest of them" (Jer. 31:34).

Why will there be this greater knowledge, victory, and power? It arises out of God's grace and mercy whereby through Christ their sins are forgiven and forgotten, and they are truly freed from the curse and its power (v. 12). The foundation for a renewed mankind and a cleansed world is the atonement by Jesus Christ. The Hebrews are told that the great victory and renewed earth foreseen by the prophets is totally dependent on Jesus Christ's high priestly work. His atonement allows the regenerating power of the triune God to complete God's creative purpose. To reject Jesus Christ as high priest is to reject His atonement and to abandon His victory.

The old covenant, v. 13 tells us, is ready to vanish away forever. The Jewish-Roman War, A.D. 66-70, destroyed Israel and the Temple. To cling to the high priesthood of Aaron was to insist on dying with that order. In the new order, God's covenant law would not be merely external but also fully internal. Clearly, in Psalm 119 the psalmist demonstrates how intensely internalized the law was before Christ. The difference was the atonement, and the radical forgiveness of sins. The nagging handicap of sin and the lingering problem of a troubled conscience give way to freedom in Christ. Antinomians see the law as a burden and penalty, rather than sin as the disappearing element, and they thereby warp the meaning of the atonement. It is not the law that disappears but the old sacrificial system and its priesthood. Christ's atonement gives freedom and power.

Chapter Eighteen
The True Sanctuary
(*Hebrews 9:1-12*)

1. Then verily the first covenant had also ordinances of divine service, and a worldly sanctuary.
2. For there was a tabernacle made; the first, wherein was the candlestick, and the table, and the shewbread; which is called the sanctuary.
3. And after the second veil, the tabernacle which is called the Holiest of all;
4. Which had the golden censer, and the ark of the covenant overlaid round about with gold, wherein was the golden pot that had manna, and Aaron's rod that budded, and the tables of the covenant;
5. And over it the cherubims of glory shadowing the mercyseat; of which we cannot now speak particularly.
6. Now when these things were thus ordained, the priests went always into the first tabernacle, accomplishing the service of God.
7. But into the second went the high priest alone once every year, not without blood, which he offered for himself, and for the errors of the people:
8. The Holy Ghost this signifying, that the way into the holiest of all was not yet made manifest, while as the first tabernacle was yet standing:
9. Which was a figure for the time then present, in which were offered both gifts and sacrifices, that could not make him that did the service perfect, as pertaining to the conscience;
10. Which stood only in meats and drinks, and divers washings, and carnal ordinances, imposed on them until the time of reformation.
11. But Christ being come an high priest of good things to come, by a greater and more perfect tabernacle, not made with hands, that is to say, not of this building;
12. Neither by the blood of goats and calves, but by his own blood he entered in once into the holy place, having obtained eternal redemption for us. (Hebrews 9:1-12)

These verses give us a summary of the Holy Place and the Holy of Holies, and some of the main items contained in them. The description does not follow the placement given in the Mosaic account but the practice of New Testament times; this is particularly true of the golden censer.

The instruments and utensils used in the rituals of atonement and their locale are cited. At this point it might be helpful to distinguish between a *liturgy* and a *ritual*; the words are close enough in terms of connotation to be confused. A *liturgy* is literally a public work or service. Religion was once a department of state, and a liturgy was a public work or service to gain the favor of the gods of the state. The origin of the word is Greek. A *rite* or a *ritual* is a carefully prescribed form whereby a service is rendered, or a kind of activity is conducted. The Latin origin of the word *rite* is related to the Greek word *arithmetic.* This helps us to understand why correct form is so important in rituals, as, for example, in the marriage ritual; among the required forms are the consenting vows of both the bride and the groom.

Here in Hebrews, the specific concern is with the act of atonement, and the high priest. But a ritual is for repetition and commemoration, whereas Jesus Christ's work of atonement cannot be repeated. The ritual of the tabernacle and the Temple ended with His act of atonement. The ritual of communion celebrates Christ's atonement, but it cannot repeat it.

A *liturgy* is related to a *rite* but is more akin to a public celebration. The rites of matrimony and communion can take place within the framework of a liturgy, but a liturgy has a broader scope. It can include a sermon, reserved last rites administered to the dying (once common among some Protestants), and more.

The concern in Hebrews is with the rite of atonement. The framework is the *first* covenant, the one going back to the patriarchs, if not earlier, and formalized in the law given to Moses. The whole liturgy of the sanctuary included much more, things like thank offerings, for example. All these various rites were meaningless if the rite of atonement were left out. The heart of the liturgy and of the sanctuary was the rite of atonement, and this was basic to the priestly calling. The sanctuary of, and in, this world had ordinances of divine service (v. 1) as decreed by God.

At this point some are tempted to see the heavenly sanctuary in terms of Plato, as the pattern or idea for the earthly one. This warps the meaning of Hebrews. The heavenly sanctuary is not simply a Platonic idea but the governing reality. The earthly sanctuary is in some way a dim reflection of the heavenly one.

The sanctuary as it existed in Israel had two key parts, the Holy Place and the Holy of Holies (vv. 2-3). The key things within these two areas are cited in vv. 2-5. The holy place was constantly used by the priests in the service of God (v. 6). The Holy of Holies was used once every year by the high priest to make atonement for himself and for the people (v. 7).

In v. 8, Hebrews tells us that the Holy Ghost Himself was speaking through and in the text of the law. He was saying, "the way into the holiest of all was not yet made manifest," as long as the sanctuary prescribed by the law was still standing. Instead of a once a year entrance into the Holy of Holies by the high priest of Aaron, in and through Jesus Christ we have continual access to the throne of grace. This is possible because of our high priest's act of atonement.

As long as the typical sanctuary, sacrifices, and priesthood remained, the access was a limited one. With Christ's sacrifice the access became a perpetual one. This therefore could be called "the time of reformation" (v. 10). Until then, the service or rite was imperfect (v. 9).

Now, having the true high priest, Jesus Christ, the old forms are abolished because the true high priest and sacrifice has come. He is a "high priest of good things to come," and He is in our heavenly sanctuary, one "not made with hands, that is to say, not of this building" (v. 11), or, more accurately, not of this creation, but of the eternal new heaven and earth.

Moreover, Christ made this efficacious atonement, not by means of animal sacrifices, "but by his own blood he entered in once into the holy place, having obtained eternal redemption for us" (v. 12). He is both sacrifice and priest, both the Son of God and the Son of Man, and His atoning work is not a ritual but also the reality of atonement. He is, moreover, not only the great High Priest but the universal King, King over all kings.

Westcott called attention to the three aspects of Christ's *present* work as High Priest, as referred to in Hebrews. *First*, Jesus Christ is our intercessor in the Trinity, according to Hebrews 7:25, "to the uttermost." We cannot *limit* His intercessory power any more than we can prescribe its operation. He is our intercessor for our sins. He is "in the presence of God for us" (Heb. 9:24).

Second, Christ carries our prayers and praise to the throne of God. Praise is, we are told, a form of *sacrifice* (Heb. 13:15). In praise we turn our attention to God's goodness towards us rather than our demands of Him, and, in this sense, praise is a surrender of our concerns to a grateful rejoicing in God.

Third, Jesus Christ secures for us perpetual access to the heavenly sanctuary because, by His atoning blood, He had made us a new creation and members of His new humanity (Heb. 4:16). We have access "in full assurance of faith" because by His work we have a cleansed conscience (Heb. 10:19-22).

We now rest, not on a ritual of atonement but upon Christ's actual atonement. The fallacy of Israel was that it gave to the Temple a fixed and unending importance, whereas the Temple signified the Coming One. One of the charges against Jesus was that He had declared Himself to be God's true Temple (Mark 14:58).

Today, too often the church sees itself as a new temple, as the goal of Christ's work rather than as His instrument. This underscores the continuing urgent relevance of Hebrews; Christ alone is the true sanctuary and Redeemer.

Chapter Nineteen
Rite versus Reality
(*Hebrews: 9-13-17*)

13. For if the blood of bulls and of goats, and the ashes of an heifer sprinkling the unclean, sanctifieth to the purifying of the flesh:
14. How much more shall the blood of Christ, who through the eternal Spirit offered himself without spot to God, purge your conscience from dead works to serve the living God?
15. And for this cause he is the mediator of the new testament, that by means of death, for the redemption of the transgressions that were under the first testament, they which are called might receive the promise of eternal inheritance.
16. For where a testament is, there must also of necessity be the death of the testator.
17. For a testament is of force after men are dead: otherwise it is of no strength at all while the testator liveth. (Hebrews 9:13-17)

Hebrews is concerned with demonstrating the finality of Christ's work. The word that best characterizes Aaron's priesthood is *repetition*. Over and over again, year after year, the sacrifice of atonement was made. The sanctuary had a required ritual in which repetition was inevitable because no full atonement was possible. However much the high priestly sacrifices were important in setting forth the meaning of atonement, and however closely the typical sacrifices tied the sacrificers to the Coming One, they were not efficacious in any final sense: they awaited the true High Priest and the true and final sacrifice who would make ultimate atonement. Repetition had to give way to the final and totally efficacious atonement. The Levitical high priest and his sacrifices were pale shadows of the reality to come. *Liturgy can never replace reality*: it can foreshadow or represent it, but it is not itself the reality it represents.

But men are often wedded to forms and shadows in preference to reality. They prefer the partial to the full reality because no room is then left for their own free activities. Men prefer the shadows of ritual to the living Presence of God.

In vv. 13-14, we are told that the Levitical sacrifices had a partial validity, not in and of themselves, but as typifying that which was to come. The reference is to the yearly sacrifices of goats and bulls on the Day of Atonement (Lev. 16), and to the sacrifice of the red heifer (Num. 19). These gave the worshipper freedom to worship and to enter into communion with the covenant God. Jesus Christ offered Himself as an unblemished sacrifice to God. His own eternal Spirit was fully involved in this sacrifice whereby He purged our conscience "from dead works to serve the living God." The reference to Christ's "eternal Spirit" tells us that, from all eternity, the atonement was Christ's calling and purpose.

This is why He is "the mediator of the new testament" (v. 15). The atonement is not an afterthought but is central to the being of God the Son. By His death, all who are called "receive the promise of eternal inheritance." His death, His blood, effects a cleansing and a renewal in us. All the transgressions of God's elect people "that were under the first testament" or covenant are wiped out. Because this letter is to the Hebrews, this pointed reference to the people of that covenant (the Greek word means both "testament" and "covenant") is to stress that all atonement with reference to the Old Testament era depends on Christ's atoning work. By the death of Christ, they "receive the promise of eternal inheritance." The choice is theirs: the signs and types of the Old Testament ritual, or the reality in Christ.

A testament requires "the death of the testator" (v. 16). When the testator dies, the inheritance then goes into effect. Without the testator's death, there is no inheritance. The death of Jesus Christ opens for us the will for His people. In Revelation, the opening of the testament also opens up the great warfare to alienate the inheritance from Christ's people, a bitter but futile war.

The force or legal status of a testament requires the death of the testator (v. 17). A will becomes effective when there is a death. Thus, for all the promises of God to men from Adam through the prophets, the will did not go into effect until Christ died. As Revelation makes clear (Rev. 5:1ff.), the will is made and is also opened up by Jesus Christ. Although contested by all the powers of this world, it is finally put into force, and the great proclamation follows: "The kingdoms of this world are become the kingdoms of our Lord, and of his Christ; and he shall reign for ever and ever" (Rev. 11:15). The crucified Christ makes the testament, and the resurrected Christ reigns triumphant with His people.

We began by calling attention to the *finality* of Christ's work. This is a basic aspect of the Gospel. There is nothing tentative about Christ's work: it is eternally efficacious. God's works are never problematical nor incomplete. In every area, His ways are total and perfect. His work of creation was "very good" (Gen. 1:31). His predestination is total, for "the very hairs of your head are all numbered" (Matt. 10:30).

What man does is tentative and partial, but not so with God. Hebrews, by here stressing the finality of Christ and of His atonement, cuts the ground out from under mediatorial groups, persons, and ministries. The Levitical priesthood could not compare with Jesus Christ. Similarly, the church cannot arrogate to itself power restricted to the Redeemer King. At issue in Hebrews is the unwarranted claim by the Temple and synagogue to a mediatorial function between God and man. The church too has at times exalted the institution over its Lord, with devastating results. Instead of a people with clean consciences before God, we have then a weakened and conscience stricken people. The church that exalts itself dishonors Christ.

Chapter Twenty

Atonement and Action
(*Hebrews: 9:18-28*)

18. Whereupon neither the first testament was dedicated without blood.
19. For when Moses had spoken every precept to all the people according to the law, he took the blood of calves and of goats, with water, and scarlet wool, and hyssop, and sprinkled both the book, and all the people.
20. Saying, This is the blood of the testament which God hath enjoined unto you.
21. Moreover he sprinkled with blood both the tabernacle, and all the vessels of the ministry.
22. And almost all things are by the law purged with blood; and without shedding of blood is no remission.
23. It was therefore necessary that the patterns of things in the heavens should be purified with these; but the heavenly things themselves with better sacrifices than these.
24. For Christ is not entered into the holy places made with hands, which are the figures of the true; but into heaven itself, now to appear in the presence of God for us:
25. Nor yet that he should offer himself often, as the high priest entereth into the holy place every year with blood of others;
26. For then must he often have suffered since the foundation of the world: but now once in the end of the world hath he appeared to put away sin by the sacrifice of himself.
27. And, it is appointed unto men once to die, but after this the judgment:
28. So Christ was once offered to bear the sins of many; and unto them that look for him shall he appear the second time without sin unto salvation. (Hebrews 9:18-28)

The references in our text to the making of the covenant are to Exodus 24 and 34. This was a testament or covenant in blood, half of which was sprinkled on the altar, and half on the people (Ex. 24:6-8). This set forth the covenant vow of both parties, God and the covenant people, to be faithful unto death to the covenant and the covenant law. This Exodus covenant is called the *first* (v. 18) because it is the first with a people as a whole and not restricted to a man and his family.

In v. 19, we are told that Moses gave "every precept" of the law to the people *before* sprinkling the book and all the people. *The book* refers to the covenant law book. This is material new to us but apparently well known, i.e., that the covenant laws, given to Moses on the mount, were also sprinkled. We are given the laws other than the Ten Commandments *after* the ratification of the covenant. Apparently the Ten Commandments, as the summary of the whole law, represented all the law. The text indicates that *every commandment had been spoken to all the people*, which may have been the case before the ratification by blood.

Moses, in so doing, declared, "This is the blood of the testament which God hath enjoined unto you" (v. 20). These words were echoed at the Last Supper by Jesus: "This cup is the new testament in my blood" (1 Cor. 11:25), and their meaning was inescapable to the disciples. This blood "God hath enjoined unto you," or, purposed for you.

Moses "sprinkled with blood both the tabernacle, and all the vessels of the ministry" (v. 21). This is partly described in Exodus 40, so we know that only when the sanctuary was first built was symbolic sprinkling done.

In v. 22, we are told that "almost all things are by the law purged with blood; and without shedding of blood is no remission," i.e., of sin. The "almost" means that in some instances, such as Exodus 19:10, purification was all that was required. (Other examples are Ex. 32:30-32; Lev. 15:5; 16:26-28; 22:6; Num. 16:46-48; 31:23f.; Ps. 32:1f.; 51:1-17.)

In v. 23, we are told that the two sanctuaries, the one on earth, and the one in heaven, require purification before men can have access to God. The earthly sanctuary can be cleansed by means of these typical sacrifices, the blood of bulls and of goats, but the heavenly sanctuary requires much more, the atoning sacrifice of Christ. The earthly sanctuary typifies access to God, while the heavenly sanctuary is the reality. Therefore only Christ's atonement effects for us the perfect access to the triune God. The penalty for sin is death. Jesus Christ, as our representative and federal head, provides Himself as our vicarious substitute, to die for our sins. The Levitical system is a shadow of the reality and cannot be given priority above Jesus Christ, our great High Priest. Neither temple nor church can make of itself either a closed door or the true access.

Verse 24 tells us that the true cleansing power belongs to the blood of Jesus Christ. The earthly sanctuary was made by hands. Christ did not enter into the Holy of Holies in Jerusalem but in heaven, to make effectual atonement for us and to represent us in the very presence of God. We are constantly and continually before God, before His very face, in the person of Jesus Christ, so that we are never forgotten, nor can be.

In vv. 25-26, we are told that, while there is perpetual intercession (v. 24), there is no continuing sacrifice as with the Levitical priesthood. The high priests of the Levitical line had to make an annual and typical atonement. They offered, not their own blood, but the blood of the sacrificial animals. Their sacrifices required repetition because they were not forever effectual. Now, at *the consummation of the ages* (M. R. Vincent), rather than "the end of the world," Jesus Christ set forth the goal, the true atonement, whereby the new human race is created and the new heavens and earth begun. Sin has been put away from us, and the power of death broken. Jesus Christ, the eternally existent one (cf. 1 Tim. 3:16), was from all eternity our appointed Redeemer.

In vv. 27-28, we are told that it is "appointed unto men once to die, but after this the judgment." Christ's redeemed people see Him "a second time" as the Sinless One who saved His people. As Judge He will award eternal salvation to His people. The fullness of salvation is brought in by His coming at the end of history.

The goal of Christ's first coming was *atonement*. Our sins are forgiven, and we are made His new human race. Our goal is now given to us, as in Matthew 28:18-20, to disciple all nations, teaching them all things which our Lord commands, and bringing all things into captivity to Christ our King. The goal of Christ's second coming is to bring in the fullness of His Kingdom.

The theology of salvation has now been given to us. Beginning in chapter 10, Hebrews goes on to apply this salvation to our daily lives. The purpose of Jesus Christ, God the Son, is not to enhance the Levitical sacrifices but to declare that atonement is the prelude to service. God therefore is *not* satisfied with the forms of sacrifice (10:5), but He tells us that our lives must reflect that of the Servant Son, who says, "Lo, I come (in the volume of the book it is written of me) to do all thy will, O God" (10:7).

We are given this strong statement and warning because the church, like the Temple and synagogue, gets easily wrapped up in its own life rather than life in Christ. The forms of worship replace faithfulness and service, and the church in effect makes an end of itself. In chapters 11-12, Hebrews strongly stresses the living faith of past saints to separate us from an institutional piety, and unto faith at work in the world. We are shown that faith is never abstracted from the context of life and its challenges and problems. The Epistle of James is rightly placed after Hebrews because both stress faith with works (James 1:22-27; 2:14-26).

Atonement leads to action, not to withdrawal and retreat.

Chapter Twenty-One

"To Do Thy Will, O God"
(Hebrews: 10:1-10)

1. For the law having a shadow of good things to come, and not the very image of the things, can never with those sacrifices which they offered year by year continually make the comers thereunto perfect.
2. For then would they not have ceased to be offered? because that the worshippers once purged should have had no more conscience of sins.
3. But in those sacrifices there is a remembrance again made of sins every year.
4. For it is not possible that the blood of bulls and of goats should take away sins.
5. Wherefore when he cometh into the world, he saith, Sacrifice and offering thou wouldest not, but a body hast thou prepared me:
6. In burnt offerings and sacrifices for sin thou hast had no pleasure.
7. Then said I, Lo, I come (in the volume of the book it is written of me,) to do thy will, O God.
8. Above when he said, Sacrifice and offering and burnt offerings and offering for sin thou wouldest not, neither hast pleasure therein; which are offered by the law;
9. Then said he, Lo, I come to do thy will, O God. He taketh away the first, that he may establish the second.
10. By the which will we are sanctified through the offering of the body of Jesus Christ once for all. (Hebrews 10:1-10)

In v. 1 reference is made to "the law." Again, this does not refer to the law as a whole but to the law of sacrifices, to atonement, and to the priesthood. The context makes it clear that the law here means the sacrificial law; to make *law* mean more than this means to falsify the Letter to the Hebrews. The reference to repetition, to the fact that the sacrifices were "offered year by year continually," makes very clear that it is wrong to see any reference here to the law as a whole, and to do so is to pervert the text.

Verse 2 reinforces this. If the sacrificial law, or, if the sacrifices, provided atonement in the full sense thereof, then the worshipper would be fully cleansed of his sins and would have a clean conscience. His status before God would be one of a full and final atonement, and no more repetition would be necessary.

The law of sacrifices, and of the priesthood, is declared to be "a shadow of good things to come" (v. 1). The use of the word *shadow* is very important. The writers are all Jews, and Paul's background was strictly so. Here, however, a line is drawn between Christianity and Judaism. As practiced and continued, Judaism is here depicted as dedicated to *shadows* rather than reality. Where a shadow religion is present, the emphasis is on the present apparency rather than the reality. Man's action then replaces God's reality, because limitation to shadows gives priority to the existing practice rather than to God's full revelation. In contemporary church life, too commonly the shadow of ritual and sacrament are allowed to predominate over the reality they are supposed to set forth. The shadows of ritual leave the worshipper dependent upon the church, whereas the reality of Christ's atonement should purge the conscience of sin (v. 2).

Verse 3 tells us, "But in those sacrifices there is a remembrance again made of sins every year." The sacrificial law's requirement of repetitive sacrifices is an acknowledgment of their limited efficacy. Their constant renewal is a reminder of their limited efficacy. But there is more: "For it is not possible that the blood of bulls and of goats should take away sins" (v. 4). While the sacrificial animals are an unblemished offering, they are not a voluntary one: the animals never volunteered themselves, nor could their sacrificial death be more than typical, not perfect and totally efficacious. Hence the necessity for repetition.

In vv. 5-7, we have Christ and His self-sacrifice contrasted to the animal offerings:

> 5. Wherefore when he cometh into the world, he saith, Sacrifice and offering thou wouldest not, but a body hast thou prepared me:
> 6. In burnt offerings and sacrifices for sin thou hast had no pleasure.
> 7. Then said I, Lo, I come (in the volume of the book it is written of me,) to do thy will, O God.

The contrast here is between the involuntary death of sacrificial animals and the voluntary self-sacrifice of Jesus Christ, who is God incarnate, truly man and truly God. God ordained the sacrificial system to set forth the meaning of atonement to mankind, but He does not see animal sacrifices as full atonement. If any assume that such sacrifices will satisfy God, their offerings will be rejected. Sin cannot be propitiated by the blood of bulls and of goats.

Instead, a body had been ordained and prepared for God the Son, in a true incarnation, so that, in fulfillment of the covenant, God rescues man as truly man yet truly God. The sacrifice made by the Son, our great high priest as well as our representative and vicarious sacrifice, is a *voluntary* one, unlike the animals sacrificed. In fact, He declares from all eternity, "Lo, I come (in the volume of the book it is written of me,) to do thy will, O God" (v. 7). His self-sacrifice is thus not only *voluntary* but also *foreordained*. The "book" is the Old Testament, and the expression "it is written" does not mean here that it is merely inscribed, but that it is the eternally true word of God. It had the same force as in Matthew 4:4,7, and 10, where our Lord cites Deuteronomy against Satan. It refers to the eternal truth of God's word and being.

Jesus Christ is chosen to exemplify the words of Isaiah 6:8, "Here am I: send me." As members of His new human race (1 Cor. 15:47ff.), we too must echo His words: "Lo, I come, to do thy will, O God." By His coming, Jesus Christ terminates the sacrificial system to establish God's own way of atonement. The reality has come.

Verse 10 sums it up: "By the which will we are sanctified through the offering of the body of Jesus Christ once for all." As Jesus declared on the cross, "It is finished," (John 19:30), it is accomplished. Atonement had been made, once and for all time.

The finality of Christ is thus emphatically set forth. There is no other way to atonement, no other way to God, no other way to freedom from sin and death. Because Jesus Christ is God the Son incarnate, He is the way to knowledge of and communion with God. Jesus Christ declares that He is the door: access to God is through Him and none other (John 10:7,9).

Many resent the exclusiveness of Christ's being, and the exclusiveness of orthodox Christian theology, but without exclusiveness there is no truth. Black is not white, nor is a dead man alive. There are not many ways to God, nor is truth *man-made*, although it can be *known* by man.

The purpose of the atonement is that, as a new creation, we serve the triune God with all our heart, mind, and being. To do the will of God is the purpose of our regeneration. Hebrews is radically oriented to a practiced faith.

Note: The cultural implications of the preference of many in the church for shadows over reality had its effect on the world at large. Instead of shadows, phantasms prevail. In the world of art, reality (not necessarily the same as realism) gave way to abstractionism in time, and an abandonment by many of reality. In literature, films, and television, the "real world" has become, at best, the shadowy world of man's imagination. In the world of business, the observation in September, 1996, of a highly successful corporate executive was, that his key to success was this: make decisions for investors because they want no responsibility. This trend first appeared in pastoral counseling after World War II: persons with a most obvious choice with regard to their future still insisted that the pastor decide for them. By so doing, they could blame him and play the victim if things failed to work out.

The world of shadows leads to irresponsibility.

When in v. 8 the prophet's denunciation of sacrifice is cited, it does not mean that God rejected the sacrificial system which He had ordained, but that He rejected men's trust in the shadow as reality. To trust in the shadow for efficacy is to deny the reality.

Chapter Twenty-Two
Remission of Sins and Freedom
(*Hebrews: 10:11-18*)

11. And every priest standeth daily ministering and offering oftentimes the same sacrifices, which can never take away sins:
12. But this man, after he had offered one sacrifice for sins for ever, sat down on the right hand of God;
13. From henceforth expecting till his enemies be made his footstool.
14. For by one offering he hath perfected for ever them that are sanctified.
15. Whereof the Holy Ghost also is a witness to us: for after that he had said before,
16. This is the covenant that I will make with them after those days, saith the Lord, I will put my laws into their hearts, and in their minds will I write them;
17. And their sins and iniquities will I remember no more.
18. Now where remission of these is, there is no more offering for sin. (Hebrews 10:11-18)

We are told, in v. 11, that every priest in Israel stood daily, as he officiated in the Temple, repeating sacrifices for the people which could "never take away sins." If the worshipper's trust was in the ritual of animal sacrifices, there was no atonement for him. Only if he recognized that the animal represented the unblemished Lamb of God, still to come, was there in any sense a remission of his sins.

Every priest *stood* in the Temple. As he officiated, he was a part of an unfinished act of atonement. The exception to this requirement to stand and serve is evident in 2 Samuel 7:18, where David, a type of Christ, *sat* before the Lord.

Verse 12 tells us that "this man," Jesus Christ, "after he had offered one sacrifice for sins for ever, sat down at the right hand of God." Atonement had been fully made, and the Great High Priest sat down on His throne in heaven, "on the right hand of God," to rule forever. As v. 13 tells us, "From henceforth expecting till his enemies be made his footstool," an image of total power and conquest. This is a remarkable challenge to all who were tempted to return to Judaism, with its Temple and Levitical priesthood. As against a priesthood with very grave limitations, in Christ there is, *first*, a High Priest at the right hand of God, ready to intercede for His people at any and all times. His atonement is fully and totally efficacious; the repetitious act is replaced by a final and eternally binding act of deliverance from the power and the penalty of sin and death. Intercession on a continual basis replaces atonement. Atonement by Christ on the cross was fully complete and final: our sins are blotted out; we are judicially declared innocent; by Christ's regenerating power, we become a new creation. Because we are His new human race, He intercedes for us.

Second, He reigns, seated at "the right hand of God the Father, ...From henceforth expecting till his enemies be made his footstool" (v. 13). He reigns, He conquers, and He rules. For men to cling to shadows is to abandon victory and triumph. The shadow-worshippers look, not to victory, but to more shadows and rites, to a form of godliness and not to the power and substance thereof.

Of our King-Priest we are told, "For by one offering he hath perfected for ever them that are sanctified" (v. 14). The perfection referred to does not mean that we are totally sanctified. Rather, the sanctified, those set apart for atonement, receive a full and perfect remission of sins. There is no need for a repetition of the act: it is complete, and forever so. The reference is to the judicial act of being declared innocent by Christ's assumption of the death penalty for us. We can never be sentenced to death for sins for which Christ paid the penalty.

Then Hebrews cites a portion of Jeremiah 31:31-34 concerning the new covenant to be established by the Messiah. There will, in a sense, be a second giving of the law once given by Moses. This time, however, it will be written in the hearts of the believers, and in their minds. It will be the same law, but now a part of the being of the true members of the new covenant (vv. 15-16).

The text is from Jeremiah, but Hebrews tells us that it came from the Holy Ghost (v. 15). This text had been previously cited in Hebrews 8:8-12, and it is also referred to in Psalm 40:7-9, where the Messiah declares, "Lo, I come, in the volume of the book it is written of me," and then continues, "I delight to do thy will, O my God: yea, thy law is within my heart." The law of God is written in all of Christ's being, and we, as His new creation, have the same law inscribed in all our being. The law is the expression of God's being, His justice or righteousness; it must be the same for us. The Holy Spirit gives both the law and the enscriptured word of God.

This giving of a new nature, a new mind and heart, goes hand in hand with the remission of all our sins and iniquities (v. 17). They are no longer chargeable to us, and God will "remember them no more."

Thus, v. 18 concludes, "Now where remission of these is, there is no more offering for sin." The Temple, the Levitical priesthood, and the sacrificial system are ended. To imagine their return in any way, as does C. I. Scofield in his Bible notes, is blasphemous.

The plain implications of this are far-reaching. Wherever either the practice or the shadow of the sacrificial system remains, there religion is past-bound. It is governed by the need to make atonement for sins. Outside the true church, in the humanistic world, it means the endless use of psychotherapy, which offers not cure but an endless churning of the mind and memory. The result is a past-bound perspective. Not surprisingly, it has been Biblical faith that has opened up freedom and progress to man by the wiping out of sins through Christ's atonement.

From the humanistic perspective, the remission of sins is only possible by man, by psychotherapy, by education, by political acts designed to salve the conscience, and so on. Sigmund Freud recognized the mental health of Christians but damned it as accepting the cosmic neurosis (God) to avoid the personal neurosis, an explanation that said nothing more than to reveal Freud's warped mind.

For us, atonement by God the Son remits our sins and frees us from the past for a future under God. This is why Hebrews is practical in emphasis. Its goal is not a new ritual or shadow but *freedom and action in Christ*. The ritual of the church must be oriented to obedience, to action. The neglect of the diaconate is evidence of the failure of the modern church.

Chapter Twenty-Three
The Call to Service
(*Hebrews 10:19-25*)

19. Having therefore, brethren, boldness to enter into the holiest by the blood of Jesus,
20. By a new and living way, which he hath consecrated for us, through the veil, that is to say, his flesh;
21. And having an high priest over the house of God;
22. Let us draw near with a true heart in full assurance of faith, having our hearts sprinkled from an evil conscience, and our bodies washed with pure water.
23. Let us hold fast the profession of our faith without wavering; (for he is faithful that promised;)
24. And let us consider one another to provoke unto love and to good works:
25. Not forsaking the assembling of ourselves together, as the manner of some is; but exhorting one another: and so much the more, as ye see the day approaching. (Hebrews 10:19-25)

Up to this point, Hebrews has developed the doctrine of Christ's royal priesthood, His work as the Great High Priest who replaces in His person the Temple, the priesthood, and the sacrificial system. Now, as Westcott pointed out, certain practical consequences necessarily follow. Because Christ redeems us by His atonement, abolishes the power and the penalty of sin over us, and pays our death penalty for us, Christians are in a privileged position. "The privileges must be used: the duties must be discharged. The faith is not for speculation but for life."[1] Personal privileges require social duties. The atonement removes us from a world of rites to a world of service and duties. Whenever Christians have seen this requirement, a great expansion of the faith and the reorganization of society through that faith have occurred.

The Christian is now empowered "to enter into the holiest by the blood of Jesus" and to do this boldly (v. 19). In the Temple rite, the Levitical high priest could enter into the Holy of Holies only once a year, but through Christ every Christian has continual access to the throne of grace. It is the atonement, "the blood of Jesus," that makes this possible.

This we do "By a new and living way, which he has consecrated for us, through the veil, that is to say, his flesh" (v. 20). Jesus Christ is truly God and truly man. He makes us members of His new humanity as our second and last Adam. Our membership in Christ is not in His deity but in His *body*, His new humanity (1 Cor. 15:45ff.). Through His flesh, His humanity, of which we are made members by His atonement and His

---

[1.] Brooke Foss Westcott, *The Epistle to the Hebrews* (Grand Rapids, Michigan: Eerdmans, (1889) 1952), 317. Originally published in 1889.

regenerating power, we now pass into the holiest place with Him as our federal head. This is "a new and living way," a matter of life because we are now members of Him who is our life, our new Adam and our Redeemer. He is the true "high priest over the house of God" (v. 21). "The house of God" refers to Christ's people, His family, as in 1 Corinthians 3:16-17, 2 Corinthians 6:16, and Ephesians 2:22.

In v. 22 we are told, "Let us draw near with a true heart in full assurance of faith, having our hearts sprinkled from an evil conscience, and our bodies washed with pure water." The reference to baptism is clear; this is the rite of admission into the Messianic covenant, replacing circumcision. The sprinkling refers to the blood of the covenant (Ex. 24:8) being sprinkled over the people to ratify the covenant. We can only draw near to God in "full assurance of faith" and "with a true heart." There can be no clinging to the old Temple as against the new Temple, Jesus Christ. The reference in vv. 26-27 to "no more sacrifice for sins" but only judgment ahead, refers to those who reject Christ's priesthood and cling to the now abolished Levitical priesthood. It does not refer to the Christian who knows the reality of the atonement, but to those Hebrews who left or planned to leave Christ for the Levitical priesthood.

In v. 23, the readers and listeners are told, "Let us hold fast the profession of our faith without wavering; (for he is faithful that promised)." "The profession of our faith" is better rendered, "the confession of our hope" (M. R. Vincent, B. F. Westcott). As Westcott noted, "Hope gives us a definite shape to the absolute confidence of Faith. Faith reposes completely in the love of God: Hope vividly anticipates that God will fulfill His promises in a particular way."[2] Where faith is lacking, there is no hope, and, as faith has receded in the twentieth century, men have lost even faith in progress and in their future. Where there is no hope, there is no future.

In v. 24, we are told, "And let us consider one another to provoke unto love and to good works." We have a duty one to another to encourage each other in the faith, "unto love and to good works." More than a few churches have found how difficult it is to overcome the cynicism and indifference of a few members. The word "provoke" is an unusual one, and in the Greek it is "paroxusmon," from whence we get our word "paroxysm." It can be used in a good or a bad sense, and here it is good. It means to stimulate or to excite. We need to have a confident excitement and confidence in the faith. Our happy excitement can stimulate the faith of others.

Then in v. 25 the counsel is, "Not forsaking the assembling of ourselves together, as the manner of some is; but exhorting one another: and so much the more as ye see the day approaching." Then as now, many church

---

[2] *Ibid.,* 323.

members were very casual about church attendance, thereby showing their hesitation to make a full commitment to the faith. Rather, they should encourage and exhort one another. The concluding phrase urges this all the more "as ye see the day approaching." This is routinely taken to mean the second coming, but it must not be so limited. "The day" means much more: the judgment of God upon His enemies, the vindication of Christ's people, the triumph of Christ's Kingdom over all His enemies (Ps. 2), and much more. All time draws us closer to Christ's victory in all its facets, and we see many preliminary triumphs, beginning with the end of Rome's persecutions.

Christ's priesthood of necessity gives His people a forward look, a substitution for a sin-bound past by a grace-empowered future. For this reason, the setting forth of Christ's priesthood is followed in Hebrews by a record of past pilgrims to Christ's future. If these persons persevered in the face of great trials without Christ's coming and His atoning death and resurrection, then we certainly should stand fast in the faith and hold faithful allegiance "without wavering" (v. 23). True, as v. 36 will tell us, we do "have need of patience," but we are called unto victory (1 John 5:4), and we must persevere.

Chapter Twenty-Four
Apostasy
(*Hebrews 10:26-39*)

26. For if we sin wilfully after that we have received the knowledge of truth, there remaineth no more sacrifice for sins,

27. But a certain fearful looking for of judgment and fiery indignation, which shall devour the adversaries.

28. He that despised Moses' law died without mercy under two or three witnesses:

29. Of how much sorer punishment, suppose ye, shall he be thought worthy, who hath trodden under foot the Son of God, and hath counted the blood of the covenant, wherewith he was sanctified, an unholy thing, and hath done despite unto the Spirit of grace?

30. For we know him that hath said, Vengeance belongeth unto me, I will recompense, saith the Lord. And again, The Lord shall judge his people.

31. It is a fearful thing to fall into the hands of the living God.

32. But call to remembrance the former days, in which, after ye were illuminated, ye endured a great fight of afflictions;

33. Partly, whilst ye were made a gazingstock both by reproaches and afflictions; and partly, whilst ye became companions of them that were so used.

34. For ye had compassion of me in my bonds, and took joyfully the spoiling of your goods, knowing in yourselves that ye have in heaven a better and an enduring substance.

35. Cast not away therefore your confidence, which hath great recompense of reward.

36. For ye have need of patience, that, after ye have done the will of God, ye might receive the promise.

37. For yet a little while, and he that shall come will come, and will not tarry.

38. Now the just shall live by faith: but if any man draw back, my soul shall have no pleasure in him.

39. But we are not of them who draw back unto perdition; but of them that believe to the saving of the soul. (Hebrews 10:26-39)

The reference in v. 26 is to Deuteronomy 17:2-7, the law of apostasy. Apostasy is treason. The apostate referred to in Deuteronomy 17:2-7 was a man in the covenant who renounced it for another allegiance, and the penalty was death. The covenant was far more than an ecclesiastical membership, or a citizenship in a nation: it was a state of grace whereby a man had been given status in God's kingdom to live in His grace and by His law. To reject the covenant was to choose an allegiance to a power working against God and His reign. Therefore,

26. For if we sin wilfully after that we have received the knowledge of truth, there remaineth no more sacrifice for sins,

99

27. But a certain fearful looking for of judgment and fiery indignation, which shall devour the adversaries.

"Truth" in v. 26 refers to the Lord's commandments, as in Isaiah 26:10.[1] Modern man's idea of truth is Hellenic: it is an abstraction, an idea, whereas the Bible sets forth the fact that truth is God and His word, His law, justice, uprightness, and purpose. To sin against the truth is here to sin against Christ and His atonement. If the Hebrews prefer the Temple sacrifices and services to Christ's atonement, no atonement is possible for them. Rather, they face God's judgment and "fiery indignation" for despising the Son. The enemies of Jesus Christ and His atonement shall be "devoured" by God's judgment.

In v. 28, the reference is again to Deuteronomy 17:2-7. The apostate receive no mercy because theirs is a sign of treason with knowledge. The reason for sin is not a lack of knowledge, but an insistence on being judge over God and on being one's own god. The deliberateness of apostasy makes it all the more fearful a sin, according to v. 29:

29. Of how much sorer punishment, suppose ye, shall he be thought worthy, who hath trodden under foot the Son of God, and hath counted the blood of the covenant, wherewith he was sanctified, an unholy thing, and hath done despite unto the Spirit of grace?

Apostasy is a sin of staggering dimensions and consequences.

As Westcott pointed out, "the act of contemptuous rejection...rests on a deliberate judgment" about the blood of the covenant, about Jesus Christ. Joined with this is a basic hostility towards God the Father.[2] Hebrews is graphic in describing the apostate's contempt: they have in effect trodden underfoot Christ's atoning blood. They have counted the blood of the covenant "an unholy thing;" the word *counted* means that a deliberate decision and judgment are involved. Moreover, they have insulted "the Spirit of grace."

Christ's blood is the blood of God's covenant. It is thus the holiest of all things holy, and to show disrespect for it by preferring the blood of bulls and goats is an act of fearful arrogance and sin.

We dare not forget that in Deuteronomy 32:35, God declares vengeance to be His prerogative, and in Psalm 50:4 we are told that God will judge His people. God does not forget judgment with the coming of Jesus Christ. Rather, there is now a sharper promise of judgment. It is, therefore, "a fearful thing to fall into the hands of the living God" (v. 31; cf. Luke 12:5).

[1] George Wesley Buchanan, *To the Hebrews* (Garden City, New York: Doubleday, 1972), 171.

[2] Brooke Foss Westcott, *The Epistle to the Hebrews* (Grand Rapids, Michigan: Eerdmans, (1892) 1952), 330f. Originally published in 1892.

The authors, led by Paul, now turn to pleading with their readers by reminding them of their past faithfulness. *First*, after joining themselves to Christ's flock, "ye endured a great fight of afflictions" (v. 32). "Fight of afflictions" may refer to the actual presence of some arena events. *Second*, many of them either suffered for their faith or were "companions of them that were so used" (v. 33). To be "made a gazingstock" means to be exhibited in the arena, a grim fact. *Third*, and here Paul speaks out clearly, they are reminded of how they "joyfully" sacrificed their goods out of compassion and apparently to rescue Paul. They did this, "knowing in yourselves that ye have in heaven a better and an enduring substance" (v. 34).

One would think that, with such a record, these Hebrews would stand fast. But in 2 Timothy 4:10, we read that Demas, long a faithful coworker with Paul (Col. 4:14; Philemon 24), forsook Paul, "having loved this present world." It is not always easy to know what is in men, and men often do not know themselves.

Paul, in his personal note, adds vv. 35-39. Their holy boldness should not now be replaced with doubt, fear, and panic. Patience in the will of God will lead to great returns in God's time (v. 36). They must do the will of God to receive the promise.

Isaiah 26:20 and Habakkuk 2:3 are now cited together in vv. 36 and 37 to encourage the readers and listeners in faith and patience. They are then reminded that the just, or the justified, live by faith, not by sight. God has no pleasure in those who turn back, who apostasize (v. 38).

Then the writers ("we") declare that, as for themselves, they are not drawing back "unto perdition," for such is the consequence of going back to the Temple, its priesthood, and its sacrifices. "We," say the writers, are "of them that believe to the saving of the soul" (v. 39). This very blunt statement obviously denies that two ways to God, Jesus Christ and the Temple, exist. The Hebrews are plainly told that salvation is by Christ alone. Very early, Peter had declared, "Neither is there salvation in any other, for there is none other name under heaven given among men, whereby we must be saved" (Acts 4:12). To deny the exclusiveness of Christ is apostasy.

Thus, Hebrews not only irrevocably ties Christ's kingship to His high priestly office, requiring of us service to manifest our obedience to the King, but also declares Him *alone* to be man's Savior. Having established these premises, Hebrews then goes on in chapter 11 to define and illustrate faith, faith with works and action, faith as a God-ordained and God-governed pilgrimage.

Because of its great importance, and because of its authorship, Hebrews has a deliberate air to it. Like a symphonic composition, it moves to great climaxes, building from one to another. It is a magnificent work, and, hopefully, its time has come.

Chapter Twenty-Five
Faith
(*Hebrews 11:1-3*)

1. Now faith is the substance of things hoped for, the evidence of things not seen.
2. For by it the elders obtained a good report.
3. Through faith we understand that the worlds were framed by the word of God, so that things which are seen were not made of things which do appear. (Hebrews 11:1-3)

These verses are commonly misunderstood and misinterpreted because faith is assumed to be human belief. A man can believe that there is a God, but this is not what our text is about. We are told in James 2:19 that the devils believe, and tremble. In Psalm 14:1, we are told, "The fool hath said in his heart, There is no God." It is no great wisdom to believe in God because any other alternative is idiotic and mad.

Thus, what Hebrews speaks of is not any wisdom or insight gained by man through his reason and observation. Paul in Ephesians 2:8 tells us, "For by grace are ye saved through faith; and that not of yourselves; it is the gift of God."

In Hebrews 10:39, Paul and the apostolic company declare, "But we are not of them who draw back unto perdition; but of them that believe to the saving of the soul." No credit is claimed for this, for faith is immediately defined as a supernatural grace: "Now faith is the substance of things hoped for, the evidence of things not seen" (Heb. 11:1). Faith is the gift of God's grace, and it gives to all who receive it a forward look; time and eternity are now seen as a dimension of our lives and our duty.

With this supernatural faith, we enter into the world of reality. The words *substance* (*upostasis*) and *evidence* (*elegmos*) make this clear. Faith has enabled us to go beyond the blindness and foolishness of unbelief and to begin to see reality. Man's faith can accomplish little, but God's supernatural gift of faith can enable man to remove mountains of difficulties (Mark 11:23).

This gift of faith gives us a forward look. It is concerned with "things hoped for" and "things not seen," which are the things to come in God's great and holy purpose. Faith is the *substance* or *assurance* of these things. What God from all eternity has decreed, we by faith know to be an assured reality. Man by his human faith can hope for certain things, but this does not make them a reality.

In v. 2, we are told that by this supernatural gift of faith, the saints of old, living in this reality of faith, received a witness of the truth of God's promises. They were not vindicated by their personal beliefs but by the promises of God they embraced and followed.

In v. 3, the first mark of this gift of faith is cited; we understand and know the fact of creation: "we understand that the worlds were framed by the word of God, so that things which are seen were not made by things which do appear." For the ungodly, any "solution" to the question of the source of the universe is preferable to acknowledging God as Creator. Over the centuries, a variety of fantastic solutions have been devised, including Charles Darwin's gnostic dream, but none are more than imaginary concepts. To imagine that all of creation developed out of nothing, or out of some primordial spark, is to credit nothingness or some original atom with all the potentiality of the universe, which makes that origin equal to God without being God. The goal of the anti-creationists is a god without God.

The eternity of matter is denied. So too is the idea of modern twentieth century scientists like Eddington and Jeans, of a Supreme Mind behind the universe that makes no claims on man or creation. Such thinking is evasive of the basic moral claim that God makes on His creatures.

Apostasy is a retreat from truth. Faith is an advance empowered by truth. Faith is Christ-centered because God's purpose in history comes to focus in Him. Apostasy weighs the factor in personal terms: which course is wisest for me? Faith, on the other hand, looks to the future in Christ. In Hebrews 11:13, we are told, "These (Old Testament saints) all died in faith, not having received the promises, but having seen them afar off, and were persuaded of them, and embraced them, and confessed that they were strangers and pilgrims on the earth." We are allowed no illusions concerning the price of faith. Faith puts us at odds with a fallen world because it is the active presence of God's power and work. Faith is a gift and a blessing, and also a burden because it separates us from other men.

Calvin noted of the ungodly, "that they assigned to fortune or chance the supremacy in the government of the world, and they made no mention of God's providence which alone rules everything."[1] Because man is fallen, and his mind darkened by his revolt against God, he is ready to deny creationism and to embrace every kind of nonsense to avoid acknowledging God.

Faith is neither a trust nor a belief in the unknown, but the firm knowledge that God is God, that He is true to His word, and, that what He has promised He will bring to pass. Therefore, the writers of Hebrews declare, we do not shrink back, "we are not of them who draw back unto perdition; but of them that believe to the saving of the soul" (10:39).

[1.] John Calvin, *Commentaries on the Epistle to the Hebrews* (Grand Rapids, Michigan: Eerdmans, 1949 reprint), 265.

E. F. Scott held that in its definition of faith, Hebrews differs from the epistles of Paul: while Paul emphasizes the object of faith as "the cross of Christ, with its supreme revelation of the gracious will of God," "The writer to the Hebrews conceives of faith in a more comprehensive manner as the power by which we hold fast to the unseen, in spite of the illusions and temptations of the passing world."[2] But the whole point of Hebrews is to set forth Jesus Christ as the Great High Priest and sacrifice. There is no retreat on the Pauline statements concerning the Cross, only a further development of their meaning to reinforce the warning against retreat.

It should be apparent that, in relation to Scripture, faith is not the human response to God, but a God-given gift. As Hebrews 11 continues, we are told how this gift of faith empowered men and women to do remarkable things. The purpose is not to tell us how much men can do but how much God has accomplished in a hostile world through persons moved by faith. We do not depend upon ourselves for strength but upon God.

---

[2] E. F. Scott, "Hebrews," in Arthur S. Peake, *A Commentary on the Bible* (London, England: T. C. & E. C. Jack, 1920), 897.

Chapter Twenty-Six
Faith: From Abel to Noah
(*Hebrews 11:4-7*)

4. By faith Abel offered unto God a more excellent sacrifice than Cain, by which he obtained witness that he was righteous, God testifying of his gifts: and by it he being dead yet speaketh.
5. By faith Enoch was translated that he should not see death; and was not found, because God had translated him; for before his translation he had this testimony, that he pleased God.
6. But without faith it is impossible to please him: for he that cometh to God must believe that he is, and that he is a rewarder of them that diligently seek him.
7. By faith Noah, being warned of God of things not seen as yet, moved with fear, prepared an ark to the saving of his house; by the which he condemned the world, and became heir of the righteousness which is by faith. (Hebrews 11:4-7)

As Hebrews 11 develops the meaning of *faith*, we see that this gift of God becomes also a part of man's being, so that God's gift and man's will become united towards the same goal. God works in man, but man is now God's redeemed person, a new creation by God, and one in whom God works His will. Thus faith is not an alien power controlling us, but the essential part of our new nature in the Lord. Paul, in 2 Corinthians 5:17, tells us, "if any man be in Christ, he is a new creature (or, creation): old things are passed away; behold, all things are become new." To be a new creature or creation means that, whereas before we sought to be our own god and law (Gen. 3:5), now we strive to be what God intended man to be on the sixth day of creation. Instead of striving to be original, hence our original sin, we are happily derivative. We know ourselves to be God's creatures, and not our own. We therefore know that not only is our faith His gift, but all our being, and also every atom of our being, is of His making.

In v. 4, we are told, "By faith Abel offered unto God a more excellent sacrifice than Cain, by which he obtained witness that he was righteous, God testifying of his gifts: and by it he being dead yet speaketh." Genesis gives much evidence that God had revealed His law to His people long before Moses. Sacrifices of atonement had to be clean animals. Cain's sacrifice was one of thanksgiving, not atonement. Abel's sacrifice was alone acceptable to God, and it alone set him apart as a righteous or just man. Jesus Himself speaks of Abel as righteous in Matthew 23:35. In 1 John 3:12, we are told that Cain's works were evil, and Abel's righteous.

While dead, Abel still speaks to us. In a fallen world, the Godly are hated, but theirs is the final victory in Christ (1 John 5:4).

107

In v. 5 we have the remarkable case of Enoch, who was transferred from this world to heaven (Gen. 5:21-24). He did not see death. We are not given the details nor the highlights of his life, other than "that he pleased God."

The time of Enoch, and of all the godly patriarchs before the Flood, was one of extremes. The conditions which marked paradise still prevailed around the world, and one consequence was longevity. Enoch, whose life did not end in death, was on earth 365 years, while his son Methuselah lived 969 years (Gen. 5:23, 27). Without the judgment of a short lifespan, man was able to indulge freely in his will to evil. In fact, for some centuries death was a rarity because of man's longevity.

At the same time, because the world was fallen, this longevity made life difficult for the Godly because the penalty of death was remote, and fallen men could be contemptuous of judgment. For this reason, we are told of three of the saints of that era, Abel, Enoch, and Noah, as examples of faith. Their stand was a lonely one, and difficult.

In v. 6 we are plainly reminded that, "without faith it is impossible to please him: for he that cometh to God must believe that he is, and that he is a rewarder of them that diligently seek him." In v. 3, we are told that creationism is essential to the life of faith. Now two things are added: faith means believing that God is, and also that "he is a rewarder of them that diligently seek him." God is unseen but He is omnipresent. To believe in God means recognizing not only His absolute determination of all things as He who is, but also His total power and presence in all things, omnipresent but never exhaustively present. He is the Creator, Governor, and Judge. Faith knows Him to be the rewarder. We do not determine the reward: He does. He sets the course of our lives and our reward in terms of His purpose, not ours.

In v. 7, we are told of Noah's faith. He heeded God's warning and prepared an ark. His act condemned a world which refused to heed God's warning and no doubt mocked Noah's faith. By this act of faith, Noah saved his family but condemned the world. He thus "became heir to the righteousness which is by faith." This is a remarkable statement because men are prone to see Noah's act in terms of the loss it entailed, the loss of kin and of possessions, in exchange for life in an empty world, with none in it save his family. But he became, we are told, "heir of the righteousness (or, justice) which is by faith." He was in God's sight now justified, righteous, and a citizen of God's new creation to come.

True, man's longevity was soon a reduced one, and sin once again had its way. The Tower of Babel lay ahead, and much, much evil. But Abraham was an heir, eternally so, of the righteousness which is by faith.

We are told of Noah that he was "moved with fear," Godly fear, and this is greatly in his favor. It is a dangerous thing to be unafraid of God, and one can question the reality of faith where there is no fear. Since all things are under God's eye, and His judgments are inescapable, the absence of a Godly fear is a deadly blindness. Others in Noah's day laughed at Noah's warnings and paid a price for it. *"Moved* with fear" can be rendered, "taking forethought." Godly fear moves wisely. 2 Peter 2:5 tells us that Noah was "a preacher of righteousness" to his age.

These few verses, vv. 4-7, carry us from the Fall to the Flood. They tell us that *faith expresses itself in obedience.* It acts in obedience to God. Again, to be "moved with fear" means far more than an emotional reaction: it means "taking forethought" because we believe that God is, and that He is both a rewarder and a punisher; we cannot evade the fact that we are here to serve God, not ourselves, and our response to Him will determine our future. Our faith is a condemnation of this present world order and an affirmation that God is, and that He alone is the Great and final Judge.

With the Fall, men began to build a world order based on man as his own god and his own source of law (Gen. 3:5). This effort still goes on. God's people in Christ represent a new human race called into being to establish God's world order, with Christ as King. What fallen man seeks to do in terms of Genesis 3:5 is *an act of faith,* but an anti-God and demonic act of faith. Our act of faith is grounded in the certainty of God as Creator, Christ as our Redeemer, and our recreation as God's ordination of a new creation in terms of His word and purpose.

Chapter Twenty-Seven
Abraham, The Man of Faith
(*Hebrews 11:8-19*)

8. By faith Abraham, when he was called to go out into a place which he should after receive for an inheritance, obeyed; and he went out, not knowing whither he went.
9. By faith he sojourned in the land of promise, as in a strange country, dwelling in tabernacles with Isaac and Jacob, the heirs with him of the same promise.
10. For he looked for a city which hath foundations, whose builder and maker is God.
11. Through faith also Sara herself received strength to conceive seed, and was delivered of a child when she was past age, because she judged him faithful who had promised.
12. Therefore sprang there even of one, and him as good as dead, so many as the stars of the sky in multitude, and as the sand which is by the sea shore innumerable.
13. These all died in faith, not having received the promises, but having seen them afar off, and were persuaded of them, and embraced them, and confessed that they were strangers and pilgrims on the earth.
14. For they that say such things declare plainly that they seek a country.
15. And truly, if they had been mindful of that country from whence they came out, they might have had opportunity to have returned.
16. But now they desire a better country, that is, an heavenly: wherefore God is not ashamed to be called their God: for he hath prepared for them a city.
17. By faith Abraham, when he was tried, offered up Isaac: and he that had received the promises offered up his only begotten son,
18. Of whom it was said, That in Isaac shall thy seed be called:
19. Accounting that God was able to raise him up, even from the dead; from whence also he received him in a figure. (Hebrews 11:8-19)

The great example of faith now cited is Abraham, who gave up the most and gained the least in his own lifetime. It is true that Abraham was apparently rich when he left Haran, and he did become very rich when he obeyed God, but his trials and sufferings were very great. God severely tested Abraham's faith. This faith was God's gift, but God tested it and refined it in the fires of affliction.

In v. 8, we are told that Abraham went out at God's command, "not knowing whither he went." He went in the direction indicated by God, leaving friends and family behind, except for Lot.

Aliens have on the whole been none too welcome over the centuries, so that to be a foreigner anywhere has been a disadvantage. Usually, people leave their homeland either to escape persecution or for an opportunity to survive or advance economically. Neither cause motivated Abraham.

When Abraham came to "the land of promise," he dwelled there in tents, as did Isaac and Jacob, who were "heirs with him of the same promise" (v. 9). All "looked for a city which hath foundations, whose builder and maker is God" (v. 10). They were promised more than a land for themselves: they expected a new society founded on God's law and word, and it was this they longed for. This new city or social order would be the *reverse* of the Tower of Babel: its purpose would be, not the glory of man, but the glory of God. The world around them gave evidence of a steady deterioration. Their pilgrimage, and that of all the saints of the Old Testament, was towards the Kingdom or City of God.

Sarah herself received supernatural strength to conceive and bear Isaac in her old age because, in spite of her initial skeptical laughter, she trusted in God (v. 11). "She judged him faithful who had promised."

Out of Isaac came to Abraham a progeny eventually as innumerable as the stars and the sand by the seashore (v. 12).

These saints "died in faith, not having received the promises, but having seen them afar off, and were persuaded of them, and embraced them, and confessed that they were strangers and pilgrims on the earth" (v. 13). Their confession of faith was that they sought the Kingdom or City of God (v. 14), one unlike any on earth. They could always have returned to their original country, but their quest was for one not yet in existence (v. 15). They sought a city whose maker and builder is God, and they sought it knowing that it is a future city. For this faith, "God is not ashamed to be called their God: for he hath prepared for them a city" (v. 16). Is God ashamed to be called our God?

Thus, faith is the gift of God, but all who receive it are then tested and refined so that both they and the city may truly be of God.

This testing of faith can be a grim one. Abraham waited a long time for the birth of his promised son, Isaac, only to have God ask that Abraham sacrifice this son. Now, in due time, God did give up His only begotten Son as a sacrifice of atonement for our sins, but Abraham had no knowledge of this. He obeyed on the basis, *first*, that God had promised that through Isaac he would have a great and innumerable progeny. *Second*, Abraham believed that God could resurrect Isaac from the dead, "from whence also he received him a figure" (v. 19).

Abraham is singled out as the great type of faith because in him we see a remarkable obedience with almost no complaining or ingratitude. All who are the people of faith are called "the children of Abraham" (Gal. 3:7). Abraham as the type of faith tells us not only of the greatness of God's gift, but also how it can be made in man a powerful transforming force which can alter man and his world.

Westcott pointed out that, in Abraham, faith entered into a new phase in its history, moving from the personal to the societal:

> Faith is treated henceforth in relation to a society, a people of God, through whom the divine blessings were to be extended to mankind. Under this wider aspect Faith is regarded in two forms as shewn by the representative founders of the ancient people in (*a*) the Faith of patient Obedience which is the foundation of the Kingdom of God, and in (*b*) the Faith of Sacrifice which is the principle of its development.[1]

It is a mark of the church's decline in our time that too little is made of Abraham and his faith.

We are plainly told in v. 8 that when Abraham began his pilgrimage, he did not know where God intended for him to go, nor are we told of his reaction to Palestine. Although then still a wooded land, and with year-round streams, it was primitive compared to the area he left. It apparently did not occur to Abraham to question God's wisdom. His faith was one of unequivocal *trust*. Moreover, v. 10 tells us, he looked, not at the Palestine of his day, but to God and the future promised by God. Abraham knew how much the world had changed from Noah's youth to his own day, and he knew that nothing was impossible for God. The Kingdom of God would be far more glorious than anything the builders of the Tower of Babel ever imagined.

Like Abraham, we too are pilgrims, but God's realm is far closer than in Abraham's day. As our day draws near, the battle intensifies, and the hostilities increase, but the Lord is no less able to deal with His enemies than at Babel and Calvary.

What is at issue is how we use the gift of faith. Ours is a great gift, one we dare not despise or abuse.

---

[1] Brooke Foss Westcott, *The Epistle to the Hebrews* (Grand Rapids, Michigan: Eerdmans, 1952), 357. Originally published in 1892.

Chapter Twenty-Eight
"By Faith Moses"
(*Hebrews 11:20-29*)

20. By faith Isaac blessed Jacob and Esau concerning things to come.
21. By faith Jacob, when he was dying, blessed both the sons of Joseph; and worshipped, leaning upon the top of his staff.
22. By faith Joseph, when he died, made mention of the departing of the children of Israel; and gave commandment concerning his bones.
23. By faith Moses, when he was born, was hid three months of his parents, because they saw he was a proper child; and they were not afraid of the king's commandment.
24. By faith Moses, when he was come to years, refused to be called the son of Pharaoh's daughter;
25. Choosing rather to suffer affliction with the people of God, then to enjoy the pleasures of sin for a season;
26. Esteeming the reproach of Christ greater riches than the treasures of Egypt: for he had respect unto the recompense of the reward.
27. By faith he forsook Egypt, not fearing the wrath of the king: for he endured, as seeing him who is invisible.
28. Through faith he kept the passover, and the sprinkling of blood, lest he that destroyed the firstborn should touch them.
29. By faith they passed through the Red sea as by dry land: which the Egyptians assaying to do were drowned. (Hebrews 11:20-29)

In v. 20, we are told, "By faith Isaac blessed Jacob and Esau concerning things to come." Our reaction, on reading the Genesis 27 account, is to focus on Isaac's false hope concerning Esau. Hebrews, on the other hand, places the emphasis on Isaac's faith in that realm whose builder and maker is God. Where men walk by sight, they have short-term vision, but to walk by faith means that we move in terms of all time and eternity. This Hebrews does not allow us to forget.

Jacob is also singled out for his faith, and for having blessed Joseph's two sons. They were thus exalted to the position lost by Reuben, the first-born. This is a curious fact, because Judah in actuality replaced Reuben. Jacob blessed Ephraim, the younger of Joseph's two sons. Why were Joseph's sons blessed? What was their relationship to the City of God? Humanly speaking, Joseph's sons, as half-Egyptian and members of a powerful family, were born rich; surely, they needed no additional inheritance. But Jacob by his blessing included them in God's promise. Their future was not to be in Egypt but in Israel (v. 21).

In v. 22, Joseph in dying looked also to God's promised realm, and he therefore instructed his family to carry his body in due time back to the Promised Land.

Moses is the focus of vv. 23-29. At age three months, he was hidden by his parents in faith and was discovered and adopted by Pharaoh's daughter, but on coming of age, he identified himself with the Hebrews rather than Pharaoh's family. His choice was affliction as against "the pleasures of sin" (v. 25). He did this, we are told, "Esteeming the reproach of Christ greater riches than the treasures of Egypt: for he had respect unto the recompense of the reward" (v. 26). Very literally, this means that any and all present contempt Moses might endure meant less to him than the very great reward, however distant and remote, that would be his from the Messiah. We are plainly told that not only was the coming great Kingdom of God very real to Moses, but so also was its King. This was logical. All kingdoms have kings, and, from the early days, God's realm had for the believer its coming King. To assume otherwise is to assume an illogical and unwarranted stupidity on the part of Moses and others. The law when given to Moses was the law of the King who reigned in heaven and was to come. The reward from this King over all kings made any other recompense trivial.

Moved by this faith, Moses "forsook Egypt, not fearing the wrath of the king: for he endured, as seeing him who is invisible" (v. 26). This took place after he killed the Egyptian (Ex. 2:13). Not a vague faith but a very specific one moved Moses. Because modern "faith" is too often vague and fuzzy, we must not assume that Moses' faith was similar. Hebrews tells us that is was specific and firm.

How specific this faith was v. 28 tells us. The death of all the first-born in Egypt was decreed by God. Israel could only avoid the judgment by recourse to the passover blood, "lest he that destroyed the firstborn should touch them." Having seen the other nine plagues, Israel obeyed God at this point and saved its first-born. *Faith requires specific action.* To limit faith to an easily held belief is a serious error. The Hebrews here had occasion to know the power of God against Egypt, and potentially against them. Israel *complied* with God's requirement as set forth by Moses, but we are told that it was Moses who through faith kept the passover. The first-born of Egypt died, but not of Israel.

In v. 29, we are told, "By faith they passed through the Red Sea as by dry land: which the Egyptians assaying to do were drowned." For Moses, the parting of the Red Sea was the act of God for Israel: therefore they could pass safely to the other shore. For the Egyptians, it was a freakish natural event that they could take advantage of, and, as a result, they were drowned. "Natural events" are not so selective!

In the wilderness, Israel whined and complained about both God and Moses. None of this is mentioned by Hebrews because its emphasis is on what God's supernatural faith accomplished for a people through one man and his submission to the Almighty. It was not Moses' faith or work that did it, but the Lord Himself; Moses was God's instrument. In Numbers 12:3 we read that "the man Moses was very meek, above all the men which were upon the face of the earth." Moses did not seem to be meek to his contemporaries, nor was he. His meekness was towards God, whom he served faithfully and well. It takes a strange arrogance for men to find fault with Moses.

Five times in six verses we read, "By faith Moses," or, "By faith he...." This strong emphasis on Moses as a man of faith is telling, for "By faith Abraham" appears only twice (vv. 8-9). Abraham held fast to faith although virtually alone. Moses demonstrated his faith against Egypt, an ungodly empire, and against Israel, a rebellious people. Like Enoch before him (Gen. 5:24), Moses walked with God, and Michael the Archangel had a part in his burial (Jude 9).

Exodus 33 and Numbers 12:7-8 tell us that Moses was closer to God than any other prophet and unique in his revelation of God to the people. He accomplished more in his lifetime than any other Old Testament saint, and it was Moses and Elijah who appeared to Jesus on the Mount of Transfiguration (Matt. 17:3). God gave His law through Moses, and Moses was also the first of the prophets.

Hebrews 11 tells us about men of faith who lived and died. The epitaph in Westminster Abbey for the Wesley brothers is a fitting one: "God buries His workmen and carries on His work." Hebrews 11 gives us a list of men who worked and died in the faith as an encouragement to us. We have no right to be discouraged, and we have been blessed by their labors. We should so live and work that others who follow us will be the richer for our efforts.

Chapter Twenty-Nine
Faith Triumphant
(*Hebrews 11:30-40*)

30. By faith the walls of Jericho fell down, after they were compassed about seven days.
31. By faith the harlot Rahab perished not with them that believed not, when she had received the spies with peace.
32. And what shall I more say? for the time would fail me to tell of Gideon, and of Barak, and of Samson, and of Jephthae; of David also, and Samuel, and of the prophets:
33. Who through faith subdued kingdoms, wrought righteousness, obtained promises, stopped the mouths of lions,
34. Quenched the violence of fire, escaped the edge of the sword, out of weakness were made strong, waxed valiant in fight, turned to flight the armies of the aliens.
35. Women received their dead raised to life again: and others were tortured, not accepting deliverance; that they might obtain a better resurrection:
36. And others had trial of cruel mockings and scourgings, yea, moreover of bonds and imprisonment:
37. They were stoned, they were sawn asunder, were tempted, were slain with the sword: they wandered about in sheepskins and goatskins; being destitute, afflicted, tormented;
38. (Of whom the world was not worthy:) they wandered in deserts, and in mountains, and in dens and caves of the earth.
39. And these all, having obtained a good report through faith, received not the promise:
40. God having provided some better thing for us, that they without us should not be made perfect. (Hebrews 11:30-40)

It is apparent by now that faith is much more than man's act of believing. As James 2:19 makes clear, the devils in hell believe in God and tremble, but mere belief is nothing. That faith which is God's gift manifests *trust*. In the face of all adverse circumstances, its trust in God remains unshaken. It requires no physical assurances of God's care but trusts wholly in His word.

We have a bold statement in v. 30: "By faith the walls of Jericho fell down, after they were compassed about seven days." It was God who brought down the walls of Jericho: the people had no idea what God would do, except that He had promised to bring down Jericho's walls (Josh. 6:1-5). They simply obeyed Him when He ordered the marches around the city. For this act of obedient faith, God, who destroyed Jericho, links it to the faith of the people.

Next, Rahab is cited. Some commentators have tried to make an innkeeper of Rahab, but we are plainly told that she was a harlot who believed and was greatly rewarded for her faith. She became also an ancestress of Jesus Christ (Matt. 1:5).

119

Hebrews then tells us that the men of faith are too many to cite. Some are mentioned in passing. From the era of the Judges, we have Barak, Samson, Jephthae, and Samuel. After that, we have David and the prophets (vv. 32f). Kingdoms were subdued, justice was enforced, men gained promises, and the mouths of lions were stopped. The latter is a reference to Daniel 6:22.

All kinds of amazing deliverance occurred. "The violence of fire" was quenched (Dan. 3:25). Men escaped death by the sword; the weak were made strong in battle, and invading armies were put to flight (v. 34).

"Women received their dead raised to life again" (v. 35). This refers to an episode in the life of Elijah, through whom the son of the widow from Sarepta regained life (1 Kings 17:22), and to Elisha's restoring the son of the Shunammite woman to life (2 Kings 4:34).

Lest we think that faith entitles us to supernatural deliverances, we are at once told that "others were tortured, not accepting deliverance; that they might obtain a better resurrection" (v. 35). Their deliverance was in the resurrection of the dead, not in a rescue.

Then, in vv. 36-37, we are told of some of the sufferings that saints of old have endured: stoning, "sawn assunder," killed by the sword, "destitute, afflicted, tormented" as they wandered homelessly, clad in animal skins for clothing. Their wanderings were "in deserts, and in mountains, and in dens and caves of the earth" (v. 38). Our faith, and our perseverance in faith, is no entitlement to an earthly reward for us, however much it serves the Kingdom.

At the same time, Hebrews says of those suffering saints that "the world was not worthy" of them (v. 38). In spite of all their sufferings, these saints did not receive "the promise," that is, the Kingdom of God. However much they suffered for Christ the Messiah-King, the Kingdom was not realized in their day. In v. 40 we are told that a fullness, perfection, or maturity of the Kingdom requires that faith be made manifest in all its richness in us as well as in them. We must embody that trust in God that leads us to develop and apply the meaning of His Kingdom, salvation, and justice to all of life.

For some, then and now, as well as in the days to come, this can mean suffering and persecution as it has in the past. For others of us, this means applying God's law to all of life; for still others, it means expanding on the works of charity and mercy required by God.

Hebrews tells us what things we must believe as Christians. Jesus Christ is not only our King but also our Savior, our Redeemer, who by His atonement makes us righteous before God. But it makes clear that faith is not merely creedal, but a mandate for action, the conquest of all things for Jesus Christ.

Hebrews begins this section, chapter 11, by telling us, *first*, that faith is a supernatural gift from God which becomes our life and our new being in Him. *Second*, it tells us that faith means the belief that God is the fiat Creator of all things (v. 3). *Third*, faith means that we "must believe that he (God) is, and that he is a rewarder of them that diligently seek him" (v. 6). *Fourth*, we are told that faith is not mere assent to articles of faith, but the faithful service to God's Kingdom and to the needs of His people.

Faith is not man-centered. We cannot assess faith as a human asset but rather as a calling from God to serve Him with all our heart, mind, and being, and to love our neighbor as ourselves. Faith replaces man as his own center and focus to make God the center. It is a draft notice to man that he has been summoned into the service of his Maker and Redeemer, and he has no option but to serve. Hebrews is thus a mandate for Christian action, and to see it merely as a theological treatise on the atonement is to limit it seriously. The atonement must be the stimulus towards a new life and a new world, one radically governed by Christ as King and High Priest, and His law-word as our mandate for conquest.

Chapter Thirty
Sons or Bastards?
(*Hebrews 12:1-11*)

1. Wherefore seeing we also are compassed about with so great a cloud of witnesses, let us lay aside every weight, and the sin which doth so easily beset us, and let us run with patience the race that is set before us,
2. Looking unto Jesus the author and finisher of our faith; who for the joy that was set before him endured the cross, despising the shame, and is set down at the right hand of the throne of God.
3. For consider him that endureth such contradiction of sinners against himself, lest ye be wearied and faint in your minds.
4. Ye have not yet resisted unto blood, striving against sin.
5. And ye have forgotten the exhortation which speaketh unto you as unto children, My son, despise not thou the chastening of the Lord, nor faint when thou art rebuked of him:
6. For whom the Lord loveth he chasteneth, and scourgeth every son whom he receiveth.
7. If ye endure chastening, God dealeth with you as with sons; for what son is he whom the father chasteneth not?
8. But if ye be without chastisement, whereof all are partakers, then are ye bastards, and not sons.
9. Furthermore we have had fathers of our flesh which corrected us, and we gave them reverence: shall we not much rather be in subjection unto the Father of spirits, and live?
10. For they verily for a few days chastened us after their own pleasure; but he for our profit, that we might be partakers of his holiness.
11. Now no chastening for the present seemeth to be joyous, but grievous: nevertheless afterward it yieldeth the peaceable fruit of righteousness unto them which are exercised thereby.
(Hebrews 12:1-11)

The imagery of v. 1f is rather startling. At this time, well before the fall of Jerusalem, it was unusual for Christians to be thrown to the animals in the arena, but the text here prepares them for such treatment. The reference to "a great cloud of witnesses" seems to be the spectators at the Roman arenas, and yet, at the same time, to the saints of old, such as those cited in Hebrews 11. This does not necessarily mean that the saints witness our sufferings, but that they stand as witnesses to the necessity of trials in a fallen world. We are not alone, nor is our own suffering meaningless. The cloud of witnesses fills the sky.

We all have our particular besetting sin which easily hampers us. We are told to lay this aside and to "run with patience the race that is set before us" (v. 1). The triune God determines our course, not we ourselves. Our duty is to do what we must, and, in so doing, to remember the grimmer course set before Jesus, "the author and finisher of our faith," our forerunner and example. He endured the cross with all its shame, which He despised. Despite His agony and suffering, He assumed His task with joy, and He is now seated at the right hand of God (v. 2).

The hostility of this sinful world against Jesus Christ far exceeds anything we might experience, and we dare not grow weary or faint, for our sufferings can never equal His (v. 3). In fact, the Christians are reminded, "Ye have not yet resisted unto blood, striving against sin" (v. 4). None of you have yet faced death for your faith.

Then, in vv. 5-11, Hebrews tells the Christian community what it means to be sons, or children, of the Father. In vv. 5-6, we have the citation of Proverbs 3:11-12:

> 11. My son, despise not the chastening of the LORD; neither be weary of his correction:
> 12. For whom the LORD loveth he correcteth; even as a father the son in whom he delighteth. (Proverbs 3:11-12)

Our sufferings are inflicted immediately by the enemies of God, but, ultimately, they have their origin in the will of God. His purpose is corrective, even as a father is eager to help properly rear a beloved son by correcting him when necessary.

Whom God loves, He chastens, even to punishing them as needed (v. 6). "If ye endure chastening, God dealeth with you as sons; for what son is he whom the father chasteneth not?" (v. 7). In other words, to be a son means to be chastened, and this is a mark of fatherly love and concern. We must therefore view our sufferings as aspects of God's fatherly love whereby we are prepared to meet our responsibilities in time and eternity.

"But if ye be without chastisement, whereof all are partakers, then are ye bastards and not sons" (v. 8). The alternatives are clearly stated: the reprobate are spared God's chastening because they are not His sons, whereas we, as sons, are prepared for our maturity in Him. If we do not suffer, we are not God's children.

Verse 9 states the alternatives bluntly. "Furthermore we have had fathers of our flesh which corrected us, and we gave them reverence: shall we not much rather be in subjection unto the Father of spirits and live?" We know that our human fathers had our own good in mind in their chastisement of us. Dare we assume that God the Father is not even wiser in His dealings with us? The "fathers of our flesh" are here contrasted with God, "the Father of spirits," not because He is not also the creator of our bodies, but because His chastening of us has an eternal spiritual consequence.

Then, in v. 10, we are told that our parental chastening was "for a few days" as compared to eternity. Our human fathers chastened us "after their own good pleasure," or, as it seemed good to them, whereas God chastens us for our profit, "that we might be partakers of his holiness." M. R.

Vincent noted, "Holiness is life," and God's chastening is preparation for our eternal life.

We are then told, in v. 11, that no chastening is pleasant when experienced. Rather, it hurts. The result, however, is "the peaceable fruit of righteousness unto them which are exercised thereby." The goal is that we be righteous or just. This means to be governed by the law-word of God, now written on the tables of our hearts.

What Hebrews here tells us is that Jesus Christ, our great High Priest who makes atonement for us, *then* proceeds to remake us by His Holy Spirit. Our sanctification requires that we be chastened and made His children. When we are born again, we have the obligation to grow and to mature in Christ. It is childish to assume that our salvation completes God's work in us. Rather, salvation is the starting point. The newly formed regenerate person must now grow into *maturity in God's service*. To believe that the goal of our salvation is heaven is to warp the Gospel. We are to seek *first* the Kingdom of God and His righteousness (Matt. 6:33). The child who after birth fails to develop his mind and understanding is at best an idiot. The churches are full of too many spiritual idiots, no-growth converts whose lives do no credit to the cause. Hebrews from beginning to end is against a simplistic theology. It is therefore very fitting that Hebrews is followed in the Bible by James' epistle. They have in common a strongly practical emphasis, one very much needed in our time as in all times.

Chapter Thirty-One

Esau
(*Hebrews 12:12-17*)

12. Wherefore lift up the hands which hang down, and the feeble knees;
13. And make straight paths for your feet, lest that which is lame be turned out of the way; but let it rather be healed.
14. Follow peace with all men, and holiness, without which no man shall see the Lord:
15. Looking diligently lest any man fail of the grace of God; lest any root of bitterness springing up trouble you, and thereby many be defiled;
16. Lest there be any fornicator, or profane person, as Esau, who for one morsel of meat sold his birthright.
17. For ye know how that afterward, when he would have inherited the blessing, he was rejected: for he found no place of repentance, though he sought it carefully with tears. (Hebrews 12:12-17)

As we have seen previously, *faith* is declared by Hebrews to be the supernatural gift of God. Faith, moreover, is God-centered. Modern Arminian teachings which present Christian faith as the solution to man's problem's, saying, "Believe in Jesus, and all your troubles will be over," are false. St. Paul's troubles began with his conversion, and this has been the experience of millions since then. In a fallen world, the man of faith finds the world warring against him. As David said, "I am for peace: but when I speak, they are for war" (Ps. 120:7).

The Christian faces a double problem. *First*, this fallen world hates him because he is a Christian. *Second*, God chastens and disciplines him as a son. It is the bastard who lacks discipline. The son is prepared for time and eternity as an adopted son of God.

Knowing these things, we who are strong are to strengthen the weak, the discouraged hands and the feeble knees (v. 12). We are to make sure that the paths of faith are straight and even in order to make the way easier for the weak and the lame. Healing rather than stumbling is the goal (v. 13). While conflict is at times necessary, normally we should "follow peace with all men," and, in relationship to God, "holiness, without which no man shall see the Lord" (v. 14).

All this is said to prepare the way for the reference to Esau in vv. 15-17. The reference to Esau is very important. Esau was the elder son and the logical heir to the blessing or the promise. The Hebrews were even more privileged than Esau: they were kinsmen, of the same nationality as the Messiah, Jesus. If they returned to the Temple and its sacrificial system in preference to Jesus, they were sinning far more flagrantly than did Esau. Esau-Edom became an apostate nation and a plague to Israel, and even as the apostolic fellowship wrote, an Idumean or Edomite family, the Herodians, were ruling. Good Hebrews hated and despised the Herodians, but here the clear implication is that their return to the Temple would make them far worse than Esau and his line. For all the care in wording, Hebrews here is very blunt in this analogy. The Hebrews who thought of returning to the Temple and forsaking Jesus were Esaus magnified.

Their sin is spelled out. *First,* "lest any man fail of the grace of God," or, fall back from the grace of God. Since grace is a gift, those who perversely reject the gift are particularly wrong. By virtue of their birth, they are the logical heirs: to receive the gift of the Messiah-Redeemer and then turn their backs on Him is a fearful offense. Bad as was the offense of the leaders of the people who crucified Jesus Christ, the sin of those who followed and then turned back was at least as infamous.

Second, their problem in apostasy was "a root of bitterness." The apostate knows himself to be a traitor, a Judas, and the result is a bitterness that consumes him. It also defiles others (v. 15).

Third, the reference to Esau now comes out openly in v. 16. "Fornicator" does not mean, as in modern usage, sexual offender, because in its Biblical usage it includes blasphemy and rebellion. It is analogous to "profane," literally someone outside the sanctuary, thus outside the faith. This means someone who is not governed by the faith. It would be absurd to say that Esau did not believe in the God of Abraham, the God of Esau's father, Isaac. He simply did not take God seriously enough to be ruled by Him. God was there to provide the over-all government and to meet Esau's needs when Esau so deemed it necessary. In other words, he was like too many churchmen.

Esau, "for one morsel of meat sold his birthright." Afterward, when Esau wanted to inherit the blessing, he could not do so, despite his tears of repentance (v. 17). "He was rejected." Esau was sorry for his act, not for his false relationship to God.

Hebrews is very hard on easy-believism, no less here than elsewhere. God would have readily accepted repentance from Esau as from any other sinner, but Esau sought to nullify what he had done rather than to repent of his sin. God does not repeal our past history: we cannot nullify the past, but we can remake the future. King Saul knew how false his course of action was, but he refused to change. He was unwilling to acknowledge God's sovereign power to replace him with David. The greatness of Jonathan was his acceptance of God's will and his readiness to help David.

Paul and the men around him were Hebrews themselves, so this was a painful statement for them to make. The whole of Hebrews is very carefully written to make as strong an appeal as possible to their fellow Hebrews to reconsider their contemplated apostasy.

It is equally applicable to the church. *Faith* was for the Hebrews an *option*, as it is for too many churchmen. As the general letter continues, the Hebrews are reminded of Mount Sinai when God gave the law to Moses. Their faith is no less a thing of power given than was the law then. The fearfulness of that mount and that occasion is far surpassed by the present. An apostate Israel then trembled before the mount, but the church does not tremble before Jesus Christ. This then is a general epistle as relevant as ever, and the church today, as well as the Hebrews then, is reminded, "our God is a consuming fire" (Heb. 12:29). This verse echoes numerous texts (Ex. 24:17; Deut. 4:24; 9:3; Ps. 50:3; 97:3; Isa. 66:15; 2 Thess. 1:8; Heb. 10:27). Failure to understand this aspect of God's being is failure to know Him.

Note: Given the bluntness of the Esau analogy, it seems likely that the apostolic fellowship was in this instance reduced to Hebrews. For non-Hebrews to participate in this rebuke might have hindered its effectiveness. Hebrews thus was probably written by Hebrew believers to Hebrews in the churches.

Chapter Thirty-Two
The Warning
(Hebrews 12:18-29)

18. For ye are not come unto the mount that might be touched, and that burned with fire, nor unto blackness, and darkness, and tempest,
19. And the sound of the trumpet, and the voice of words; which voice they that heard intreated that the word should not be spoken to them any more:
20. (For they could not endure that which was commanded, And if so much as a beast touch the mountain, it shall be stoned, or thrust through with a dart:
21. And so terrible was the sight, that Moses said, I exceedingly fear and quake:)
22. But ye are come unto mount Sion, and unto the city of the living God, the heavenly Jerusalem, and to an innumerable company of angels,
23. To the general assembly and church of the firstborn, which are written in heaven, and to God the Judge of all, and to the spirits of just men made perfect,
24. And to Jesus the mediator of the new covenant, and to the blood of sprinkling, that speaketh better things than that of Abel.
25. See that ye refuse not him that speaketh. For if they escaped not who refused him that spake on earth, much more shall not we escape, if we turn away from him that speaketh from heaven:
26. Whose voice then shook the earth: but now he hath promised, saying, Yet once more I shake not the earth only, but also heaven.
27. And this word, Yet once more, signifieth the removing of those things that are shaken, as of things that are made, that those things which cannot be shaken may remain.
28. Wherefore we receiving a kingdom which cannot be moved, let us have grace, whereby we may serve God acceptably with reverence and godly fear:
29. For our God is a consuming fire. (Hebrews 12:18-29)

Verses 18-21 hark back to the revelation of the law on Mount Sinai. It was then forbidden to all to even touch the mountain, surrounded as it was with fire, blackness, and tempest (v. 18). Israel then heard the blasts of a trumpet, a voice, and a warning that for man or beast to touch the mountain meant death (v. 19f). A presumptuous people were warned against presuming on God's mercy. Moses himself said, "I exceedingly fear and quake" (v. 21). The context of this statement is very important (Deut. 9:11-21). Moses was sent down by God to confront a people that had made a golden bull calf, a fertility cult symbol, and were worshipping it with fertility cult rites. Moses' great fear was that God would judge and obliterate Israel, as it deserved, and he prayed earnestly and fearfully for Aaron and Israel.

131

In all this, Paul and the company obviously had Israel's sins in the desert in mind. Israel wanted to return to bondage in Egypt, to the security of slavery. The Hebrews in the church wanted to return to Jerusalem, but the Christians were beginning to see the earthly Jerusalem as another Egypt, even a Sodom, for crucifying Jesus Christ (Rev. 11:8). The Hebrews who wanted a return to the Temple saw themselves as Godly, but Hebrews here implies that they are the people of Egypt and Sodom if they defect.

In the person of Jesus Christ, they face the incarnate God, their King and Savior. To turn their backs on Him is worse by far than the sin of Israel in the desert. In Him they have come to the true mount Zion, to the great City of God, the goal of their forefathers' pilgrimage. This is the *heavenly* Jerusalem, not the crucifying earthly one, and they have come "to an innumerable company of angels" (v. 22). As Christians, they have these heavenly hosts as allies. Will they seek the fellowship of those who crucified the Messiah? Even if they rejected Jesus Christ as the great High Priest, if they saw him still as Messiah, how could they join His murderers?

In Jesus Christ, the Messiah Redeemer, they were part of "the general assembly and church of the firstborn, which are written in heaven." "Congregation" or church is "ekklesia," the governing body; "general assembly" is "paneguris," from *pan*, all, and *agora*, assembly. These terms *exclude* the earthly Jerusalem because the totality of the true Israel of God is in Christ, in His true church. Will they cut themselves off from the true Israel of God?

Here and here alone, in Christ and His congregation, are they in the company of "God the Judge of all, and to the spirits of just men made perfect" (v. 23). To separate themselves from Christ is to separate themselves from salvation and to invoke the judgment of God.

It is also a separation from Jesus Christ, from the Messiah; He cannot be *our* King if He is not our Savior, our High Priest. His blood speaks of mercy, grace, and atonement, whereas the blood of righteous Abel can speak only of the need for vengeance, judgment, and death against the murderer, against all who break God's law (v. 24).

We must therefore not refuse Him who speaks, namely, God. If judgment followed on all who refused to hear Moses, how much more so will judgment fall on all who refuse to hear God? (v. 25). The words of our Lord are clearly identified as the very words of God. He speaks, in effect, "from heaven," from whence He came, and He must be heard.

In fact, v. 26 declares the words of the Father, the Son, and the Holy Spirit to be one. There is a declared continuity between the words spoken to Moses on Mount Sinai and the words spoken by Jesus Christ. At Sinai, that voice shook the earth; now, in terms of Haggai 2:6-7, all things are again being shaken (v. 26). This is a continuous shaking to the end of the world, and its purpose is to shake down all things so that only those things which cannot be shaken may remain (v. 27).

History is thus a time of shaking in order to bring down all things whose foundation is not the Rock, Jesus Christ. Clearly, this echoes our Lord's final words in the Sermon on the Mount (Matt. 7:24-27). He alone is the unshakable foundation which can withstand the earthquakes and floods of history. Anything without Him as the foundation will perish.

Because we are citizens of a kingdom "which cannot be moved," we must cling to grace whereby we stand, in order to "serve God acceptably with reverence and godly fear" (v. 29). History will not spare those who equivocate and who avoid an unqualified stand. Because history is of God's ordination, it moves to eliminate all that is against Him, and all that is not clearly for Him.

In A.D. 60, Judaea was clearly far ahead of the nations of its day in its morality and its general caliber. Yet God judged Jerusalem and the Jews before He judged Rome, and far more severely. "Judgment must begin at the house of God" (1 Peter 4:17) because its offense is far greater, being done in the name of God.

"Our God is a consuming fire" (v. 29; see Ex. 24:17; Deut. 4:24; 9:3; Ps. 50:3; Isa. 66:15; 2 Thess. 1:8). History cannot be understood apart from this fact. There is no escaping this God. Either we are purged by His fiery love of all our dross and impurity, or we are consumed by Him. His fire can be the security of His protection, as with Shadrach, Meshach, and Abednego (Dan. 3:20-30), or it can destroy us and all our pretensions. The potentially defecting Hebrews are warned that their future is not theirs to determine, i.e., the *good* is not what they choose but what God determines. Judgment is not in their hands but in God's, and He is the Judge.

Chapter Thirty-Three
The Conclusion
(Hebrews 13:1-25)

1. Let brotherly love continue.
2. Be not forgetful to entertain strangers: for thereby some have entertained angels unawares.
3. Remember them that are in bonds, as bound with them; and them which suffer adversity, as being yourselves also in the body.
4. Marriage is honorable in all, and the bed undefiled: but whoremongers and adulterers God will judge.
5. Let your conversation be without covetousness; and be content with such things as ye have: for he hath said, I will never leave thee, nor forsake thee.
6. So that we may boldly say, The Lord is my helper, and I will not fear what man shall do unto me.
7. Remember them which have the rule over you, who have spoken unto you the word of God: whose faith follow, considering the end of their conversation.
8. Jesus Christ the same yesterday, and to day, and for ever.
9. Be not carried about with divers and strange doctrines. For it is a good thing that the heart be established with grace; not with meats, which have not profited them that have been occupied therein.
10. We have an altar, whereof they have no right to eat which serve the tabernacle.
11. For the bodies of those beasts, whose blood is brought into the sanctuary by the high priest for sin, are burned without the camp.
12. Wherefore Jesus also, that he might sanctify the people with his own blood, suffered without the gate.
13. Let us go forth therefore unto him without the camp, bearing his reproach.
14. For here have we no continuing city, but we seek one to come.
15. By him therefore let us offer the sacrifice of praise to God continually, that is, the fruit of our lips giving thanks to his name.
16. But to do good and to communicate forget not: for with such sacrifices God is well pleased.
17. Obey them that have the rule over you, and submit yourselves: for they watch for your souls, as they that must give account, that they may do it with joy, and not with grief: for that is unprofitable for you.
18. Pray for us: for we trust we have a good conscience, in all things willing to live honestly.
19. But I beseech you the rather to do this, that I may be restored to you the sooner.
20. Now the God of peace, that brought again from the dead our Lord Jesus, that great shepherd of the sheep, through the blood of the everlasting covenant,
21. Make you perfect in every good work to do his will, working in you that which is wellpleasing in his sight, through Jesus Christ; to whom be glory for ever and ever. Amen.

22. And I beseech you, brethren, suffer the word of exhortation: for I have written a letter unto you in few words.
23. Know ye that our brother Timothy is set at liberty; with whom, if he come shortly, I will see you.
24. Salute them that have the rule over you, and all the saints. They of Italy salute you.
25. Grace be with you all. Amen. (Hebrews 13:1-25)

B. F. Westcott divided Hebrews 13 into three sections: 1) social duties, vv. 1-6; 2) religious duties, vv. 7-17; and 3) personal instructions from the writer, vv. 18-25. This is an apt division, but a most impressive fact is present in all three. These "exhortations to faith and Godliness" are as warm and kindly as the preceding chapters are often stern. Hebrews is not addressed to one particular congregation planning to defect to the Temple system, but to the Hebrews in all the churches. At that time, most Christians were still Jewish converts. In the various churches, *some* Jews had apparently considered defection, but *all* Jewish Christians were instructed and armed to cope with the problem. This kindly tone reflects the fact that the faithfulness of most was unquestioned.

In. vv. 1-6, the "social duties" are cited. Brotherly love among the Christians must continue. Some who were in error and astray in their views of sacrifice and atonement must now be forgiven if they recant, and they must be treated as brethren in the faith.

In that era were also brothels, and prostitutes commonly came with the room. Hence Christians provided hospitality to traveling Christians in order to avoid ungodly situations. Paul, for example, went to synagogues to see if any would invite him home after he spoke. Abraham entertained strangers, not knowing at first that they were angels. The likelihood of any believers entertaining angels was, of course, minimal, but the moral duty was the same: hospitality to the saints (v. 2).

The saints in bondage are to be remembered even as we would want to be remembered when also imprisoned (v. 3).

Pagan and ascetic ideas are to be avoided. Sex within marriage "is honorable in all, and the bed undefiled," but it is "whoremongers and adulterers (whom) God will judge" (v. 4). Paganism associated sex with sin and spirituality with asceticism, and falsely so.

Our behavior is to be without covetousness. We are to be content with what we have, for God's promise is this: "I will never leave thee nor forsake thee, so that we can boldly say, The Lord is my helper, and I will not fear what man shall do unto me" (v. 5f.). These words are based on Deuteronomy 31:6 and Joshua 1:5 (cf. Gen. 28:15). With this assurance, we should be of good courage.

The "religious duties" of vv. 7-17 begin with a reminder to be thoughtful and grateful to the church's faithful leaders. We are to follow their faith and the goal of their lives, the primacy of Jesus Christ, "the same yesterday, and to day, and for ever" (vv. 7-8).

We should be steadfast in the faith and avoid being influenced by strange teachers and teachings. These would be novel doctrines about Jesus Christ, and about meats offered to idols (v. 9).

Our altar, sacrifice, and high priest is Jesus Christ, and those who are still tied to the old sacrificial system have no right to eat of the communion offerings (v. 10).

On the Day of Atonement and on the consecration of a priest (Ex. 29:14), the sacrifice was to be burned outside the camp. Similarly, Jesus Christ was sacrificed outside the gate (vv. 11-12). We must therefore go outside the camp, leaving old Israel behind, to join Jesus Christ, whatever the reproach (v. 13). "For here we have no continuing city, but we seek one to come" (v. 14). Jerusalem, which crucified Jesus Christ, is not the City of God.

God wants from us "the sacrifice of praise;" we must be grateful and thankful (v. 15).

In relationship to men, we are to *do good and to communicate*, i.e., we must be merciful and faithful in providing charity. These are the sacrifices pleasing to God (v. 16).

We are to be obedient and appreciative of all who are in positions of religious authority; give them thereby joy in their service to us (v. 17).

Then, in vv. 18-25, we have some final comments, and, in vv. 20-21, a prayer. There is in v. 18 a request for prayer for the writers. They want to work with a good conscience before God. Then, a personal note from one, Paul, asks for prayers that he be restored to them, perhaps from prison, soon.

In v. 20, the prayer begins by stressing Jesus Christ, *first*, as the resurrected Messiah; *second*, He is the great Shepherd, i.e., King, of the sheep; *third*, the everlasting covenant had been made in His blood. The prayer in v. 21 calls for their maturity in Christ's service. May God work in them what is "wellpleasing in his sight, through Jesus Christ; to whom be glory for ever and ever. Amen."

The conclusion thus states that Timothy is now free, and he will visit the churches shortly (v. 23). Greetings from the saints of Italy are sent to all the churches (v. 25), and the letter concludes, "Grace be with you all. Amen" (v. 25).

The serenity of this conclusion tells us that the writers, whatever the wavering Hebrews might do, were confident of the outcome: God's King and Kingdom would triumph. The defection of foolish and sinful men could not alter the outcome.

JAMES

Introduction

The letter of James has not received the attention it deserves from the church. In fact, James Hope Moulton spoke of it as not "a treatise destined for permanence."[1] It supposedly survived only because it was generally accepted that James was a brother of Jesus.

William Hendriksen called attention to the many echoes of Christ's Sermon on the Mount: Matt. 7:7 (James 1:5); Matt. 7:11 (James 1:17); Matt. 7:24 (James 1:22); Matt. 5:3 (James 2:5); Matt. 7:12f; 22:39 (James 2:8); Matt. 5:7 (James 2:13); Matt. 7:16 (James 3:12); Matt. 9:9 (James 3:12); Matt. 7:1 (James 4:11); Matt. 6:19 (James 3:2).[2] This by no means exhausts the relationship, however. The concern of James is the true Israel of God (Gal. 6:16; James 1:1), God's Kingdom, Christ's Lordship, the law of God, and the necessity of a vital faith, along with works.

The neglect of this book or epistle is startling. How else can we explain the failure to take the matter of unction seriously, and to see its relationship to old and new Israel, and to church history? (See chapter 15, "Unction.")

James is careful, for example, to trace speech to its origin in man's being, to his heart. Speech, he insists, is revelatory of what we are. Why, then, the very casual treatments of this?

Hebrews stresses the necessary relationship between *faith* and *life*, *faith* and *works*. When James says that faith without works is *dead*, he tells us that faith is not a mere matter of words, but it is of necessity a matter of life. We are dead men if we no longer can breathe, and we are spiritually dead if our faith is unaccompanied by works. Too many churches are like graveyards because too many members have no living faith.

The Christian cannot be, James holds, double-minded, or, as contemporary psychiatry would say, schizophrenic. The schizophrenic is a non-functioning person; so too is the double-minded churchman.

"Pure religion and undefiled" requires Christian charity and action. Anything short of this is a self-delusion.

James' letter is a corrective the church needs badly.

---

1. James Hope Moulton, "James," in Arthur S. Peake, editor, *A Commentary on the Bible* (London, England: T.C. & E.C. Jack, 1920), 903.
2. William Hendriksen, *Bible Survey* (Grand Rapids, Michigan: Baker Book House, 1947), 326f.

Chapter One
James, the Servant
(James 1:1)

1. James, a servant of God and of the Lord Jesus Christ, to the twelve tribes which are scattered abroad, greeting. (James 1:1)

The author of the Epistle of James is said to be, by some scholars, the brother of Jesus. William Hendriksen saw "striking similarities" between the Sermon on the Mount and James' Epistle. There are indeed close resemblances.[1] Some scholars see it as the first written of New Testament writings.

R.C.H. Lenski dated the letter between A.D. 35 and 52 and held the author to be the Apostle James, one of the Twelve. Lenski did not believe that Mary had any child other than Jesus, and he asserted that the reference to Jesus' brothers in Matthew 12:46 could refer to Joseph's sons by an earlier marriage.[2]

John Wick Bowman suggested that the ascription to James, the brother of Jesus, may be perhaps the best answer.[3]

According to R.V.G. Tasker:

The authorship of James the brother of the Lord is not only consonant with the note of authority which sounds throughout the Epistle, and with the possible echoes of the speech of James at the council of Jerusalem, but also with the extent to which the writer has obviously been profoundly impressed by the teaching of Jesus as we know it today in the Sermon on the Mount.[4]

Alexander Ross pointed out that there are only three men in the New Testament bearing the name of James. *First*, there is the disciple, James, the son of Alphaeus. We know little about him. *Second*, there is James, the son of Zebedee, who was martyred in the year 44 (Acts 12). *Third*, there is James, the brother of the Lord. His status bore authority, and he here writes authoritatively.[5]

James, the brother of Jesus, was martyred in A.D. 62, and this letter was probably written much earlier. F. Bertram Clogg said it was "the earliest book in the New Testament."[6]

---

[1] William Hendriksen, *Bible Survey* (Grand Rapids, Michigan: Baker Book House, 1947), 326f.

[2] R.C.H. Lenski, *The Interpretation of the Epistle to the Hebrews and of the Epistle of James* (Columbus, Ohio: Wartburg Press, 1946), 506f.

[3] John Wick Bowman, *The Letter to the Hebrews, The Letter of James, The First and Second Letters of Peter* (Richmond, Virginia: John Knox Press, 1968), p. 93f.

[4] R.V.G. Tasker, *The General Epistle of James* (Grand Rapids, Michigan: Eerdmans, 1982 reprint), 28.

[5] Alexander Ross, *Commentary on the Epistles of James and John* (Grand Rapids, Michigan: 1954), 14.

In v. 1, James writes: "James, a servant of God and of the Lord Jesus Christ, to the twelve tribes which are scattered abroad, greeting." This is an unusual beginning, unlike all other epistles. "Greeting," the concluding word, is the Greek word for *rejoice*. In Acts 15:23, we encounter its only other New Testament use, and both instances are connected with James.

The reference to "the Lord Jesus Christ" is here and in James 2:1. We find here an interesting fact in that, *first*, the letter assumes without question or argument the lordship of Jesus Christ. It is neither an open question nor a matter of debate. All the people of the twelve tribes everywhere are addressed by the Lord's brother, a strict keeper of the law and widely respected, by James, "a servant of God and of the Lord Jesus Christ." The line of division between the Temple and the church was not yet clearly drawn, and James was regarded by all as a holy man of the nation.

Second, James writes his epistle with a full sense of continuity with the Old Testament. The lordship of Jesus Christ and the revealed Scriptures are seen as a unit and assumed to be so throughout the letter.

A.T. Robertson called attention to the use of the word *Lord*, *kurios* in the Greek. In the Septuagint, it was used for either *Elohim* or *Jahweh*, for God. The Romans applied it to their emperor in emperor worship. The letter is addressed to the twelve tribes, "Israel in its fullness and completeness."[7] Because the letter addresses the Jews of the Diaspora as well as the Palestinian Jews, it was written in Greek.

There is a tremendous presupposition in this verse. All Israel is addressed in the name of the Messiah-King. *This means that to separate oneself from Jesus Christ, or to repudiate Him, was implicitly to separate oneself from Israel.* In Galatians 6:16, Paul refers to the church as the Israel of God. This is implicit in James 1:1.

In James 2:2, the word *assembly* is the Greek form of *synagogue*, the earliest name for the Christian Church. Again we see the assumption of continuity. If the Temple and its people reject Jesus Christ, then they depart from God's chosen people, Israel, and the true synagogue.

In Hebrews, the rejection of Christ's high priestly status is stated to be the point of departure. In James, probably the earlier epistle, the true Israel of God is totally tied to the person of Jesus Christ. This fact, as well as the insistence on the moral requirement of faith with action, connects James and Hebrews. They make a common appeal for a living faith.

Israel in its fullness cannot exist now without its Messiah and Lord, Jesus Christ. James goes on immediately to speak of the trials and troubles that

---

6. F. Bertram Clogg, *An Introduction to the New Testament* (New York, New York: Charles Scribner's Sons, 1937), 150.

7. A.T. Robertson, *Word Pictures in the New Testament*, vol. VI (Grand Rapids, Michigan: Baker Book House, reprint, n.d.), 10.

befall them, and yet his essential word to them is, "greeting," or *rejoice*. Their great Redeemer-King has come. M.R. Vincent cites as James' "key words," *rejoice, joy, patience, perfect*.[8]

In v. 1, James calls himself a "servant of the Lord Jesus Christ." *Doulos*, meaning servant, is a term used by the apostles and their associates to describe themselves in relationship to Jesus Christ. James never uses his relationship to the Lord to claim any honor. It is his privilege to be a *servant*.

In the Epistle of Jude, v. 1, Jude identifies himself as "the servant of Jesus Christ, and brother of James." In Mark 6:3, we are told that James and Jude were two of Mary's four sons. We thus have two portions of the New Testament apparently written by two brothers of our Lord who did not mention this relationship to Him. James and Jude saw their standing in relationship to Him as one of grace and service. Unlike later churchmen, they made no claims on the basis of blood and in fact avoided them. They identified themselves as *servants* of Jesus Christ and saw in this their dignity and honor. The status of James in the earliest days of the church was central and powerful, but it rested entirely on his service, not on blood. Because the church and its leaders represented God's new human race on earth, their status and dignity rested on God's grace, and no more.

---

8. M. R. Vincent, *Word Studies in the New Testament*, vol. I (MacDill AFB, Florida: MacDonald Publishing Co., reprint, n.d.), 344.

Chapter Two
Faith and Wisdom
(James 1:2-7)

2. My brethren, count it all joy when ye fall into divers temptations;
3. Knowing this, that the trying of your faith worketh patience.
4. But let patience have her perfect work, that ye may be perfect and entire, wanting nothing.
5. If any of you lack wisdom, let him ask of God, that giveth to all men liberally, and upbraideth not; and it shall be given him.
6. But let him ask in faith, nothing wavering. For he that wavereth is like a wave of the sea driven with the wind and tossed.
7. For let not that man think that he shall receive anything of the Lord. (James 1:2-7)

James in these verses deals with a familiar theme in Old Testament thought, in Proverbs in particular, and that is *wisdom*. Wisdom is in the Hebrew perspective not a natural fact but the result of intense and disciplined living and studying. It was seen as a product of *discipline* and *teaching*. Such teaching began in the family and continued under teachers. Above all, it was from God. We see this same idea in such psalms as 1 and 37. (Wisdom is in Hebrew, *hokhmah*). Above all, God is wise, and wisdom is not only a personal attribute of God, but also is God in action in His works and creation.

In the New Testament we have echoes of the perspective of Proverbs and Psalms, i.e., Psalm 104:24; 117:1-2; and 107:7 in such verses as Ephesians 3:10; Hebrews 9:10; and Revelation 15:3-4. In Matthew 11:19, Jesus Christ identifies Himself as wisdom. Wisdom is not an abstract concept, but rather the Person of God at work, expressing His nature and being. Wisdom, i.e., the wisdom of God, is also a communicable attribute of God, and it must be sought.

James thus has done two things in his letter, in 1:1-7. *First*, his starting point is "the Lord Jesus Christ" (v. 1), so that his comments about wisdom are linked to the Godhead. *Second*, he begins on ground familiar to all Hebrews, because wisdom literature was at that time very popular.

He then declares, *first*, that we should *count* it "all joy when ye fall into diverse temptations" (v. 2) or trials. Very early, James shows his emphasis by his use of certain key words, i.e., *rejoice, joy, patience*, and *perfect*. The goal of the trials we endure is a God-ordained one; we shall gain wisdom and joy, and be made perfect or mature.

This process can be a painful one; we therefore cannot *feel* it as joy, but we can *count* it as such.

The testing of our faith results in patience (v. 3). Your faith is tested in the fires of affliction and refined by fire. James Moffatt commented, "The true view of faith is that any sort of trial,...hardship, or misfortune of any kind or degree, is an opportunity for proving our mettle....James indicates that the ordeal of *faith* brings out *endurance*, the staying power of life."[1]

The word *faith* here carries the same meaning as in Ephesians 2:8: "it is the gift of God," and it tests and develops us as it works in us. Similarly, "patience" is not a passive word here: in French's words, "it does not mark merely passive endurance but the brave patience with which the Christian contends against various hindrances, persecutions and temptations that befall him in his conflict with the outward and inward world."[2]

Patience has as its active and perfecting work our preparation to be "perfect and entire, wanting nothing" (v. 4). Life for us must not be a series of miscellaneous events, but a purposeful sequence to prepare us for our responsibilities in time and eternity. The wisdom is from above (1:5; 3:17), and so too are our trials and testings.

Therefore, "If any of you lack wisdom, let him ask of God, that giveth to all men liberally, and upbraideth not; and it shall be given him" (v. 5). Wisdom comes from God, and it is He whom we should ask for it. There is no qualification. Anything else we ask for is subject to God's judgment, but if we truly ask for wisdom, we shall get it. The price to us is testing and adversity. Most people are unwilling to pay the price for wisdom. But, if we do ask for wisdom, we must "ask in faith, nothing wavering. For he that wavereth is like a wave of the sea driven with the wind and tossed" (v. 6). The waves are acted upon by the wind rather than themselves acting. So too are men who are fearful of being men of faith and wisdom. Too many churchmen are concerned with self-salvation rather than the service of the Lord. The wavering man is in conflict with himself, not with the world. Where the world is concerned, he is like a cork floating on the waves, as someone has observed. Such a man, James tells us, will get nothing from the Lord (v. 7). This is a very blunt statement, as indeed so much in James is. Prayer must be "in faith, nothing wavering" (v. 6).

The surviving stories about James are often exaggerations, but they do tell us of a man of strong and uncompromising faith, a staunch and resolute leader, and a champion of God's law. James strongly emphasizes a personal faith and commitment. Storms and troubles come from without; faith and wisdom come from within. Both come from the hand of God, whose purpose for us is altogether righteous and holy. Most men want to be spared from the storms of life, but James makes it clear that every faith shall be tested. It is therefore impossible for a man to survive without *faith and wisdom*.

---

[1] James Moffatt, *The General Epistles, James, Peter, and Judas* (New York, New York: Harper, n.d.), 9.

[2] Cited by Alexander Ross, *Commentary on the Epistles of James and John* (Grand Rapids, Michigan: Eerdmans, 1954), 27.

James' teaching on wisdom is tied to the Messiah, "the Lord Jesus Christ" (1:1). The very early date of the book of James is in part likely because the whole of the revelation of the Old Testament and the coming of the Messiah are assumed to be an unbroken unity. In effect, James says that if a division be made, it will be made by others, and it will result in their own judgment. Such persons will be unstable and worthless. Hence, James' contemptuous conclusion: "let not that man think that he shall receive any thing from the Lord" (v. 7). "The Lord" is Jesus Christ. The crucified One requires decision and sacrifice from His followers.

An important fact emerges. The exclusive stressing of faith in the church today is valid with respect to salvation but not sanctification. James insists that true faith is marked by *works*. In other words, faith without wisdom and works can be both stupid and dead.

Chapter Three

The Double Minded
(James 1:8-18)

8. A double minded man is unstable in all his ways.

9. Let the brother of low degree rejoice in that he is exalted:

10. But the rich, in that he is made low: because as the flower of the grass he shall pass away.

11. For the sun is no sooner risen with a burning heat, but it withereth the grass, and the flower thereof falleth, and the grace of the fashion of it perisheth: so also shall the rich man fade away in his ways.

12. Blessed is the man that endureth temptation: for when he is tried, he shall receive the crown of life, which the Lord hath promised to them that love him.

13. Let no man say when he is tempted, I am tempted of God: for God cannot be tempted with evil, neither tempteth he any man:

14. But every man is tempted, when he is drawn away from his own lust, and enticed.

15. Then when lust hath conceived, it bringeth forth sin: and sin, when it is finished, bringeth forth death.

16. Do not err, my beloved brethren.

17. Every good gift and every perfect gift is from above, and cometh down from the Father of lights, with whom is no variableness, neither shadow of turning.

18. Of his own will begat he us with the word of truth, that we should be a kind of firstfruits of his creatures. (James 1:8-18)

These verses can be divided as follows: 1) in v. 8, James issues a general warning calling for a clear-cut faith, one without reservations; 2) in vv. 9-11, riches are revealed as a curse when given priority; 3) in v. 12, we have a beatitude pronounced on all who are righteous or just; 4) in vv. 13-15 the meaning of temptation is set forth; 5) in vv. 16-18, we are told that God's gifts to us are only good.

First, in this letter, James is writing to ostensible believers. Given the early date, we can understand why he is concerned with double-mindedness. There was a choice to be made, Christ or the Temple? For many, the requirement to choose was unwelcome. They wanted the best of all worlds, but James insists on a decision. If Jesus Christ is indeed Lord (as stated in 1:1 and 2:1), He must be followed and obeyed unequivocally.

The "double-minded man" is described as radically "unstable in all his ways" (v. 8), not merely in his thinking about Jesus Christ. Our faith expresses the core of our being, so that more than mental indecision or reservation is involved. Our commitment to the "Lord" (v. 7) governs every aspect of our being, so that our faith is either unreserved, or it is dangerous in the instability it gives us.

In the *second* section, vv. 9-11, James tells us that if we seek out stability in wealth we in effect seek it in sand. This may be an echo of Matthew 7:26-27, where the ruin of the man whose life has a false foundation is described. Wealth is transient; a true faith is not. The man who trusts in his wealth rather than God is "double-minded," and his prayers will get him nothing from the Lord.

The brevity of life, like the short duration of green grass, leaves the rich naked and dead before they know it. "All flesh is grass" (Isa. 40:6). It cannot take the heat of life as God ordains it.

Third, we have the beatitude of v. 12: "Blessed is the man that endureth temptation; for when he is tried, he shall receive the crown of life, which the Lord hath promised to them that love him." The reward is the crown which is life. The fullness of life, eternal life now and forever, is God's gift to all who endure testing. It is testing, the refining fire of adversity, that God ordains for us. A distinction is made here and in v. 13 between trials and temptations to sin.

The beatitudes of the Bible are not intended to be comforting thoughts; rather, they are promises from God of the consequences of certain stands and actions on our part. A beatitude is thus an assurance of God's faithfulness to the faithful.

Fourth, in vv. 13-15, as against trials or testings of our faith, we now have a statement concerning temptation, or the urge to stray, or to commit sin. We cannot legitimately say that God tempts us to sin. To say, "I am tempted of God," is wrong, "for God cannot be tempted with evil, neither tempteth he any man" (v. 13). Because God is all-holy, He cannot be tempted to do evil: He is untemptable. God gives man the freedom to do good or evil, but this does not mean that He is tempting man.

"But every man is tempted, when he is drawn away of his own lust, and enticed" (v. 14). We are responsible for our own sins. James makes no reference to the devil, because we have no moral ground for blaming him. Whatever the part of other persons or of the devil, we ourselves are responsible for our own sins, and we cannot legitimately blame anyone else, God, man, or the devil. The sin of Adam and Eve was not only to succumb to temptation, but also to blame God, the devil, and, in Adam's case, Eve as well. The imagery of v. 15 is of desire, leading to conception, leading to the birth of sin, and sin brings forth or gives birth to death. As against righteousness or justice, sin is abnormal and leads to death.

In the *fifth* section, vv. 16-18, we are warned again (v. 16) against blaming God for our sin. God's *gift* to us is then cited: it is "good" and it is "perfect." God is "the father of lights," not of darkness, and with Him there "is no variableness, neither shadow of turning" (v. 17). All things else change and are variable, but not so God. He is the unchanging and changeless One (Mal. 3:6), "the same yesterday, and today, and for ever" (Heb. 13:8).

Verse 18 tells us, "Of his own will begat he us with the word of truth, that we should be a kind of firstfruits of his creatures." God "begat" us, brought us forth, or created us, that, like the firstfruits cited in His law, we should be dedicated and consecrated to His service (Rom. 8:23; 16:5; 1 Cor. 15:20, 23; Rev. 14:4). As in v. 15, we have again the metaphor of birth, but this time in a good sense.

No less than Hebrews, James calls for a decision between the Israel of the past and the new Israel of God. The historical crisis that Hebrews had to confront is here in its infancy, and it is presented as a moral one. The choice is between being double-minded and unstable, or strong and single-minded in allegiance to the "Lord Jesus Christ" (1:1; 2:1). This is ever the choice, from James' day to our own.

Double-mindedness has been the curse of the church over the centuries. Certainly *Hebrews* indicates that the double-minded existed in the early church. We do not know how many of the double-minded and unstable remained in the church of that day: but certainly in our time the churches are full of people who are unwilling to give an unwavering and unequivocal allegiance to Jesus Christ, and the church is often paralyzed by their double-mindedness.

Chapter Four

"Pure Religion and Undefiled"
(James 1:19-27)

19. Wherefore, my beloved brethren, let every man be swift to hear, slow to speak, slow to wrath:
20. For the wrath of man worketh not the righteousness of God.
21. Wherefore lay apart all filthiness and superfluity of naughtiness, and receive with meekness the engrafted word, which is able to save your souls.
22. But be ye doers of the word, and not hearers only, deceiving your own selves.
23. For if any be a hearer of the word, and not a doer, he is like unto a man beholding his natural face in a glass:
24. For he beholdeth himself, and goeth his way, and straightway forgetteth what manner of man he was.
25. But whoso looketh into the perfect law of liberty, and continueth therein, he being not a forgetful hearer, but a doer of the work, this man shall be blessed in his deed.
26. If any man among you seem to be religious, and bridleth not his tongue, but deceiveth his own heart, this man's religion is vain.
27. Pure religion and undefiled before God and the Father is this, To visit the fatherless and widows in their affliction, and to keep himself unspotted from the world. (James 1:19-27)

In James 1:19-27, we are plainly told, *first*, that our Christian faith does not make us into judges over other men but enables us to grow, to improve ourselves. He thus begins, in v. 19f, "Wherefore, my beloved brethren, let every man be swift to hear, slow to speak, slow to wrath: For the wrath of man worketh not the righteousness of God." Men are quick to spot the evils of others, but not their own.

James Moffatt said of vv. 19 and 20:

> When James, like Peter, hastens to urge the moral and spiritual activities of Christians, he passes from the idea of the regenerating *word* to the conception of the *Word* as seed which has to be cared for, if it is to thrive; indeed, he develops the metaphor more definitely than Peter. Give the divine seed a clean soil.[1]

The condition whereby the word of God is properly received is *humility*. The word must be received with humility, with *meekness* (v. 21). James does not flatter his readers. He summons them to "lay apart all filthiness and superfluity of naughtiness and receive with meekness the engrafted word, which is able to save your souls" (v. 21). Lenski's translation reads: "Wherefore, by putting away all shabbiness and what there is of a lot of

---

[1] James Moffatt, *The General Epistles, James, Peter, and Judas* (New York, N.Y.: Harper, n.d.), 24.

baseness, accept with meekness the implanted Word that is able to save your souls!"

Second, in vv. 22-25, James tells the readers how humility is to be used. It is not something that is limited to an attitude, but is rather *active obedience*. The believers are to be doers of the word, not hearers only, for to be hearers only is to deceive or to cheat one's own self.[2]

Then, in vv. 23-25, James gives us an unusual illustration, a mirror. Those who are hearers only, and not doers of the word of God, are like a man who looks into a mirror to see if he is pleased with himself. Having done this, and having satisfied himself that his hair is properly combed, his clothing in place, and his general appearance pleasing, he moves on. He is not mindful of "what manner of man he is." However, the man who makes God's law-word his mirror tries to conform himself to the image God requires of him. God's law is "the perfect law of liberty" (v. 25), and it impels man to be "a doer of the word." Such a man is blessed in his deed or doing.

James thus insists that our true spiritual mirror is the law-word of God. To neglect this mirror is to reject seeing ourselves as God sees us.

If we use God's law as our mirror, we shall be blessed in what we do (v. 25). This blessing has reference to time present. Here and now God blesses those whose mirror is His law, because they are the doers of His law.

Third, in vv. 26-27, we see the conclusion of this matter: the result of humility, and obedience to God's law, is a morality that is God-shaped, a morality that leads to social and personal righteousness or justice.[3]

The man whose mirror is only glass is wrapped up in himself. The man whose mirror is society may manifest social concerns, but their basis will be humanistic rather than Godly. James insists on the law of God as our only true mirror because it alone sets forth the righteousness or justice of God.

True religion, James says, easily manifests itself in our speech. It is not sound religion to be unbridled or uncontrolled in our speech (v. 26). In chapter 3, James has more to say about speech, about the tongue. It is a barometer of our faith; it tells others how seriously, or how lightly, we take our faith. James is very much concerned about the use of intemperate or harsh language, and he sees it as an important test of the reality and seriousness of our faith. If anyone *seems* to be religious, or appears to be a devout Christian, but does not bridle his tongue, that person deceives his or her own heart, and his or her "religion is vain" (v. 26). This is blunt

---

2. R.C.H. Lenski, *The Interpretation of the Epistle to the Hebrews and of the Epistle of James* (Columbus, Ohio: Wartburg Press, 1946), 553.
3. John Wick Bowman, *The Letter to the Hebrews, The Letter of James, and the First and Second Letters of Peter* (Richmond, Virginia: John Knox Press, 1968), 103f.

language and is intended to be taken very seriously. James says plainly that much piety on the surface is belied by an unbridled tongue, and he thereby requires a self-examination that begins with our speech.

James then proceeds to define, in v. 27, "pure religion and undefiled." He has already cited intemperate language as the enemy of "pure religion and undefiled." Now he gives us the positive side of his definition. It is "To visit the fatherless, and widows in their affliction, and to keep himself unspotted from the world" (v. 27).

In Acts 6:1-7, we learn that the early church, in Jerusalem, had many widows as members. James, as a resident there, was very familiar with their needs. Acts 6 tells us that these widows were fed, but James goes beyond that to ask or require that they be visited. The care of widows and orphans is basic to God's law, and God Himself uses it first as a test of man. James' concern reveals how thoroughly he is a man of the law, a man for whom God's law is his mirror.

This law of God is "the perfect law of liberty" (v. 25; 2:12). Freedom is under God, not man. James summons us, as the servant of the Lord Jesus Christ (1:1), to a life of freedom in Him. It is Christ who set us free from sin and death (John 8:34-36), and His law is the perfect law of liberty.

The goal of the Christian is "to keep himself unspotted from the world" (v. 27). This means to continue morally unblemished, not necessarily perfect, but always growing in the right direction.

Chapter Five
"Respect of Persons"
(James 2:1-13)

1. My brethren, have not the faith of our Lord Jesus Christ, the Lord of glory, with respect of persons.
2. For if there come unto your assembly a man with a gold ring, in goodly apparel, and there come in also a poor man in vile raiment;
3. And ye have respect to him that weareth the gay clothing, and say unto him, Sit thou here in a good place; and say to the poor, Stand thou there, or sit here under my footstool:
4. Are ye not then partial in yourselves, and are become judges of evil thoughts?
5. Hearken, my beloved brethren, Hath not God chosen the poor of this world rich in faith, and heirs of the kingdom which he hath promised to them that love him?
6. But ye have despised the poor. Do not rich men oppress you, and draw you before the judgment seats?
7. Do not they blaspheme that worthy name by the which ye are called?
8. If ye fulfil the royal law according to the scripture, Thou shalt love thy neighbor as thyself, ye do well:
9. But if ye have respect to persons, ye commit sin, and are convinced of the law as transgressors.
10. For whosoever shall keep the whole law, and yet offend in one point, he is guilty of all.
11. For he that said, Do not commit adultery, said also, Do not kill. Now if thou commit no adultery, yet if thou kill, thou art become a transgressor of the law.
12. So speak ye, and so do, as they that shall be judged by the law of liberty.
13. For he shall have judgment without mercy, that hath shewed no mercy; and mercy rejoiceth against judgment. (James 2:1-13)

James speaks again of "our Lord Jesus Christ," and he refers to Him as "the Lord of glory" (v. 1). In v. 5, as in 1:12, he refers to Christians as those who love God. His purpose is to encourage them in their love and service. To call Jesus "the Lord of glory" is to declare Him to be the manifested presence of God among His people (1 Sam. 4:22; Isa. 6:3; John 1:14).

To believe in Jesus Christ as the Lord of glory is not consistent "with respect of persons" (v. 1). Such a partiality to persons because of their status, whether rich or poor, is forbidden by God (Deut. 1:17). In this instance, what is involved is favoritism to the rich. The Christian "assembly" is, in the Greek text, the *synagogue*. This was the earliest name for the church. The Christian synagogue, because it held strictly to the Old Testament revelation, saw itself, not as a new group, but as the true vessel of the ancient faith. It attracted, especially in its earliest days, more than a few persons of note who were curious about this messianic synagogue. When such persons attended the Christian synagogue, much attention was paid to them. Late comers sat on the floor, but these important, curious persons were given good seats rather than the floor space (vv. 2-4). This could be called courtesy, but, at the same time, poor visitors had no such courtesy extended to them. They were told to sit on the floor. Such partiality James calls *evil* (v. 4). Paul, in 1 Corinthians 1:1ff., makes a like point, condemning partiality on the basis of status. The fact was that, while many prominent Greek and Roman converts were early made, for some years the notable Jewish thinkers stayed outside the Christian fold, no matter how great their curiosity. God, James reminded the church, was confounding the wisdom of the wise and choosing "the poor of this world" as "heirs of the kingdom," a kingdom "promised to them that love Him" (v. 5). To show partiality to the cultured despisers of Jesus Christ is to go against the Lord.

Already these powerful leaders were oppressing and arresting Christians, and having them taken to court for trial (v. 6). Their treatment in court would not be lightened by their courtesy in church, for these leaders were heartless men. "Do they not blaspheme that worthy name by which ye are called?" (v. 7). In other words, their presence at the church was at times intended only to silence the Christians and to facilitate their arrest.

James did *not* call for discourtesy to these visitors. Rather, he insisted on the same Godly treatment of all in terms of "the royal law," "Thou shalt love thy neighbour as thyself" (v. 8; Lev. 19:18; Matt. 22:39; Rom. 13:8-9; Gal. 5:14, 6:2).

James then makes an important point with respect to the law: it is a unity, not a collection of miscellaneous texts. To break a regulation of the state with respect to some rule about the disposal of trash does not make us guilty or lawless men in reality. There are enough statist regulations enacted, of which we are ignorant, to convict us all many times over. God's law is different. It is a unity, and its purpose is justice. If we violate the law at any point, we have chosen injustice. We have broken the law. If we exercise daily and then take poison, the poison negates our exercise. So, James says, we must keep the whole law to avoid being a transgressor of the law (vv. 9-11). God's law is "the law of liberty" (v. 12), but sin is slavery (John 8:34). To break God's moral law at any point is to move from freedom into slavery.

Statist criminal law is having trouble disengaging itself from this Biblical premise. However exemplary a man's life may be otherwise, if he commits murder, he is sentenced for murder. However, social factors are increasingly being weighed before sentence is pronounced.

Instead of being governed by social factors and the status of men, we must be governed by God's law, "the law of liberty" (v. 12).

James' conclusion is important: "For he shall have judgment without mercy, that hath shewed no mercy; and mercy rejoiceth against judgment" (v. 13). We are not to be hard-hearted. The fact that the prosperous visitors to the meeting may be enemies of Christ does not give us the right to be merciless or unkind. The Golden Rule still must govern us. To show grace and mercy towards enemies will bring mercy and grace to us from our God.

A.T. Robertson pointed out that, as late as the fourth century, there are references to the church as the "synagogue."[1]

The reference to gold rings is better translated as "a gold-ringed man," i.e., having many rings. One of these would be the signet ring. Greeks and Romans wore many rings, often more than one on a finger, but never on the right hand. After the battle of Cannae, Hannibal sent as a trophy to Carthage three bushels of gold rings taken from the Roman dead.

Early Christians for some generations wore rings adorned with symbols of the faith, such as the cross, the anchor, the monogram of Christ, etc.[2]

St. Paul, in 1 Corinthians 1, echoes James on respect of persons and calls attention to the false starting points of Jewish and Greco-Roman thought. Jesus Christ is the only true premise of thinking, and those who reject Him are, despite their claims of wisdom, fools and sinners.

---

[1] Archibald Thomas Robertson, *Word Pictures in the New Testament*, vol. VI (Grand Rapids, Michigan: Baker Book House, 1933 reprint), 28.

[2] M. R. Vincent, *Word Studies in the New Testament*, vol. I (Macdill AFB, Florida: MacDonald Publishing Co., reprint, n.d.), 351.

Chapter Six
Faith and Works
(James 2:14-26)

14. What doth it profit, my brethren, though a man say he hath faith, and have not works? can faith save him?
15. If a brother or sister be naked, and destitute of daily food,
16. And one of you say unto them, Depart in peace, be ye warmed and filled; notwithstanding ye give them not those things which are needful to the body; what doth it profit?
17. Even so faith, if it hath not works, is dead, being alone.
18. Yea, a man may say, Thou hast faith, and I have works: shew me thy faith without thy works, and I will shew thee my faith by my works.
19. Thou believest that there is one God; thou doest well: the devils also believe, and tremble.
20. But wilt thou know, O vain man, that faith without works is dead?
21. Was not Abraham our father justified by works, when he had offered Isaac his son upon the altar?
22. Seest thou how faith wrought with his works, and by works was faith made perfect?
23. And the scripture was fulfilled which saith, Abraham believed God, and it was imputed upon him for righteousness: and he was called the Friend of God.
24. Ye see then how that by works a man is justified, and not by faith only.
25. Likewise also was not Rahab the harlot justified by works, when she had received the messengers, and had sent them out another way?
26. For as the body without the spirit is dead, so faith without works is dead also. (James 2:14-26)

This may well be the most controversial text in all the Bible. Many avoid James' epistle because they will not face up to this text.

We need to recognize that much can be separated in analysis that cannot be separated in life. We can and of necessity do analyze the human respiratory system and the circulatory system separately, but neither can exist without the other. *Faith* in theology is tied to the doctrine of salvation, and works to sanctification, but, just as breathing is necessary for the life of the heart, so too are works to a living faith. This is why James can say, "Ye see then how that by works a man is justified, and not by faith only" (v. 24). Those who would separate faith and works can only do so theologically, and they should do so, but in life the two are inseparable. To take a theological distinction and assume that in life what is an otherwise valid and necessary difference is a radical separation of one from the other is to confuse dissection with life.

James confronts us with this fact: "What doth it profit, my brethren, though a man say he hath faith, and have not works, can faith save him?" (v. 14). Can a man live with a heart only, and not lungs?

James then uses a very practical illustration of the interconnection of faith and works. Given the need for charity in the Jerusalem Christian synagogue, and like churches elsewhere, his example is both blunt and real. If a fellow believer is naked and hungry, and if we simply say, "Depart in peace, be ye warmed and filled," or, "we will pray for you," and nothing more, what good is all this? Such a professed faith, having no works, is dead. It is dead because faith cannot stand alone: it manifests itself in works (vv. 15-17).

James is *not* anti-theology; what he is against is the separation of theology from life, the reduction of faith to easy-believism, and the negation of action as the expression of faith. Neither valid faith nor valid works can be separated one from another. How can any man demonstrate a valid faith without works? Faith is shown by works (v. 18).

Simple belief saves no man. "Thou believest that there is one God; thou doest well: the devils also believe, and tremble" (v. 19). A more blunt and telling statement of the case cannot be imagined. Those in hell, beginning with the very devils, believe that God is; the knowledge makes them tremble, *but it does not save them.*

"But wilt thou know, O vain man, that faith without works is dead?" (v. 20). Such a man is called *vain* by James. The word is *kenos*, meaning empty, foolish, senseless, purposeless; it is highly uncomplimentary. James does not dignify the position as one of valid dissent: it is a fool's opinion.

Then, in vv. 21-24, James turns to Abraham, the covenant father, revered alike by Jews and Christians. He says without qualification that Abraham was "justified by works, when he had offered Isaac his son upon the altar" (v. 21). The reality of Abraham's faith was manifested in his readiness to obey God, even to binding Isaac to the altar (Gen. 22:9). God waited until Abraham's faith was shown by his works before He delivered Isaac.

James continues, "Seest thou how faith wrought with his works, and by works was faith made perfect" (v. 22). Literally, James says, "faith worked with his works." Faith became works, a realization of itself. Faith expressed itself, or revealed itself, in works. There is an essential connection between the two.

This, James says, is what the Scripture means when it says, "Abraham believed God, and it was imputed unto him for righteousness: and he was called the Friend of God" (v. 23).

It is in 2 Chronicles 20:7 that Abraham is called God's "friend for ever." In Genesis 15:6, we are told that Abraham "believed in the LORD; and he counted it to him for righteousness." Paul cites this verse in Romans 4:3 and

Galatians 3:6. Paul uses the text to criticize the idea of salvation through works, James to call attention to the emptiness of faith without works. It was Paul who, in Romans 3:31, said, "Do we then make void the law through faith? God forbid: we establish the law." Above all, our Lord in Matthew 7:16-23 makes totally clear that "Ye shall know them by their fruits," i.e., by their works.

It is plain, James insists, that a man is justified by his works, not by faith only (v. 24). Works manifest the reality of a man's faith, so that his justification is shown to be real by his works, not by his faith only.

James then gives another illustration, Rahab. The account in Joshua makes obvious the terror of the people of Jericho. They knew what God had done to other peoples, so that they believed that the Hebrew's God was working to destroy their enemies. Only Rahab *acted* on that faith; her works alone showed the reality of her faith. Hence, James says, she was *justified* by her works, i.e., her justification was manifested in her works.

Very clear in all that James has to say is that both faith and works have reference to God and to His law. The Council of Trent related faith to assent to the church, and too many Protestant groups have in practice tended to do the same. Both faith and works must be seen as essentially a trust in and obedience to God and His inscriptured word.

James concludes with another blunt statement: "For as the body without the spirit is dead, so faith without works is dead also" (v. 26). James does not say it is *weak*, but rather that it is *dead*. Here again, as in the Sermon on the Mount, and all the Gospels and epistles, we are told how to "judge righteous judgment" (John 7:24). There are many who follow ancient Greek thinking to say that we cannot know a man's heart and therefore cannot judge him, whereas our Lord says plainly, "by their fruits ye shall know them" (Matt. 7:20). Works are faith in action, faith made manifest.

Chapter Seven

The Tongues of Leaders
(*James 3:1-5*)

1. My brethren, be not many masters, knowing that we shall receive the greater condemnation.
2. For in many things we offend all. If any man offend not in word, the same is a perfect man, and able also to bridle the whole body.
3. Behold, we put bits in the horses' mouths, that they may obey us; and we turn about their whole body.
4. Behold also the ships, which though they be so great, and are driven of fierce winds, yet are they turned about with a very small helm, whithersoever the governor listeth.
5. Even so the tongue is a little member, and boasteth great things. Behold, how great a matter a little fire kindleth! (James 3:1-5)

The entire third chapter of James takes up again the problem of speech, of verbal sinning. The works of faith mean not only Godly actions but also Godly speech. This was a matter of importance, and a moral question, in Jewish society, as it is in ours. In civilized and more or less orderly societies, men are more prone, because it is safer, to unleash hatred and hostility by their tongues than by aggressive action. In many backward societies, men are often very careful to speak guardedly because ugly words can mean their death. At least one people still have no word for "no" because rejection is dangerous. Women have a reputation for being looser with their tongues, but this is unusual when they do not confront the world directly, but do so only through a father or a husband. Speech is a means of aggression and war, and it is more likely to be used, and more safely used, in an orderly society. James thus wrote to a people living in an orderly context, and this is therefore especially true for church peoples in our time.

He begins by warning, "My brethren, be not many masters," or, better, teachers, i.e., rabbis or pastors. The honor of the position is far outweighed by its liabilities, the chief of which is the greater condemnation for sins by the Lord. R. V. G. Tasker commented:

> Not unnaturally James follows the statement *faith without works is dead* by the reminder that works are not to be limited to actions. Words are also works. Indeed, much of the work of the world is accomplished through the medium of words. This is particularly true of the work of teachers. Hence James sounds the warning 'Let not many of you become teachers' (R.S.V.). Often the words of teachers leave an indelible impression for good and evil upon receptive and immature minds....

167

Teachers are continually engaged in passing judgments, both moral and intellectual.[1]

In viewing the callings of men, whether husbands, employers, or teachers, we tend to see only the advantages, not the liabilities before God and man.

All of us, either as fallen men or as sinners saved by grace, offend others. We all offend. The man who does not offend by word is a mature man who has learned to bridle his tongue. We all offend others "in many things." However, the man who does not offend by his speech is a mature man because he has learned to keep his tongue in check (v. 2).

Speech is thus presented as a criterion of character. It is one of the key works, at the very least, that indicates what we are. It reveals what we think, both about ourselves and about others. Because speech is often a form of back-stabbing, it is very deadly. Our Lord repeatedly speaks of the evil of the unbridled tongue, as in Matthew 12:33-37:

> 33. Either make the tree good, and his fruit good; or else make the tree corrupt, and his fruit corrupt: for the tree is known by his fruit.
> 34. O generation of vipers, how can ye, being evil, speak good things? for out of the abundance of the heart the mouth speaketh.
> 35. A good man out of the good treasure of the heart bringeth forth good things: and an evil man out of the evil treasure bringeth forth evil things.
> 36. But I say unto you, That every idle word that men shall speak, they shall give account thereof in the day of judgment.
> 37. For by thy words thou shalt be justified, and by thy words thou shalt be condemned.

These are not words that can be spiritualized away.

In vv. 3-5, James compares the tongue, *first*, to the bit in a horse's mouth whereby the horse, larger and more powerful than a man, is controlled. *Second*, a large ship is directed in the face of the fiercest winds by a very small helm, controlled by a helmsman. *Third*, a small fire can create a gigantic blaze and destroy much property.

Speech, James tells us, is similar. Its power is very great. In the *first* illustration, a powerful horse is controlled by man for good and a direction given by the rider or driver. Similarly, the tongue is a controlling force for good or for evil. It provides leadership and direction. To use the tongue, created with so noble a purpose, for evil is to abuse a power given to us. *Second*, the life of those aboard a ship depends in a storm especially on the helmsman. His command of the helm brings life or death to all on board. We must remember that, in these early verses, James speaks of potential teachers or pastors. Their use of the tongue can either save or shipwreck the

---

[1] R. V. G. Tasker, *The General Epistle of James* (Grand Rapids, Michigan: Eerdmans, 1982 reprint), 72.

congregation. *Third*, the analogy of fire is used. A small spark can burn down a house or destroy a forest.

We must again remember that James was writing to Jewish Christians who, like modern ones, had the security of a somewhat orderly society. No man would have a knife at his throat if he spoke slanderously or carelessly. Then as now, congregations were torn apart by petty talk and grievances. In Phillipians 4:2, we see Paul plead with two women "that they be of the same mind in the Lord." An essentially good church was disturbed by their conflict. Too often people allow their petty likes and dislikes to prevail over the peace and unity of Christ's congregation.

James begins by speaking to leaders and would-be leaders in the church. He then broadens the scope to speak to everyone, because the tongue is a problem with everyone.

In my youth, a pastor, speaking on James 3, said that a tongue was either the last thing to be converted, or else what first revealed a person's unconverted status: he was not sure which! In any case, it is serious.

A missionary in my youth spoke on the various diseases common to his mission field. Some were unknown to an American community but so common in that out of the way area as to be taken for granted. What sickened his listeners was an accepted fact of everyday life in his field. We have come to accept irresponsibility in speech as easily as the natives accepted that field live with diseases, for example.

James began with the leaders and prospective leaders. Today we too often hear of the rash and irresponsible comments of pastors and of prominent churchmen, and it is important to remember that James describes the tongue as a potentially destructive force in all of life, in church, home, workplace, and society. Words like a small fire can set alight a great conflagration. Moreover, God holds us accountable for every idle word.

Chapter Eight
The Tongue and Self-Revelation
(James 3:6-12)

6. And the tongue is fire, a world of iniquity: so is the tongue among our members, that it defileth the whole body, and setteth on fire the course of nature; and it is set on fire of hell.
7. For every kind of beasts, and of birds, and of serpents, and of things in the sea, is tamed, and hath been tamed of mankind:
8. But the tongue can no man tame; it is an unruly evil, full of deadly poison.
9. Therewith bless we God, even the Father; and therewith curse we men, which are made after the similitude of God.
10. Out of the same mouth proceedeth blessing and cursing. My brethren, these things ought not so to be.
11. Doth a fountain send forth at the same place sweet water and bitter?
12. Can the fig tree, my brethren, bear olive berries? either a vine, figs? so can no fountain both yield salt water and fresh. (James 3:6-12)

In Leviticus 19:16, we have a law against "talebearers," i.e., gossips. It has no human-imposed required penalty; it is God who punishes us for it. Certainly what James has to say comes under Leviticus 19:16, but it goes much further.

Speech, says James, is revelational of man. Its tells us what the nature of a person is. When we speak, we reveal ourselves. Speech is a very important fact. Animals can communicate certain things, but they cannot speak. Speech is an attribute limited to man, and to angelic and demonic beings. The supreme Speaker is God, whose speech is always His revelation.

To speak is therefore a privilege, and one that must not be lightly used. We are known by what we say as well as what we do.

Two of the Ten Commandments govern speech: "Thou shalt not take the name of the LORD thy God in vain: for the LORD will not hold him guiltless that taketh his name in vain" (Deut. 5:11), and, "Neither shalt thou bear false witness against thy neighbor" (Deut. 5:20). Obviously, speech is very important to God; it is a communicable attribute which He shares with man.

The tongue is revelational of man. Because man is fallen, the tongue "is a fire, a world of iniquity." Our speech reveals what we are, and, in fallen man, it reveals the depravity of our being. In fact, James says, the tongue "is set on fire of hell," so that it defiles the body and the whole course of nature (v. 6).

James echoes Christ's teaching: "Out of the abundance of the heart the mouth speaketh" (Matt. 12:34); and, "Out of the heart proceed evil thoughts, murders, adulteries, fornications, thefts, false witness, blas-phemies; these are the things which defile a man" (Matt. 15:19).

All kinds of animals, James continues, are tamed by men. In that era, amazing acts of animal taming existed, and James was aware of them (v. 7). As against this, James declares, no man has been able to tame the fallen man's tongue. It is "an unruly evil, full of deadly poison" (v. 8). Man being evil, his tongue is evil. Like a rattlesnake, the tongue of man is full of venom and is ready to strike at any provocation.

In vv. 9-10, James cites the abuse of speech. We bless God, and we curse men made in His image. The same mouth both blesses and curses, and this is very wrong. We play the judge, which is to usurp God's prerogative. In Scripture, to curse is to condemn *religiously*; it is not normally an individual's prerogative to do so because we are not God.

Then, in vv. 11-12, James uses some illustrations from the natural world. These echo Matthew 7:16-20, which tell us that only a good tree can bear good fruit. James says that a fountain cannot at one and the same time send forth both good water and bitter water (v. 11). This is an orderly world, and there is a consistency in things. The meaning is that a tongue that lets loose both good and evil must be hypocritical in its pretense to goodness. The heart reveals itself, despite the protective coloration of piety, in its evil expressions.

"Slips of the tongue" are likely to be slips of the heart, revealing the man.

A fig tree cannot bear olives, nor a vine figs. "So can no fountain both yield salt water and fresh" (v. 12). Again we have an echo of the Sermon on the Mount, Matthew 7:16-20. Speech is revelational, and we had better recognize it as such.

What James gives us is more than a warning against gossip. Rather, he tells us to examine ourselves, or, our speech, because it reveals to others what we are.

The Renaissance was an aggressive, immoral, and degenerate era on the whole, and this was made manifest in its gross, foul speech. John Calvin was unusual in the plainness and cleanness of his writings. Vituperative language was common on all sides.

It is an interesting thing to study other religions because, before imitations of biblical faith came into vogue, there were no written revelations. Speech was not highly regarded in such religions. Many looked to dice, bones, strange natural events, and the like for hints from the spirit world, or from the gods. If oracles spoke, it was in strange and incoherent ways.

In the Bible, the prophet *speaks*, and he gives to man a word from God, a plain word, such as, "Thou art the man" (2 Sam. 12:7). Because God is totally self-conscious, perfect in all His Being and without any darkness in

His "mind" or nature, His speech is clear and unequivocal. Failure to understand is due to our blindness and deafness, not His word.

Whenever Christianity is faithful and strong, it creates a culture which stresses and gives clarity to the word, written and spoken: it honors and purifies speech. Too commonly, in apostate or fallen cultures, speech is a tool of aggression, not communication or community. Speech and writing are used to propagandize and to deceive, not to enlighten. Perjury becomes a common practice, and men like Nietszche declare that a lie is often more useful than the truth.

What James is telling us involves more than disapproval of gossip or bad language. We are told that language reveals our nature to both God and to man. We are warned that speech tells everyone what our professions of the faith are worth. Our speech betrays us. The tongue *cannot* be tamed unless the person is tamed and made a new creation by Christ. The tongue reveals what we are, and to whom we belong.

Chapter Nine
Two Kinds of Wisdom
(James 3:13-18)

13. Who is a wise man and endued with knowledge among you? let him shew out of a good conversation his works with meekness of wisdom.
14. But if ye have bitter envying and strife in your hearts, glory not, and lie not against the truth.
15. This wisdom descendeth not from above, but is earthly, sensual, devilish.
16. For where envying and strife is, there is confusion and every evil work.
17. But the wisdom that is from above is first pure, then peaceable, gentle, and easy to be intreated, full of mercy and good fruits, without partiality, and without hypocrisy.
18. And the fruit of righteousness is sown in peace of them that make peace. (James 3:13-18)

In v. 1, James began this section by speaking of masters or teachers in the Christian synagogue. In v. 13, he again speaks to the leaders, but, like the rest of his letter, it is also counsel for all Christians.

James Hope Moulton commented on this text:

"Who is enlightened among you, and a man of knowledge? Let him exhibit the fruits of it by a noble life, with the humility that true enlightenment brings." We must be careful to remember that "meekness" in popular usage has lost its nobility: the Greek word describes a strong man's self-discipline and a wise man's humility. One who is strong, and knows it, is not jealous of rivals, or frenzied with partisanship for a cause that God will prosper.[1]

In a fallen world, even words tend to depreciate in meaning, and *meekness*, which in origin means controlled or harnessed through strength, has come to imply mousiness.

A wise man who to his wisdom adds knowledge will demonstrate what he is not only by his words, but also by his works (v. 13). Men reveal themselves by their words *and* their works. The "meekness of wisdom" means that they are aware of their strength in God. As Moulton noted, they know that in the Lord their victory is certain. They do not face the hostilities, oppositions, and frustrations of this world alone or in isolation and weakness. It is an aspect of wisdom to know that God is always with us.

The contentious leader (or member) will be a frustrated man, with "bitter envying and strife" in his heart. R. C. H. Lenski rendered v. 14 thus: "But if you have bitter zeal and selfishness in your heart, do not be boasting

---

[1] James Hope Moulton, "James," in Arthur S. Peake, editor, *A Commentary on the Bible* (London, England: T. C. & C. C), 905.

and lying against the truth!" A false zeal will not be joyful but rather bitter. Zeal in itself is not a mark of truth nor grace.

There are two kinds of wisdom. *First*, there is the wisdom that comes from God. The Bible's "wisdom literature" indicates how practical Godly wisdom is, whereas humanistic wisdom is abstract and unrelated to living. Proverbs 8:36 is a telling and illustrative statement of Godly wisdom.

Second, man's wisdom, worldly wisdom, or humanistic wisdom can be any number of things: scientific, economic, political, and so on, but it is separate from morality because it is in essence separated from God, and this is purported to be its practicality and virtue. James in v. 15 says, in Lenski's translation, "This wisdom is not one coming down from above, but is earthly, sensual, demoniacal. For where there is zeal and selfishness, there is disturbance and every bad thing."[2]

This is necessarily so, "For where envying and strife is, there is confusion and every evil work" (v. 16). This is an eschatological statement. It tells us that evil in all its forms is self-defeating. The man who truly believes in the triune God knows that he is called to victory, and he will work with patience and confidence.

As against this humanistic wisdom, Godly wisdom "is first pure, then peaceable, gentle, and easy to be entreated, full of mercy and good fruits, without partiality, and without hypocrisy" (v. 17). Again, this and v. 18 are eschatological. The consequence of false wisdom is destruction and death, whereas Godly wisdom leads to the benefits of a triumphant certainty and victory. Whether we like it or not, the wisdom we cultivate can reveal itself in all our being. The blessed meek are God's nobility: they know their calling is to victory (1 John 5:4), and they move in that grace and confidence.

"And the fruit of righteousness is sown in peace of them that make peace" (v. 18). The assurance of victory marks the wise. Their radical dedication to God's righteousness or justice marks them in the peace they communicate in all their being.

We fail to appreciate the extent to which our faith shapes us. An intelligent and talented woman who was totally without a Christian faith saw only a growing disaster in American life, in every area of activity and thinking. A talented musician, she ceased playing either her piano or her organ because one should not be joyful in a dying culture. She died miserably and alone, too painful to be near.

At the same time, another woman of confident faith drew people to herself because her serenity was so contagious. Except for a few, people were unaware of the horrors and griefs she had experienced. Psalm 84:5-7

---

2. R. C. H. Lenski, *The Interpretation of the Epistle to the Hebrews and the Epistle of James* (Columbus, Ohio: Wartburg Press, 1946), 616.

speaks of those persons who go through the valley of Baca, a desert place, and make it a well, an area with pools of refreshing water, because they create their own climate by their faith.

Language is a central part of the human climate, and it surrounds us daily. Even if we are entirely alone, our innermost thoughts are verbal, and we thereby create a good or a bad climate to live in.

Thus language is not only a privilege which on earth is restricted to mankind, but it is also basic to self-communication. We are in constant communion with our own souls, and we determine the nature thereof. We can poison ourselves with our thoughts, or we can bless ourselves by relying on, and often by reciting to ourselves, the word of God. We then manifest wisdom from on high. Of course, we can choose to poison ourselves by thoughts which are bitter and which isolate us from God as well as man. It is the wisdom of James to confront us with the great and grave importance of language and speech.

Chapter Ten
Problems and Growth
(*James 4:1-6*)

1. From whence come wars and fightings among you? come they not hence, even of your lusts that war in your members?
2. Ye lust, and have not: ye kill, and desire to have, and cannot obtain: ye fight and war, yet ye have not, because ye ask not.
3. Ye ask, and receive not, because ye ask amiss, that ye may consume it upon your lusts.
4. Ye adulterers and adulteresses, know ye not that the friendship of the world is enmity with God? whosoever therefore will be a friend to the world is the enemy of God.
5. Do ye think that the scripture saith in vain, The spirit that dwelleth in us lusteth to envy?
6. But he giveth more grace. Wherefore he saith, God resisteth the proud, but giveth grace unto the humble. (James 4:1-6)

These verses give us a very different portrait of the early church from the idealized accounts. They contain a very blunt indictment of certain, sinful tendencies. We are told, *first*, of wars and fightings, traced to the lusts or desires at war in their members. *Second*, we are told that they desire things they do not have. *Third*, they "kill," or they wish others dead, for actual murder would have brought the Romans onto the scene. *Fourth*, James says, ye "desire to have, and cannot obtain." *Fifth*, "ye fight and war, yet ye have not, because ye ask not." They do not ask of God because they perhaps know that their hopes are ungodly. *Sixth*, when they do pray, their prayers are wrong: "Ye ask, and receive not, because ye ask amiss, that ye may consume it upon your lusts" or pleasures. *Seventh*, James calls them "adulterers and adulteresses" in relationship to God, to whom they are faithless. *Eighth*, they fail to recognize that friendship with the world is enmity towards God. In fact, to be the world's friend is to be God's enemy (vv. 1-4).

To whom is James speaking? To just the church, or more than the church? We must remember that Judea at that time was in turmoil over various issues. Many were expecting the Messiah. Others felt that war against Rome would bring Judea heavenly and miraculous help. The country was deeply involved in intense factionalism, which Josephus recorded. These various factions divided the people, and the Christian synagogues were infected by the same vain hopes, so that James' indictment mirrors the Jewish scene, both Christian and non-Christian. The intensity of popular feelings severely limited the scope of action and intelligent analysis. Josephus revealed the horror of a man who saw intelligent decisions ruled out by fanatical imperatives. The early Christians were people of their times. The fact that they survived the national judgment came from the impact of Matthew 24 and probably also James 4:1ff. Between the ascension and the outbreak of the Jewish-Roman War in A.D. 66, the Christians had slowly but surely disentangled themselves from the fanaticisms of popular eschatology.

Thus, James 4:1ff reflects the national scene as it impinged upon the church, or the Christian synagogue. But this passage also tell us about the nature of man and the source of his problems and his religious failures.

In v. 1, we are told that the conflicts of nations have their origins in man's fallen being. As sinful men, we create sinful societies. No arrangement of powers and forces in any society can undercut the impact of man's sin. To blame on some other agency the guilt for our society's evils is conspiracy thinking such as Adam and Eve indulged in to account for their sin. The Godly will say with David, "Against thee, thee only, have I sinned, and done this evil in thy sight: that thou mightest be justified when thou speakest, and be clear when thou judgest" (Ps. 51:4). Evil begins in man's heart and then embodies itself in life, in men, and in institutions. The modern view is that evil begins outside of men, in economic arrangements, in religions, in families, and so on and on.

In v. 2, James calls attention to the perpetual frustrations of sinful men. Their lips may profess faith and virtue, but in practice they negate these things.

God rejects their prayers because, however good the ostensible purpose of their requests, their actual motivation is not Godly (v. 3). They want what is not possible, peace with God at the same time as peace with a fallen, God-hating world. This compromising position means enmity with God.

The Holy Spirit, whom the Lord gave to dwell within us, yearns jealously to make us the Lord's (v. 5). The Lord gives greater grace to those who seek it. God resists the proud but gives grace to the lowly (v. 6). We must therefore be meek and lowly before the Lord, acknowledging our sins and our needs.

What James gives us is a very important analysis. He requires us to recognize how much we are children of our time, and how deeply our world has shaped us. The members of the Christian synagogues of James' day were not inferior to us. Their survival in the Jewish-Roman War of A.D. 66-70 tells us that they learned and grew in terms of Godly teaching and the Spirit's leadings. Their sins were very real, but their grace was even greater. If James' epistle does not accomplish a like work in our time, we have only ourselves to blame.

The locale of sin is the human heart. We cannot without sin neglect that fact. The bitter conflicts within Judaean society in our Lord's day and up to the War were seen by the people as occasioned by the Roman overlordship. Their doctrines of sin and responsibility were very defective, as are ours.

We can understand the blinding effect of sin by looking at the reception of James' letter in the churches. It should provoke us to self-examination, to confession, to repentance, and to renewed service. A proud people and generation will not be heard by God. The heavens become deaf and like stone to the prayers of those who want answers but will not repent.

As James later says (vv. 13-15), we whose lives are so ephemeral too readily assume that there is no end, that there is neither judgment nor accountability, when in truth all our days are forever held to an accounting. James calls for the intensity of faith of a Job, or an Elijah (5:11, 17-18).

Chapter Eleven

The Holy War
(James 4:7-10)

7. Submit yourselves therefore to God. Resist the devil, and he will flee from you.
8. Draw nigh to God, and he will draw nigh to you. Cleanse your hands, ye sinners; and purify your hearts, ye double minded.
9. Be afflicted, and mourn, and weep: let your laughter be to turned to mourning, and your joy to heaviness.
10. Humble yourselves in the sight of the Lord, and he shall lift you up. (James 4:7-10)

It is apparent by now that James is concerned with the springs of human action. His analysis places him at odds with our present culture of victimhood and environmentalism. The origins of human conflict, personal and national, are traced to our own nature. Being at war within ourselves, we are also at war with one another. We may profess peace, but we are more inclined to conflict and war than anything else. History is a reflection of man's inner nature and turmoil. Sophisticated rationalizing simply masks the actual roots of conflict within human nature. The fall of man created warfare between man and God, between man and man, and within man's own being.

The solution, says James, sounds simple but is in reality drastic: "Submit yourselves therefore to God. Resist the devil, and he will flee from you" (v. 7). "Submit yourselves," in the Greek a form of *hupotasso*, means to put into subjection, subordinate, or submit to, to be under the authority of. We must place ourselves under the authority and rule of the triune God. God cannot be viewed as merely an available resource when needed, but must be viewed always and only as the ultimate power, authority, and lawgiver. In Robert Johnstone's words, this means, "'Submit yourselves unto the Lord,' then, brethren — to His grace and to His law, whether in regard to being or doing."[1] As H.A.W. Meyer noted, "submission to God means resistance to the devil."[2]

Although not now a popular concept, *submission* is a fact of life. We have today, as often in history, a slavish submission to the popular culture and a strong resistance to God. Moral standards are reversed, and the tyranny of the mob is seen as freedom because it expresses hatred for, and a revolt against, God. In 1 Peter 5:8-9, submission to the devil means the temptation to apostasy, to a compliance with the world against Jesus Christ. According

---

[1]. Robert Johnstone, *The Epistle of James* (Grand Rapids, Michigan: Baker Book House, 1954 reprint), 321.
[2]. H.A.W. Meyer, *James, Peter, John, and Jude* (Peabody, Massachusetts: Hendriksen Publishers, 1983), 134. Originally published in 1883.

to the *Shepherd of Hermas*, "The Devil can fight, but he cannot conquer; if, therefore, thou dost withstand him, he will flee from thee, beaten and ashamed." We must submit to God, not sit in judgment over Him. Luther said, "God gave us his law, not that we should censure it, but keep it."[3]

Verse 8 declares, "Draw nigh to God, and he will draw nigh to you. Cleanse your hands, ye sinners; and purify your hearts, ye double minded." What James has in mind is man's total moral purification: our hands (our actions), our hearts (our motives), and our minds (our thoughts) must be cleansed and purified. In Exodus 30:20, the washing of hands by the priests before beginning their sacrificial duties is mandatory, and James' requirement echoes it. Men must see themselves as sinners when they approach God, for they stand by virtue of God's grace, not their works. James addresses us all as "ye sinners." In James 1:6-8, we are reminded of the instability of the double minded: such men receive nothing from the Lord.

James' requirement of us is stated in v. 10: "Humble yourselves in the sight of the Lord, and he shall lift you up." "Lift you up" can be rendered, "He shall exalt you." This humility must be before God: it is not to be displayed before men. Too often in the history of the church elaborate displays of humility before men have occurred as a part of ascetic disciplines. As vv. 11ff make clear, James obviously calls for is an inner humility before God, an obedience to God's law in respect to our brethren. It is then a call for a practical humility, a working obedience to God's law towards others.

James clearly has no use for the parade of piety by the Pharisees and others, neither in the church community nor out of it. Hypocrisy and pretense are alien to true faith, which is marked by works. James makes it clear that he is weary of religious people who are strong on professions of faith and low on works.

Hypocrisy is pretending to be something we are not, and it is a very common and popular human failing. The solution is not to express our evil propensities, but to obey God. In the 1940s, I heard members of one cult, given to bad language and coarse speech, defend their practice as honest because they spoke without pretense. Their speech was routinely offensive to others. But this is not the solution. We are not to pursue evil in any form, but to pursue righteousness. If we indulge in foul language, why not evil conduct? The cult members had no answer to that.

The presupposition of James, and the whole Bible, is that a holy war is under way, and man, in his every word, thought, and deed, is involved in that war. He can, in one way or another, give aid and comfort to the

---

[3]. Cited by John Peter Lange, *Commentary on the Holy Scriptures, James, Jude* (Grand Rapids, Michigan: Zondervan, reprint of 1867 edition), 124.

enemy, or he can resist him. "Resist the devil, and he will flee from you" (v. 7). Resistance is half the battle won.

The battlefield in this warfare is in the life of man. James requires us, by his plain speaking, to recognize this fact, and to recognize that the first step to victory is resistance. James' epistle is a call to resistance and to holy warfare, one with the clear assurance of victory. We are not victims in this battle, but a people called to and promised victory.

Chapter Twelve

Law and Time
(James 4:11-17)

11. Speak not evil one of another, brethren. He that speaketh evil of his brother, and judgeth his brother, speaketh evil of the law, and judgeth the law: but if thou judge the law, thou art not a doer of the law, but a judge.
12. There is one lawgiver, who is able to save and to destroy: who art thou that judgest another?
13. Go to now, ye that say, To day or to morrow we will go into such a city, and continue there a year, and buy and sell, and get gain:
14. Whereas ye know not what shall be on the morrow. For what is your life? It is even a vapour, that appeareth for a little time, and then vanisheth away.
15. For that ye ought to say, If the Lord will, we shall live, and do this, or that.
16. But now ye rejoice in your boastings: all such rejoicing is evil.
17. Therefore to him that knoweth to do good, and doeth it not, to him it is sin. (James 4:11-17)

There are two sections in our text: *first,* vv. 11-12 call for humility by recognizing that the law comes from God, not from us; therefore, He, not we, is the Judge. *Second,* we cannot command the length of our life or the future; therefore, we must humbly trust in God, and leave the judging to Him (vv. 13-17).

In v. 11, James returns once again to speech, to the lawless tongue, and he now carries his argument a step further. His argument is a very important one. To speak evil of one's brother, a fellow believer, is to break God's law. The commandment in Leviticus 19:16 forbidding tale-bearing does not allow us the freedom to bear tales that are true. Any kind of tale-bearing is forbidden because we must be a community, not a panel of judges. Both church and state have their jurisdictions here, and we have none. We are usurping God's prerogative of judgment, both through His appointed judges and on His own, by playing the judge. In Jude 8-10 we are told that even Michael the archangel *dared not* accuse Satan directly, but simply said, "The Lord rebuke thee." Our ready but ungodly judgments presume upon God's prerogative.

For us to pass our private judgments on others is to assume that God and His law cannot function without us. We then speak evil of the law and judge the law, and, implicitly, the Law-giver, God. "But if thou judge the law, thou art not a doer of the law, but a judge" (v. 11).

James then declares, "There is one lawgiver," an emphatic statement in the original, meaning, there is *only* one Law-giver, God. He can both save and destroy. Man and the state can only destroy; they cannot save, nor make alive. "Who art thou that judgest another?" (v. 12). *The prerogative of judgment is not ours, although God permits judgments within the limits of His law to His appointed judges.* Such judgments by men are only valid when they are within the limits of God's law. If God-ordained judges are limited, what right have we to judge casually and freely?

We are not gods, although it is our sin to try to be gods (Gen. 3:5). Can we truly ordain and govern our future? We are creatures of time, and we cannot ordain the length of our days and years. Thus, to plan without God, to assume that our future is ours to ordain, is foolishness (v. 13). We do not know what tomorrow will bring. A backward look will often tell us how unforeseen our days often are. To reckon our future, its buying and selling, without God is foolishness (v. 14). Life is transitory, like a vapor. Men are here today and gone tomorrow.

We ought, therefore, to plan always with the premise, "if God wills." We cannot guarantee ourselves a future by our willing; God alone determines our days (v. 15).

Law and time, like all things else, are alike given by God. In the *first* section of this text, we are reminded that the *law* is given by God. In the *second* section, we are bluntly told that *time* is also God's gift to us. Luther said of the former, "God gave us His law, not that we should censure it, but keep it (Deut. 7:11)."[1]

How can man claim to be the maker of the law when he cannot create time or the world? The law was given by God for an order He created. Man apart from God makes laws for a world he plans to remake. This is insanity and absurdity.

Our perspective should rather be this: "If the Lord will, we shall live, and do this, or that" (v. 15). This was long embodied in Christian speech. *Deo volante* in the Latin, *Dehr gahmehnah* in the Armenian, once familiar to most, and now forgotten.

This humility is gone now, James says. Once a part of a devout Jew's vocabulary, it is now replaced with a boastful confidence in one's ability to be one's own determiner and god (v. 16).

"Therefore to him that knoweth to do good, and doeth it not, to him it is sin" (v. 17). This verse seems out of place if it is read only in terms of v. 16. Rather, it sums up all that James has said up to this point. By his teaching, he has shown them God's way. He has stressed the law of God, and its application to human speech. He has left them *without excuse.*

So too every pastor who declares the law-word of God leaves his listeners without excuse. They have been charged with the law-word of God, and

---

[1] John Peter Lange, *James, Jude* (Grand Rapids, Michigan: Zondervan, reprint, n.d.), 124.

cannot neglect it without sin. To hear, and to pay no heed, means that the guilt is ours, and our own blood is on our heads (Ezek. 33:5-8).

James leaves people without excuse. Their own sin leads them into trouble, and their arrogant independence from God is their undoing. To profess faith is meaningless if it means no more than believing that *God is*: "The devils also believe, and tremble" (James 2:19). Faith requires a total trust in and dependence upon God as Lord, and it means living by every word that comes from the mouth of God (Matt. 4:4). What Satan tried to do in the temptation of our Lord was to offer another governing premise for mankind and to persuade our Lord of its validity: he had successfully tempted the first Adam, and now, the second Adam being man also, as well as God incarnate, he hoped to tempt Him into adopting the same premise, another word from the creature god (Gen. 3:5). James sees this temptation at work in the minds of all men, and his concern is to uproot it.

Chapter Thirteen
Judgment on the Rich
(James 5:1-6)

1. Go to now, ye rich men, weep and howl for your miseries that shall come upon you.
2. Your riches are corrupted, and your garments are motheaten.
3. Your gold and silver is cankered; and the rust of them shall be a witness against you, and shall eat your flesh as it were fire. Ye have heaped treasure together for the last days.
4. Behold, the hire of the labourers who have reaped down your fields, which is of you kept back by fraud, crieth: and the cries of them which have reaped are entered into the ears of the Lord of sabaoth.
5. Ye have lived in pleasure on the earth, and been wanton; ye have nourished your hearts, as in a day of slaughter. (James 5:1-6)

Without a knowledge of Acts 6:1-8, it is almost impossible to understand our text. In Acts 6:1ff, we see, *first*, that the early church, following and improving on the synagogue's practice, took care of all needy widows. *Second*, the deacons were appointed to carry out this duty. In Greco-Roman practice, rich patrons commonly took care of poor clients in return for praise and adulation from them. Statist welfarism was supplanting this practice. In Judaism, the care of the needy was a *religious* duty, and it was fulfilled by the Christian synagogue or church.

This was, however, an era of transition, and many converts, Jews and Gentiles alike, felt liberated from old requirements. The growing emphasis on individualism within the Empire left many unready to maintain the old requirements of God's law, or Greco-Roman practice.

Not only was the requirement of *charity* neglected, but the law of Leviticus 19:13 regarding prompt compensation was also set aside: there was neither *charity* nor *justice*.

For James, this meant that judgment was on the way, as indeed it was. We find that the early church developed a strong faithfulness to charity and justice, and, no doubt, James' letter contributed greatly to this change. For the present, however, the situation was an evil one.

James is unsparing. He tells the rich who are unjust and uncharitable to "weep and howl" because of the miseries that will soon overwhelm them (v. 1). This is strong language, but strong too was the judgment that came.

James' indictment, *first*, is that their wealth shall turn to rust and be devoured by moths (vv. 2-3). We can understand that costly woolen garments can be moth-eaten, but gold and silver do not rust, and James knew that full well. This is therefore a startling image. What James says is that the most secure forms of wealth and security will be turned against them by God's judgment. Their plans for security have experience behind them, but James' warning has God's judgment behind it. Their gold and silver will eat their flesh "as it were fire. Ye have heaped treasure together for the last days" (v. 3). A sound plan for security that leaves out God becomes a death-dealing fire.

Second, they have been unjust in their treatment of their workers (v. 4). They have held back the wages of workers, paying them as late as possible. The cries of their defrauded workers have been heard by "the Lord of Sabaoth," by the Lord of Hosts, literally, but the term means, by the omnipotent God. Are they so foolish to think that the all-powerful and omnipotent God will not judge them? Their treatment of poor workers shows contempt not only for these poor people, but also for the God who *commanded* that justice be done them.

Because the workingman then was a day laborer, he was to be paid by the day. Now men work by the week or month, and they must be paid accordingly. The point of Leviticus 19:13 is that the worker must be paid faithfully as contracted.

Then, *third,* James declares that these rich men have been mindless of their evil and their self-indulgence. They have lived wantonly and in terms of pleasure, as though nothing would ever change. They have been like cattle which, up to the time of their butchering, eat and are mindless of their coming slaughter (v. 5). They have condemned and murdered the just man, a man who was in no way resisting them. It was a Hebrew idiom to characterize the exploitation of the poor as a form of murder. It killed their ability to survive, and it reduced them to a position near to death.

James deals very bluntly with the problem of irresponsible wealth. He does *not* offer a political solution; it is not the duty of the state to take care of the poor. Had he thought so, he could have appealed to the then current example of Rome and its state welfarism. *He sees poverty not as a political problem but as a moral one.* Paul states it as a *commandment,* "that if any would not work, neither shall he eat" (2 Thess. 3:10). Those who could not work were to be provided for by the people of God.

James thus was attacking those who felt liberated from the law and who disregarded their religious and moral obligation to be members one of another (Eph. 4:25). Perhaps they assumed that, because the world was changing, so too their regard for and obedience to God's ancient law had changed. Moral relativism in any age is corrosive of law and society. Moral relativism too often seeks to take off what it sees as the rough edges of God's law, but, in doing so, it supplants God's word with man's. Erosion then sets in to destroy the whole of the law.

James is thus correct in condemning the arrogance of the rich. They have replaced God's law with their convenience, and the consequence will soon be judgment unless they repent.

Before long, we see Paul collecting funds for the famine in Judea from churches in other countries. Clearly, James' letter had prepared the way for this, because there were no dissenters to this moral obligation to be members one of another.

Christian charity grew rapidly to include the care, not only of needy fellow members, but of all needy peoples. Its faithfulness to the extent of God's law was notable. One of the aspects of the early church that commended it to unbelievers was its remarkable concern for and care of people in need, both Christian and non-Christian alike.

We need the letter of James once again to revivify the church in this respect. There are already evidences of a renewed emphasis on Christian works of mercy.

Chapter Fourteen

Judgment
(James 5:7-9)

7. Be patient therefore, brethren, unto the coming of the Lord. Behold, the husband-man waiteth for the precious fruit of the earth, and hath long patience for it, until he receive the early and latter rain.
8. Be ye also patient; stablish your hearts: for the coming of the Lord draweth nigh.
9. Grudge not one against another, brethren, lest ye be condemned: behold, the judge standeth before the door. (James 5:7-9)

In these three verses, James turns to the subject of judgment. Among many groups, the Last Judgment is the sole concern when this matter of judgment is discussed. Certainly the Last Judgment is important, and it is clearly the subject in Matthew 25:31-46. In Isaiah, however, we have a series of judgments pronounced on the nations of the day. God's judgments began in Eden; in the Flood, at the Tower of Babel, and during other events, we see His judgments on men and nations. God's judgments come in history to restore order by bringing about condemnation and destruction of sinful men and nations. When we pray, "Thy kingdom come. Thy will be done in earth, as it is in heaven" (Matt. 6:10), we are praying, among other things, for judgment. Jesus Christ is the Prince of Peace because He is the Lord of judgment. His coming in clouds is referred to in Isaiah 19:1 to signify judgment, so that the clouds of judgment do not have exclusive reference to the Last Judgment.

James, in speaking of the coming and very near judgment, had apparently Matthew 24 in mind, i.e., the approaching judgment on Jerusalem and Judea. "The last days" of v. 3 do not refer to the end of the world but to the end of the Judean order which condemned and crucified Christ.

From the biblical perspective, history is a series of judgments, great and small, culminating in the Last Judgment. Failure to recognize this fact is a failure to learn. Surely the twentieth century has seen a series of judgments; men's failure to see the wars and catastrophes as judgments becomes a failure to repent and to grow, and this only leads to more judgments.

Judgments are "the coming of the Lord" (v. 7) as King to bring conviction to evil-doers and justice to the world. Indeed, many "innocent men" die in these judgments, but a secularized world must be judged because it has forsaken justice. In v. 7, *patience* is urged until "the coming of the Lord." The Jewish-Roman War of A.D. 66-70 was unrivaled in its horrors, and, though Christians, being forewarned, survived it, they lost their homes and relatives. James uses a clearly startling image to describe the coming judgment. A harvest requires "the early and latter rain." The farmer patiently waits on the rains because he wants a harvest. So too must we wait on God's judgments as revivifying rain. The alternative to this is the continuation of injustice, and its triumph.

As with Egypt, upon whom judgment after judgment fell with increasing severity in the ten plagues, so too the people of the twentieth century refuse to learn and to be spared further judgments. In all this, God is breaking up ground to sow His seed.

James urges, therefore, "Be ye also patient; establish your hearts: for the coming of the Lord draweth nigh" (v. 8). Everything that these Jewish Christians loved, their land and its people, was about to be destroyed in this coming, and James, in vv. 7 and 8, urges *patience*, a very remarkable counsel.

In v. 9, the counsel is, "Grudge not one against another, brethren, lest ye be condemned: behold, the judge standeth at the door." The judgment is inevitable on a people who crucified their King, the Lord of glory. They are not to involve themselves in grudges, murmuring, or in intense recriminations. The deed is done. It is now time to think of the future, not the past. When the Judge stands at the door with His decreed judgment, it is too late to try to relive the past. As people of the past, they will then be judged; if they think in terms of the King's work, as people of the future, they will have a future.

The *coming* of the Lord is His *parousia*. This word, according to Alexander Ross, is found in the Egyptian papyri and means "royal visit."[1] The judgments of history are God's royal visits to the world. The word *parousia* appears in v. 7, in the reference to the coming of the Lord, and again in v. 8.

Instability marks a time of judgment, and therefore in both vv. 7 and 8 *patience* is urged. James knows that living in an age of crisis is painfully difficult. His letter never deludes us into thinking that it is an easy thing to go through times of upheaval and judgment. We are never told that a pseudo-piety can enable us to survive like Stoics in a time of destruction. Jeremiah's Lamentations, for one, militates against the idea that Stoicism is Godly.

James urges *patience* because the conclusion of God's judgments is good, however painful. In a sinful world, God's judgments are necessary, and they are, in their conclusions, a blessing. Patience means that our perspective is not existential but providential. We know by God's grace His purposes for His Kingdom, for history, and for us. Patience can be a mark of grace, a trust in God's purposes, and a knowledge that "we know that all

---

[1] Alexander Ross, *Commentary on the Epistles of James and John* (Grand Rapids, Michigan: Eerdmans, 1954), 92.

things work together for good to them that love God, to them who are the called according to his purpose" (Rom. 8:28).

Patience means recognizing that there can be no peace without judgment. Peace without justice would be no more than hell, an unchanging and everlasting state of evil. History is a series of judgments to prepare the way for the new creation. However difficult and painful, these judgments are to be welcomed.

Chapter Fifteen
Unction
(James 5:11-20)

10. Take, my brethren, the prophets, who have spoken in the name of the Lord, for an example of suffering affliction, and of patience.
11. Behold, we count them happy which endure. Ye have heard of the patience of Job, and have seen the end of the Lord; that the Lord is very pitiful, and of tender mercy.
12. But above all things, my brethren, swear not, neither by heaven, neither by the earth, neither by any other oath: but let your yea by yea; and your nay, nay; lest ye fall into condemnation.
13. Is any among you afflicted? let him pray. Is any merry? let him sing psalms.
14. Is any sick among you? let him call for the elders of the church; and let them pray over him, anointing him with oil in the name of the Lord.
15. And the prayer of faith shall save the sick, and the Lord shall raise him up; and if he have committed sins, they shall be forgiven him.
16. Confess your faults one to another, and pray one for another, that ye may be healed. The effectual fervent prayer of a righteous man availeth much.
17. Elias was a man subject to like passions as we are, and he prayed earnestly that it might not rain: and it rained not on the earth by the space of three years and six months.
18. And he prayed again, and the heaven gave rain, and the earth brought forth her fruit.
19. Brethren, if any of you do err from the truth, and one convert him;
20. Let him know, that he which converteth the sinner from the error of his way shall save a soul from death, and shall hide a multitude of sins. (James 5:11-20)

Our text is a very important one and very much a unit. Very early in his letter to the Christian synagogues, James called attention to their persecution by the unconverted Jews, and he summons believers to faith and patience in their difficulties. He reminds them of two men who had undergone great troubles, Job and Elijah. Job had been reduced from wealth to sickness and poverty. Elijah, like them, was persecuted by his own people, the supposedly chosen people, for his unswerving faith. The members of the Christian synagogues were similarly hated and persecuted. They are to take these men, and all the prophets, as examples "of suffering affliction, and of patience" (v. 10). Those who endure are happy or blessed. God's goal is seen plainly, and in time, with Job. God's compassion and mercy are clearly shown (v. 11).

In facing their own trials of patience, they must guard their tongues. Especially when we are under the stress of troubles and opposition, it is easy to speak rashly. In appealing to God and to man for help in great adversity, we can emphasize the extremity of our condition by using extravagant language and swearing by God (v. 12). This is to risk condemnation. If we are God's people, the simple word is enough; as the people of the Truth, we need no more than our simple *yea* and *nay* to substantiate our word.

We do not need others to be heard of God. If we are in trouble, we can pray, and God will hear us; if we are blessed and thriving, we can sing God's praise (v. 13).

We are reminded of the power of God, and therefore we are urged to pray. Elijah, a man with our own passionate and emotional nature, prayed to God for a judgment on Israel, and a drought lasting three years and six months ensued; then he prayed for rain, and it rained (vv. 17-18).

In vv. 14-16, we have a very important statement closely tied to all of the letter, and especially to the verses of our text. There are no satisfactory interpretations of these verses because Protestants see the Catholic doctrine of extreme unction derived from this text, and they are determined to avoid it. Catholics in turn associate this with extreme unction, for them a sacrament. A sacrament is a means of grace instituted by Christ. Not all means of grace, e.g., prayer, confession, etc., are sacraments. It was late in the eighth century when extreme unction became a sacrament.

To understand this text, we must go back to the Old Testament rite of unction, of anointing with oil. This anointing was done to the first in the line of high priests, to kings, and, on occasion, to a prophet, as in the case of Elisha (1 Kings 19:16).

In all instances, it is clear that the unction or anointing is ordained by God (2 Sam. 1:21 and Isa. 21:5 are listed by one scholar as *possible* exceptions). Lepers who were pronounced clean and whole were anointed on the eighth day. At the very least, anointing marked a change of status.[1]

In the New Testament, the believer is plainly said to be what the Old Testament implies, *a royal priesthood*. The fact that in Revelation 1:6 Christians are told that they have been made "kings and priests unto God and his Father" by Jesus Christ is especially important. Persecuted and martyred Christians are reminded of their high calling and status in Christ.

In extreme unction, the form of the anointing varied in different traditions. For the Roman Ritual, it was the five external senses (eyes, ears, nostrils, lips, and hands), and, where death was very near, on the forehead only. This was accompanied, in its briefest form, by the statement,

---

[1.] Jozeph Milchman, "Anointing," in *Encyclopedia Judaica*, vol.3 (Jerusalem, Israel: Keter Publishing House, 1971), 27f.

"Through this holy unction may the Lord pardon thee whatever sins and faults thou hast committed."[2]

Thus far, certain things are clearly in view: *first*, the origin of this unction is in the consecration into their office and calling of priests, prophets, and kings. *Second*, this unction marks all Christians. According to 1 John 2:20, "But ye have an unction from the Holy One and ye know all things." The meaning of all things in their essence is known to the believer. *Third*, this unction is related to Christ's triple functions or offices as priest, prophet, and king. *Fourth*, in Christ and under His ministry through us, we share in these three offices, strictly in terms of His word. *Fifth*, we find in Mark 6:13 that the disciples cured a number of sick people by anointing them with oil. Thus, unction was clearly associated with healing *some* sick people.

In v. 15, the Authorized Version reads, "and if he have committed sins, they shall be forgiven him." "Him," the sick one, is in the Greek a form of *kamno*, to be sick, exhausted, under an unrelenting strain. This is not an ordinary ailment, and *it is associated with sin and the need for forgiveness.* How then must we understand this text?

The early church for centuries faced a deeply entrenched paganism which did not disappear with conversion. There were temptations, often taken, to defect. Then, often, as death approached, there was repentance.

In this century, missionaries working in a pagan context have found that, facing death, defectors from the faith would summon the pastor with deep repentance. One man, who sinned in many ways, and deliberately so in order to accentuate his break with Christ, confessed most humbly to his sin and to Christ's refusal to let him go. This was a problem in the early church, and over the centuries to the present day.

The persecuted members of the early church did at times defect. Some, when seriously ill, made their peace with God by confessing to the elders and to the pastor. With unction, the anointing with oil, they were restored to their status as kings, priests, and prophets in Christ. Can any other explanation do more than confuse the issue?

In v. 16, James urges all of them, "Confess your faults one to another, and pray one for another, that ye may be healed. The effectual fervent prayer of a righteous man availeth much." The example of Elijah is then cited.

All believers have this status as priests, kings, and prophets if they will but exercise it in total faithfulness to Christ's word, and in humility. The tongue, instead of being used for criticism, can be used for prayer.

---

2. P.J. Toner, "Extreme Unction," in *The Catholic Encyclopedia*, vol.V (New York, N.Y.: The Encyclopedia Press, 1913), 716-730.

Polycarp wrote that the elders in particular should be merciful and work to bring back all who had gone astray. James 2:13 declares: "For he shall have judgment without mercy, that hath shewed no mercy; and mercy rejoiceth against judgment." The goal with regard to those who have strayed is restoration.

The unction described by James refers to the priesthood of all believers, and their calling to be prophets and kings in Christ. By this act, the repentant sinner was visibly reminded of his restoration. The anointing described by James was apparently reserved for the sick or dying and repentant former members of Christ's synagogues. It was a beautiful ceremony of restoration, and an act of the Christian synagogue through the persons of its elders. Faithful members had no need for it, but, for the straying, it was a visible reminder of the grace of the Lord Jesus Christ.

A few centuries later, the problem recurred when the Donatists refused to allow the restoration of any who had apostasized during persecution. In time, this Phariseeism destroyed the Donatists.

JUDE

Chapter One

The Enemy
(*Jude 1-4*)

1. Jude, the servant of Jesus Christ, and brother of James, to them that are sanctified by God the Father, and preserved in Jesus Christ and called:
2. Mercy unto you, and peace, and love, be multiplied.
3. Beloved, when I gave all diligence to write unto you of the common salvation, it was needful for me to write unto you, and exhort you that ye should earnestly contend for the faith which was once delivered unto the saints.
4. For there are certain men crept in unawares, who were before of old ordained to this condemnation, ungodly men, turning the grace of our God into lasciviousness, and denying the only Lord God, and our Lord Jesus Christ. (Jude 1-4)

The Epistle of Jude is a general letter by a man who identifies himself as "the servant of Jesus Christ and the brother of James" (v. 1). Matthew 13:55 and Mark 6:3 identify a Jude, together with James, as brothers of Jesus. J.E. Huther said, "That the Judas who wrote this Epistle was one of the four brothers, and not cousins of Jesus, is probable." In fact, he held, "it is beyond any considerable doubt."[1]

This is a brief and an obscure letter, i.e., not widely known or studied, but its purpose is an important one. False teachers were perverting the faith, and Jude of necessity spoke out. By identifying himself as Jude, the brother of James, he indirectly notifies the reader that he writes with authority as the brother of James and Jesus. He does this, not to gain personal prestige, but to stress the urgency of his message. Those whom he addresses are those "sanctified by God the Father, and preserved in Jesus Christ, and called" (v. 1). These are the elect of God, persons who will heed Jude's warning. They have been made holy by God's grace and preserved from falling away by Jesus Christ because they are the called of God.

"Mercy unto you, and peace, and love, be multiplied" (v. 2). This triple benediction is very biblical. In v. 1, the triple description is sanctified, preserved, and called. Jude not only wants this rich blessing on the saints, but he also wants it "multiplied." We must not take this benediction as a merely formal and courteous one. The churches were facing a serious problem in infiltration by alien groups who saw in the success of Christianity an opportunity to capture a vigorous faith for their very different purposes. Throughout church history, infiltration has been a common problem. Very early, it was Gnosticism, later Albigensianism,

---

[1.] J. E. Huther, *Critical and Exegetical Handbook to the General Epistles of James, Peter, John, and Jude* (Peabody, Massachusetts: Hendrickson Publishers, 1981), 824.

Hellenic philosophies, humanism, and more. These alien faiths have had in common the desire to merge into Christianity with a facade of agreement while working to remake the faith in their own image.

Jude felt an urgent necessity to alert Christians everywhere against this threat to "the common salvation" (v. 3). The common or general salvation is one known to all: Jesus Christ, God incarnate, had made atonement for the sins of His people. This they all knew, but now men were promoting supposedly new insights into the faith, and higher truths. Therefore "it was needful for me to write unto you, and exhort you that ye should earnestly contend for the faith which was once delivered unto the saints" (v. 3). Men were determined to improve on the faith and modernize Jesus to conform to contemporary science and philosophy. This effort was the Gnostic movement, which sought to capture Christianity. Gnosticism represented the new and higher learning of its day. It is now almost incomprehensible, and one can only marvel at the credulity of learned men. Contemporary philosophy and evolutionary science bear a strong resemblance to ancient Gnosticism.

The Christian faith needs no improving, and it needs no new revelations: it is complete, once and for all time "delivered unto the saints." We must "earnestly contend" to defend and preserve that faith.

"For there are certain men crept in unawares," i.e., they have insinuated their way into the church as supposed leaders and wise men who seek to preserve the faith. These are men who, in God's predestination, were ordained to this evil purpose *and* to condemnation. They are "ungodly men, turning the grace of our God into lasciviousness," and this can only be done by antinomianism, which marked the old Gnostics and also the new. This lasciviousness is identified for us in 1 Peter 4:3 and 2 Peter 2:19. It was simply a contempt of the law in the name of a higher spirituality, and this claim to a higher spirituality then marked Gnosticism, as it does now.

The faith is not an evolving matter. It was "delivered unto the saints" in its full and final form with Jesus Christ (v. 4). The growth of the faith is in *application*, not in content. In application, the believer obeys and serves his Lord; he does not develop or alter the content of the faith. Such men are "denying the only Lord God, and our Lord Jesus Christ" (v. 4).

The Gnostics saw themselves as the truly enlightened ones, as more spiritual than those whose faith was simply to *believe and obey*. Gnosticism so thoroughly adapted itself to the thought of its age that it died with that age in its then existing form. Then as now, orthodox Christianity, biblical Christianity, has been thoroughly out of tune with the wisdom of its day. This has usually been true over the centuries, and it is true now. The faithful believer has commonly been seen as an impediment to the "progress" of the faith, and he has commonly been treated with contempt.

Jude's letter is a general warning against all attempts to improve upon Christianity by making it more palatable to modern man.

Jude's warning thus has relevance to more than a passing movement of his day. The fallen world order hates Jesus Christ and His people. It has always done whatever is possible to capture and revise biblical faith. Jude's letter is a warning against this enemy.

Chapter Two
Examples of Apostasy
(*Jude 5-7*)

5. I will therefore put you in remembrance, though ye once knew this, how that the Lord, having saved the people out of the land of Egypt, afterward destroyed them that believed not.
6. And the angels which kept not their first estate, but left their own habitation, he hath reserved in everlasting chains under darkness unto the judgment of the great day.
7. Even as Sodom and Gomorrha, and the cites about them in like manner, giving themselves over to fornication, and going after strange flesh, are set forth for an example, suffering the vengeance of eternal fire. (Jude 5-7)

Jude's concern is with the influx of alien faith and influences into Christianity. Because we have today, as over the centuries, false and evil doctrines and religions masquerading as true Christianity, what Jude has to say is important for us.

Paul not only denounces all heresies, but also calls attention to their errors. Jude's approach is different: he tells his readers, "You should earnestly contend for the faith which was once delivered unto the saints" (v. 3). Before Jude, other men, like Paul and John, had sharply and clearly drawn the line between the faith and heresies. Now Jude says, you have the truth: fight for it and defend its purity.

In v. 5, Jude grimly reminds them that Israel had been miraculously delivered out of the land of Egypt. Israel's deliverance was a spectacular one, far more notable than was their own redemption. All the same, because Israel showed ingratitude and rebelliousness, God destroyed almost the whole nation. One miracle succeeded another in Israel's years in the wilderness, but God still destroyed a carefully protected people because of their unbelief. Why then should He spare the early church? Obviously, this was written *before* the fall of Jerusalem, or else Jude certainly would have cited that as the great example of God's judgment on unbelief. "Though ye once knew this" is more accurately translated, "though ye know all things once and for all" (M.R. Vincent and A.T. Robertson). They cannot plead ignorance. It was a temptation to say of the Hebrews who left Egypt that they were slaves and not as enlightened as the present generation. The problem, however, was not an intellectual one but a moral matter. The people of the Exodus, like the present generation, trusted more in their own understanding than in the Lord.

The new teachers, the Gnostics, stressed intellectual understanding and denigrated moral issues as simplistic. Their writings, in fact, lacked moral content and were more metaphysical than ethical.

The Lord had "saved the people out of the land of Egypt," and this Israel had conveniently chosen to neglect, or to treat as their due because they were the chosen people. It is all too easy for Christians to see themselves as a chosen people who deserve only the best from God, when the calling of the elect is to serve God in the war against the City of Man, the new Tower of Babel. Instead of realizing how much we owe God, we tend to think more of what God should give to us.

Thus, Jude's *first* example of ingratitude and apostasy is Israel after its deliverance from Egypt. His *second* example is the company of fallen angels. They refused to keep their first estate or principality. Created by God for a high and holy purpose and place, they sought apparently more power. The references in Romans 8:38 and Ephesians 1:21 are to angelic spheres of authority and service. This dignity they forsook, and, in rebelling against God, they lost all their privileged status. The fallen angels a) did not remain in their proper place, or office, and b) they left their proper habitation. As a result, they are now "in everlasting chains under darkness unto the judgment of the great day" (v. 6).

The emphasis here is *not* on the fallen angels but on the Christians who may fall or go astray. They are a more privileged group than were the Hebrews of the Exodus, and even the fallen angels. Jude is thus saying in effect: If these things can happen to them, why not to you? You are *the most privileged* people because of Jesus Christ.

Jude's *third* example is Sodom and Gomorrha and the other cities of the plains. They were privileged to have so rich and fertile a land-base, well watered and lush in growth. These are set forth by God as an example of His judgment, "suffering the vengeance of eternal fire" (v. 7). Two sins in particular are cited: a) "giving themselves over to fornication," and b) "going after strange flesh." The word *fornication* in the original Greek covers more than sexual acts, although this is a part of the meaning. It means lasciviousness, blasphemous attitudes, and more. "Strange flesh" has reference to homosexuality. The cities were wealthy, proud, and arrogant. It has been said of urban life that men there see more of man's work than God's, and they accordingly become too prone to seeing man in independence from God. With such a perspective, they become ungrateful and apostate.

The Gnostics saw themselves as men who advanced the faith because they were in harmony with the philosophy and science of their age. They were living, it was felt, in a golden era of mankind, with government, philosophy, science, technology, and human thought generally at its highest. For men to resist merging their simple biblical faith into the highest of men's wisdom was absurd.

Jude's requirement is simple: "ye should earnestly contend for the faith which was once delivered unto the saints" (v. 3). The thinkers of the City of Man were contemptuous then, as they are now, of God's revelation. They have their own word of truth. Hans Jonas wrote of "the resemblance between Gnostic myth and the myth of Neo-Darwinian biology."[1] The mythology of Darwin has great prestige as against the Bible. This will help us to understand what the early church faced. The wisdom of that era found the Christian revelations to be wanting. Time has disposed of the wisdom of that era, but we face a new generation of self-styled wise men. Hence the timeliness of Jude.

[1.] Joan P. Couliano, *The Tree of Gnosis* (New York, New York: Harper San Francisco, 1992), 262.

Chapter Three
Righteous Judgment
(*Jude 8-16*)

8. Likewise also these filthy dreamers defile the flesh, despise dominion, and speak evil of dignities.

9. Yet Michael the archangel, when contending with the devil he disputed about the body of Moses, durst not bring against him a railing accusation, but said, The Lord rebuke thee.

10. But these speak evil of those things which they know not: but what they know naturally, as brute beasts, in those things they corrupt themselves.

11. Woe unto them! for they have gone in the way of Cain, and ran greedily after the error of Balaam for reward, and perished in the gainsaying of Core.

12. These are spots in your feasts of charity, when they feast with you, feeding themselves without fear: clouds they are without water, carried about of the winds; trees whose fruit withereth, without fruit, twice dead, plucked up by the roots;

13. Raging waves of sea, foaming out their own shame; wandering stars, to whom is reserved the blackness of darkness for ever.

14. And Enoch also, the seventh from Adam, prophesied of these, saying, Behold, the Lord cometh with ten thousands of his saints,

15. To execute judgment upon all, and to convince all that are ungodly among them of all their ungodly deeds which they have ungodly committed, and of all their hard speeches which ungodly sinners have spoken against him.

16. These are murmurers, complainers, walking after their own lusts; and their mouth speaketh great swelling words, having men's persons in admiration because of advantage. (Jude 8-16)

Irreverence is the sin Jude now cites as basic to the ungodly, in particular those who pretend to be true believers and are not. In v. 8, the Authorized Version reads "*filthy* dreamers;" the word *filthy* is not in the Greek, but the word as used here implies a loss of reality that is of a sinful nature. Their dreaming, or fallen imagination, leads to, *first*, a contempt of the flesh, or of man's humanity; they want to see man as far more than man. *Second*, they "despise dominion." *Dominion, Kuriotes* in the Greek, refers to angelic offices (Eph. 1:21; Col. 1:16; 2 Peter 2:10). These alien peoples in the church want authorities other than the God-given ones. *Third*, *dignities* refers to other authorities in the biblical scheme of things, again despised by these enemies of the faith, who speak evil of them.

In vv. 9-10, we find a clear statement about the use of language which ties in clearly with what James had to say about the tongue. When the archangel Michael was contending with the devil about the body of Moses, he did not dare make a "railing accusation" against the devil, simply saying, "The Lord rebuke thee." Judgment is the prerogative of God; where God

213

empowers us and requires us to render judgments, we can do so; otherwise, like Michael, we leave it to God. Very clearly, judgment is to be exercised only as God permits it, and Michael's restraint here is very telling and instructive.

The enemies of Christ within the church are very ready to speak evil "of those things which they know not" (v. 10). Their only source of knowledge is, like that of animals, simply a physical one. They have no religious insight, and, in their judgments on others, "they corrupt themselves."

In v. 11, Jude says that such people run frantically and wildly in the very ways of Cain, Balaam, and Korah. These three are examples of men who should have known the truth clearly but were totally wedded to error by their sin. Cain is a type of unrighteousness, Balaam of deceit and covetousness, and Korah of rebellion against Godly authority.[1] Such people are against all Godly authority because they refuse to acknowledge any authority except their own.

They are also a blot on the church scene. Their presence at the church love feasts or dinners is an ugly one. Apparently they fed themselves gluttonously although unwilling to help. They were clouds without water, i.e., ostensibly promising rain or nourishment while bringing drought. They were dead trees, without fruit, twice dead because rootless (v. 12). The reference to "feeding themselves without fear" is to Ezekiel 34:2-8; as pretended leaders, they were to feed the flock, not to be parasites on it. In their self-importance they felt entitled to whatever they wanted.

In v. 13, Jude continues his description of these pretenders to the faith. In their false claims to wisdom, they are comparable to "raging waves of the sea, foaming out their own shame." They are thus a troublesome hindrance to the church. They are also like "wandering stars, to whom is reserved the blackness of darkness for ever" (v. 13). The reference is to dead heavenly bodies, lifeless and barren, which are visible in the sky but useless.

Then, in vv. 14-15, Jude refers to a statement by Enoch, "the seventh from Adam," who "prophesied of these, saying, Behold, the Lord cometh with ten thousands of his saints, To execute judgment upon all and to convince all that are ungodly among them of all their ungodly deeds which they have ungodly committed, and of all their hard speeches which ungodly sinners have spoken against him" (vv. 14-15).

At this point, it is important to call attention to the fact that, in v. 9, we have a reference to Michael which appears only in *The Assumption of Moses*, and here, vv. 14-15, a reference to Enoch which appears in the *Book of Enoch*; both are apocryphal books. Was Jude quoting from them? Or, rather, was Jude citing two historical statements which were well known

---

[1] David H. Wallace, in "Jude," in Charles F. Pfeiffer and Everett F. Harrison, editors, *The Wycliffe Bible Commentary* (Chicago, Illinois: Moody Press, 1972), 1041f.

and used by the apocryphal writers also? We know that apocryphal "gospels" did quote from the legitimate ones. Jude was citing a source used by others as well.

Jude then summarizes his view of these heretics. "These are murmurers, complainers, walking after their own lusts; and their mouth speaketh great swelling words, having men's persons in admiration because of advantage" (v. 16). Their priorities are man-centered.

J. E. Huther noted that Jude depicts these intruders as teachers of the worst sort and as destructive in nature; "these words (v. 14) indicate their emptiness, and the fact that, being thus empty, they are borne along anywhither, and consequently are unsafe to follow."[2] These are men whose goal is personal advantage.

At this point, it is important to contrast what Jude says here with what Michael said to Satan, vv. 9-10. Michael says to Satan, simply, "The Lord rebuke thee," whereas Jude very bluntly condemns the false teachers. We must recognize that through Jude, by inspiration, God Himself is rebuking these Gnostic teachers. Jude's words are more than his own.

Jude calls attention to the evil character of these false leaders. *First*, they are grumblers, complainers, whose pretense to greater holiness is based on their supposed sensitivity. Nothing pleases them except themselves. *Second*, they are malcontents whom nothing pleases because they believe nothing and are determined to bring down the faith. *Third*, their sole guide is their passionate love of advantage.[3] "Righteous judgment" is thus necessary (John 7:24).

---

[2] J.E. Huther, *Critical and Exegetical Handbook to the General Epistles of James, Peter, John, and Jude* (Peabody, Massachusetts: Hendrickson Publishers, 1984), 830. Originally published in 1883.

[3] David H. Wallace, "Jude," in Charles F. Pfeiffer, Everett F. Harrison, editors, *The Wycliffe Bible Commentary* (Chicago, Illinois: Moody Press, 1971), 1043.

Chapter Four

The Battle
(*Jude 17-25*)

17. But, beloved, remember ye the words which were spoken before of the apostles of our Lord Jesus Christ;
18. How that they told you there should be mockers in the last time, who should walk after their own ungodly lusts.
19. These be they who separate themselves, sensual, having not the Spirit.
20. But ye, beloved, building up yourselves on your most holy faith, praying in the Holy Ghost,
21. Keep yourselves in the love of God, looking for the mercy of our Lord Jesus Christ unto eternal life.
22. And of some have compassion, making a difference:
23. And others save with fear, pulling them out of the fire; hating even the garment spotted by the flesh.
24. Now unto him that is able to keep you from falling, and to present you faultless before the presence of his glory with exceeding joy,
25. To the only wise God our Saviour, be glory and majesty, dominion and power, both now and ever. Amen. (Jude 17-45)

Faced by false teachers in the church, many are easily discouraged. They leave large churches that have gone astray, only to find problems in smaller, reform-minded congregations. Their despairing attitude is, what's the use? Jude now warns against this danger. What can they expect? Will the enemy lie down and die because they have come to the truth? Will he not, in fact, rage all the more?

In vv. 17-20, Jude reminds his readers that the apostles predicted such a development. Jesus Christ created a new human race by His atoning death and resurrection, and by His regenerating power (1 Cor. 15:45-50; John 3:3). They are involved in the great war of the ages, and it will not be settled at once nor in their lifetime. Therefore, "remember the words which were spoken before of the apostles of our Lord Jesus Christ" (v. 17). Verse 18 refers to "the last days," meaning, as does every such reference, the time from Christ's resurrection to the general resurrection at the end of time. These are the last times in which all Christians live. These last times are marked by *mockers*. Their purpose is to put down Christ, His Kingdom, and His people by *mockery*. In v. 15, the word *ungodly* is used four times to describe Christ's enemies; it is used here again in v. 18. History now evidences that mockery, a savage contempt and hostility to Christ and His people.

Holiness is a separation unto God, but the ungodly have their own form of separation to unholiness. These ungodly peoples, "having not the Spirit" (v. 19), separate themselves to a purely sensual or physical existence.

217

Meaning for them is radically personal, not cosmic, man-centered and not God-centered.

Jude tells his readers that, as against this, they must grow and build themselves up "on your most holy faith, praying in the Holy Ghost" (v. 20). As against the self-righteousness of their enemies, they grow by prayer. prayer is a recognition of our needs and of our dependence on the triune God. Knowing our sins and shortcomings, we keep ourselves "in the love of God, looking for the mercy of our Lord Jesus Christ unto eternal life" (v. 21). Our salvation is an act of mercy and grace on Christ's part, and Jude reminds Christians of this fact. They must not presume on the Lord's grace by assuming, once saved, that they are now a members of a deserving group. From start to finish, they are entirely dependent on the Lord's grace and mercy.

In v. 22, Jude, having spoken very plainly about the heretics, false teachers, and troublemakers, now makes a distinction. Some are not of the same sort as others, but are in fact redeemable. Have compassion, then, and make a difference between them.

This does not mean being less clear about their errors and sins. Like firemen, pull them out of the fire. As we do so, we must be fearful of the contagion of sin; thus, our kindliness to them is not an indifference to their sin. "Hating even the garment spotted by the flesh" (v. 23) refers to the care of someone with a contagious disease. Our concern for their recovery does not blind us to the need of care lest we be infected.

In vv. 24-25, we have a superb benediction much used over the generations. It tells us, *first*, that God preserves His own; He keeps us from falling. This is the doctrine of the preservation of the saints. *Second*, God shall present us in time to the very fullness of His glory "with exceeding joy." Therefore, *third*, we must ascribe "To the only wise God our saviour,...glory and majesty, dominion and power, both now and ever. Amen." (v. 25). For all eternity, God will be joyfully praised. God is our infinite, almighty, and omniscient resource, and His praise is a wellspring of life and joy.

In v. 3, Jude speaks of "our common salvation," i.e., the same for all. The Gnostics had an elitist faith reserved for intellectuals who could follow their scientific and philosophical thinking into strange byways. Antinomianism marked them, because their faith was *metaphysical and not ethical.* For Marcion, God being superior meant that He did not judge![1] We can see why Jude's condemnation, inspired by the Holy Spirit, is so sharp. We can also understand contemporary Gnosticism, whether called New Age thinking, theosophy, Aquarian Age ideas, or anything else, because all

---

[1.] Joan P. Couliano: *The Tree of Gnosis* (New York, New York: Harper/San Francisco: 1992), 153.

seek to live beyond good and evil, beyond morality. As against contemporary faiths which bypass morality as the Bible defines it in exchange for worship of life and Nature, Jude's brief letter is a devastating indictment. A more wretched and beggarly faith than Gnosticism is hard to imagine, and yet, in each new form, century after century, its followers have been legion. Their passion is for anything but the truth, and anyone other than Jesus Christ. Those who love the truth (John 14:6) will be hated by all who love and believe in a lie, and such people are now very many. The direction of antinomianism is religion without morality, another "spiritual" Gnosticism.

Scripture Index

Genesis
1:26-28 — 16, 19, 27
1:31 — 27, 80
2:2 — 27, 32
3:5 — 21, 69, 107, 109, 188–189
5:21-24 — 108
5:23 — 108
5:24 — 117
5:27 — 108
14 — 59
14:18-24 — 56
14:19 — 59
15:6 — 164
22:9 — 164
27 — 115
28:15 — 136

Exodus
2:13 — 116
19:10 — 84
24 — 83
24:6-8 — 83
24:8 — 96
24:17 — 129, 133
25:40 — 69
29:14 — 137
30:20 — 184
32:30-32 — 84
33 — 117
34 — 83
40 — 84

Leviticus
9:7-17 — 40
15:5 — 84
16 — 79
16:6-19 — 40
16:26-28 — 84
16:30 — 40
19:1 — 160
19:13 — 191–192
19:16 — 171, 187
22:6 — 84

Numbers
11:20 — 28
12:3 — 116
12:7 — 24
12:7-8 — 117
14:4 — 28
16:44-48 — 84
19 — 79
31:23 — 84

Deuteronomy
1:17 — 159
4:24 — 129, 133
5:11 — 171
5:20 — 171
7:11 — 188
9:3 — 129, 133
9:11-21 — 131
17:2-7 — 99–100
25:13-16 — 60
31:6 — 136
32:35 — 100

Joshua
1:5 — 136
6:1-5 — 119

1 Samuel
4:22 — 159

2 Samuel
1:21 — 200
7:18 — 91
12:7 — 172
24:24 — 35

1 Kings
17:22 — 120
19:16 — 200

2 Kings
4:34 — 120

2 Chronicles
20:7 — 164
26:16-23 — 36

Psalms
  1 — 147
  2 — 97
  2:7 — 36, 41
  8 — 16–17
  14:1 — 103
  22:22 — 20
  32:1 — 84
  37 — 147
  40:7-9 — 92
  50:3 — 129, 133
  50:4 — 100
  51:1-17 — 84
  51:4 — 180
  84:5-7 — 176
  95:7-11 — 29
  97:3 — 129
  97:7 — 12
  102:2 — 65
  102:26-28 — 13
  104:24 — 147
  107:7 — 147
  110 — 1, 33, 44, 56, 61
  110:1 — 13
  110:4 — 43, 59, 65
  117:1-2 — 147
  119 — 73
  120:7 — 127
Proverbs
  3:11-12 — 124
  8:36 — 176
  19 — 52
Isaiah
  6:3 — 159
  6:8 — 88
  8:17 — 20
  11:9 — 73
  19:1 — 195
  21:5 — 200
  26:10 — 100
  26:20 — 101
  40:6 — 152
  57:20-21 — 27

  66:15 — 129, 133
Jeremiah
  31:31-34 — 71–72, 92
  31:34 — 73
Ezekiel
  21:27 — 1
  33:5-8 — 189
  34:2-8 — 214
Daniel
  3:20-30 — 133
  3:25 — 120
  6:22 — 120
  7:14 — 6
Amos
  9:7 — 56
Habakkuk
  2:3 — 101
Haggai
  2:6-7 — 132
Zechariah
  6 — 1
Malachi
  3:6 — 153
Matthew
  1:5 — 119
  3:17 — 35, 41
  4:4 — 88, 189
  4:7 — 88
  4:10 — 88
  5:3 — 141
  5:7 — 141
  6:10 — 195
  6:19 — 141
  6:33 — 17, 25, 36, 48, 125
  7:1 — 141
  7:7 — 141
  7:11 — 141
  7:12 — 141
  7:16 — 141
  7:16-20 — 172
  7:16-23 — 165
  7:20 — 165

7:24 — 141
7:24-27 — 133
7:26-27 — 152
9:9 — 141
10:30 — 80
11:19 — 147
11:27 — 6
12:33-37 — 168
12:34 — 171
12:46 — 143
13:1-9 — 47, 49
13:55 — 205
15:19 — 172
16:28 — 20
17:3 — 117
22:39 — 141, 160
23:35 — 107
24 — 180, 195
25:31-46 — 195
25:40 — 52
27:51 — 60
28:18 — 6
28:18-20 — 9, 36, 60, 85

Mark
2:27 — 32
6:3 — 145, 205
6:13 — 201
9:1 — 20
11:23 — 103
14:58 — 77

Luke
1:32 — 7
3:22 — 12
9:27 — 20
9:35 — 35, 41
12:5 — 100

John
1:3 — 20
1:14 — 159
1:36 — 72
3:3 — 217
3:16 — 48
3:35 — 7

5:17 — 28, 32
6:63 — 33
7:24 — 165, 215
8:34 — 160
8:34-36 — 157
8:52 — 20
10:7 — 89
10:9 — 89
14:6 — 219
15:1-6 — 72
15:16 — 54
19:30 — 89

Acts
4:12 — 101
6 — 157
6:1-7 — 157
6:1-8 — 191
6:7 — 65
7:53 — 16
12 — 143
15 — 5, 60
15:23 — 144
21:23-26 — 51

Romans
3:31 — 165
4:3 — 164
8:17 — 9
8:23 — 153
8:28 — 197
8:38 — 210
11:15-24 — 72
13:1 — 14
13:8-9 — 160
14:9 — 7
16:5 — 153

1 Corinthians
1 — 161
1:1 — 160
1:18-31 — 19
3:16-17 — 96
6:1 — 20
11:25 — 84
15:20 — 153

15:23 — 153
15:24-28 — 17
15:27 — 7–8
15:43 — 20
15:45 — 41, 73, 95
15:45-50 — 217
15:47 — 54, 88

2 *Corinthians*
 5:17 — 107
 6:16 — 96

Galatians
 3:6 — 165
 3:7 — 112
 3:19 — 16
 5:5 — 54
 5:14 — 160
 6:2 — 160
 6:16 — 141, 144

Ephesians
 1:10 — 7
 1:21 — 210, 213
 2:8 — 103, 148
 2:22 — 96
 3:10 — 147
 4:25 — 192

Philippians
 2:9-11 — 7

Phillipians
 4:2 — 169

Colossians
 1:5 — 54
 1:16 — 213
 4:14 — 101

2 *Thessalonians*
 1:8 — 44, 129, 133
 3:10 — 192

1 *Timothy*
 3:16 — 85
 6:15 — 1

2 *Timothy*
 4:10 — 101

Titus

2:13 — 54

Philemon
 24: — 101

Hebrews
 1:1-12:29 — 33
 1:1-2 — 7, 9
 1:1-3 — 34
 1:1-4 — 5
 1:2 — 6, 8–9, 12, 24, 65
 1:3 — 8–9
 1:4 — 8
 1:4-14 — 11
 1:4-2:18 — 34
 1:6 — 12
 1:5 — 12, 24
 1:5-6 — 12
 1:7 — 12
 1:7-9 — 12
 1:8 — 12, 14
 1:10 — 65
 1:10-12 — 12–13
 1:13 — 13
 1:14 — 13
 2:1 — 5, 15, 24–25
 2:1-4 — 34
 2:1-8 — 15
 2:2 — 16
 2:3 — 16
 2:4 — 24
 2:5 — 16, 25
 2:6 — 16–17
 2:7 — 16
 2:7-11 — 24
 2:7-19 — 25
 2:8 — 16
 2:9 — 16, 20
 2:9-18 — 19
 2:10 — 20
 2:11 — 20
 2:12 — 20
 2:13 — 20, 25
 2:14 — 21, 24
 2:15 — 21

2:15-19 — 25
2:16 — 21
2:17 — 21
2:18 — 21
3:1 — 24–25, 34
3:1-19 — 23
3:10-4:13 — 34
3:12 — 5
3:17-19 — 32
4 — 13
4:1-2 — 28
4:1-5 — 27
4:2 — 28–29
4:3 — 28
4:5 — 29
4:6-16 — 31
4:8 — 32
4:9 — 31
4:10 — 27, 32
4:11 — 33
4:12 — 32
4:13 — 33
4:14 — 34
4:14-13:3 — 34
4:14-16 — 33–34
4:15 — 34
4:16 — 33–34, 77
5:1 — 36, 39
5:1-10:18 — 33
5:1-5 — 35, 39
5:1-7:28 — 34
5:2 — 36, 40
5:3 — 36, 40
5:4 — 36, 40
5:5 — 35, 41
5:6-14 — 43
5:7 — 43
5:7-8 — 43
5:8 — 43
5:9 — 44
5:10 — 44
5:11 — 44
5:11-14 — 44

5:11-6:20 — 33
5:12 — 44
5:13 — 44
5:13-14 — 5
5:14 — 44
6:1 — 48, 52
6:1-2 — 48
6:1-8 — 47
6:2 — 49
6:4-6 — 48
6:6 — 48
6:7 — 49
6:7-8 — 47
6:8 — 49
6:9 — 52
6:9-10 — 51
6:9-11 — 54
6:9-20 — 51
6:11 — 52
6:12 — 52, 54
6:14 — 53
6:15 — 53
6:16 — 53
6:17 — 52
6:18 — 53
6:19 — 53
6:20 — 53
7:1-6 — 55
7:2 — 55
7:3 — 55
7:4 — 56
7:5-6 — 56
7:7 — 55, 59
7:7-14 — 59
7:8 — 59
7:9-10 — 59
7:11 — 60
7:12 — 60
7:12-14 — 60
7:13 — 61
7:14 — 61
7:15 — 63
7:15-28 — 63

7:16 — 63–64
7:17 — 63
7:19 — 64
7:20-22 — 64
7:22 — 64
7:23 — 64
7:24 — 64
7:25 — 64, 77
7:25-28 — 64
7:26 — 65
7:28 — 40, 65
8:1 — 67–68
8:1-13 — 34
8:1-5 — 67
8:2 — 67
8:3 — 68
8:4 — 68
8:5 — 68
8:6 — 71
8:6-13 — 71
8:8 — 72
8:8-12 — 92
8:9 — 72
8:10 — 72
8:12 — 73
8:13 — 73
9:1 — 76
9:1-12 — 34, 75
9:2-5 — 76
9:6 — 76
9:7 — 76
9:8 — 76
9:9 — 77
9:10 — 147
9:11 — 77
9:12 — 77
9:13-10:18 — 34
9:13-14 — 79
9:13-17 — 79
9:15 — 80
9:16 — 80
9:17 — 80
9:18 — 83

9:18-28 — 83
9:19 — 83
9:20 — 84
9:21 — 84
9:22 — 84
9:23 — 84
9:24 — 77, 84
9:25-26 — 84
9:27-28 — 85
10:1 — 87
10:1-10 — 87
10:2 — 87–88
10:3 — 88
10:4 — 88
10:5 — 85
10:5-7 — 88
10:7 — 85, 88
10:8 — 89
10:10 — 89
10:11 — 91
10:11-18 — 91
10:12 — 91
10:13 — 91–92
10:14 — 92
10:15-16 — 92
10:17 — 92
10:18 — 92
10:19 — 95
10:19-12:30 — 34
10:19-22 — 77
10:19-25 — 95
10:20 — 95
10:21 — 96
10:22 — 96
10:23 — 96
10:24 — 96–97
10:25 — 96
10:26 — 99
10:26-27 — 96, 100
10:26-39 — 99
10:27 — 129
10:28 — 100
10:29 — 100

10:31 — 100
10:32 — 101
10:33 — 101
10:34 — 5, 101
10:35-38 — 101
10:36 — 97, 101
10:36-37 — 101
10:36-39 — 29
10:38 — 101
10:39 — 103–104
11 — 6, 101
11-12 — 85
11:1 — 103
11:1-3 — 103
11:2 — 103
11:3 — 104, 108, 121
11:4 — 107
11:4-7 — 107, 109
11:5 — 108
11:6 — 108, 121
11:7 — 108
11:8 — 111, 113
11:8-19 — 111
11:8-9 — 117
11:9 — 112
11:10 — 13, 112–113
11:11 — 112
11:12 — 112
11:13 — 104, 112
11:15 — 112
11:16 — 112
11:19 — 112
11:20 — 115
11:20-29 — 115
11:21 — 115
11:22 — 115
11:23-29 — 115
11:25 — 116
11:26 — 116
11:28 — 116
11:29 — 116
11:30 — 119
11:30-40 — 119

11:32 — 120
11:34 — 120
11:35 — 120
11:36-37 — 120
11:38 — 120
11:39 — 6
11:40 — 120
12:1 — 123
12:1-11 — 123
12:2 — 124
12:3 — 124
12:4 — 124
12:5-11 — 124
12:6 — 124
12:7 — 124
12:8 — 124
12:10 — 124
12:11 — 125
12:12 — 7, 127
12:12-17 — 127
12:13 — 127
12:14 — 127
12:15 — 128
12:15-17 — 127
12:16 — 128
12:17 — 128
12:18 — 131
12:18-21 — 131
12:18-29 — 131
12:21 — 131
12:22 — 132
12:23 — 132
12:24 — 132
12:25 — 132
12:26 — 6, 132
12:27 — 133
12:28 — 6
12:29 — 6, 129, 133
13:1-25 — 136
13:1-6 — 136
13:2 — 136
13:3 — 136
13:4 — 136

13:5 — 136
13:7-17 — 136
13:7-8 — 137
13:8 — 153
13:9 — 137
13:10 — 137
13:11-12 — 137
13:13 — 1, 137
13:14 — 137
13:15 — 77, 137
13:16 — 137
13:17 — 137
13:18-25 — 136–137
13:20 — 137
13:20-21 — 137
13:23 — 6, 137
13:25 — 137

James
1:1 — 141, 143–145, 147, 149,
    151, 153, 157
1:1-7 — 147
1:2 — 147
1:2-7 — 147
1:3 — 147
1:4 — 148
1:5 — 141, 148
1:6 — 148
1:6-8 — 184
1:7 — 148–149, 151
1:8 — 151
1:8-18 — 151
1:9-11 — 151
1:12 — 151–152, 159
1:13 — 152
1:13-15 — 151–152
1:14 — 152
1:15 — 152–153
1:16 — 152
1:16-18 — 151–152
1:17 — 141, 152
1:19 — 155
1:19-20 — 155
1:19-27 — 155

1:22 — 141
1:22-25 — 156
1:22-27 — 85
1:23-25 — 156
1:25 — 156–157
1:26 — 156
1:26-27 — 156
1:27 — 157
2:1 — 144, 151, 153, 159
2:1-13 — 159
2:2 — 144
2:2-4 — 160
2:4 — 160
2:5 — 141, 159–160
2:6 — 160
2:7 — 160
2:8 — 141, 160
2:9-11 — 160
2:12 — 157, 160
2:13 — 141, 161, 202
2:14 — 164
2:14-26 — 85, 163
2:15-17 — 164
2:18 — 164
2:19 — 103, 119, 164, 189
2:20 — 164
2:21 — 164
2:21-24 — 164
2:22 — 164
2:23 — 164
2:24 — 163, 165
2:26 — 165
3 — 169
3:1 — 175
3:1-5 — 167
3:2 — 141, 168
3:3-5 — 168
3:6 — 171
3:6-12 — 171
3:7 — 172
3:8 — 172
3:9-10 — 172
3:11-12 — 172

3:12 — 141, 172
3:13 — 175
3:13-18 — 175
3:14 — 175
3:15 — 176
3:16 — 176
3:17 — 148, 176
3:18 — 176
4:1 — 180
4:1-4 — 179
4:1-6 — 179
4:2 — 180
4:3 — 180
4:5 — 180
4:6 — 180
4:7 — 183, 185
4:7-10 — 183
4:11 — 141, 184, 187
4:11-12 — 187
4:11-17 — 187
4:12 — 188
4:13 — 188
4:13-15 — 181
4:13-17 — 187
4:14 — 188
4:15 — 188
4:16 — 188
4:17 — 188
5:1 — 191
5:1-6 — 191
5:2-3 — 191
5:3 — 192, 195
5:4 — 192
5:5 — 192
5:7 — 195
5:7-8 — 196
5:7-9 — 195
5:8 — 196
5:9 — 196
5:10 — 199
5:11 — 181, 199
5:11-20 — 199
5:12 — 200

5:13 — 200
5:14-16 — 200
5:15 — 201
5:16 — 201
5:17-18 — 181, 200

1 Peter
4:3 — 206
4:17 — 133
5:8-9 — 183

2 Peter
2:5 — 109
2:10 — 213
2:19 — 206

1 John
2:20 — 201
3:4 — 12
3:12 — 107
5:4 — 6, 97, 107, 176

Jude
1 — 145, 205
1-4 — 205
2 — 205
3 — 206, 209, 211, 218
4 — 206
5 — 209
5-7 — 209
6 — 210
7 — 210
8 — 213
8-10 — 187
8-16 — 213
9 — 117, 214
9-10 — 213, 215
10 — 214
11 — 214
12 — 214
13 — 214
14 — 215
14-15 — 214
15 — 217
16 — 215
17 — 1, 217
17-20 — 217

17-45 — 217

18 — 217

19 — 217

20 — 218

21 — 218

22 — 218

23 — 218

24-25 — 218

25 — 218

Revelation

1:6 — 200

5:1 — 80

11:8 — 132

11:15 — 80

14:4 — 153

15:3-4 — 147

Index

A.D. 70, 6, 73, 195
Aaron, 36, 39–41, 56–57, 60–61, 67,
    131
Abel, 107–108, 132
Abraham, 13, 21, 43, 52–54, 55–56,
    59, 72, 108, 117, 128, 163–164
    faith of, 111–113
abstractionism, 89
accreditation, 55–57
Adam, 29, 41, 180, 189, 214
    the sin of, 152
age to come, 6–7, 9
Albigensianism, 205
anchor, 53, 161
angels, 8, 11, 13, 15–17, 20–21, 24,
    136, 210, 213
    worship of, 11–13
anointing, 13, 200
antinomianism, 32, 60, 73, 206,
    218–219
apocryphal books/writings, 11,
    214–215
apostasy, 41, 49, 99–101, 104, 128,
    183, 210
    examples of, 209–211
apostles, the, 72
Apostlic Constitutions, 48
archangel, Michael, 213–215
arena, 101, 123
Arminianism, 127
ascension, 51
assembly, 144
atonement, 8, 16, 19, 21, 27, 33, 35–
    37, 40–41, 54, 57, 60, 63–64,
    71–73, 84, 87–89, 91–93, 100,
    107, 112, 120–121, 125, 132,
    206, 217
    and action, 83–85
    and community, 21
    and God's law, 60
    and society, 19–21

privileges and duties of, 95–96
purpose of, 37, 89
rites of, 60, 75–77, 79–80

Babel, tower of, 112–113
Baca, valley of, 177
Badcock, F. J., 5
Balaam, 213–214
baptism, 49, 96
Barak, 120
Barclay, William, 9
bastards, 124, 127
battle of Cannae, 161
Battle, the, 217–219
benediction, 205, 218
Bible (word of God), 33
bitterness, 177
blasphemy, 25, 41, 92
Book of Enoch, 214
Bowman, John Wick, 143, 156
Buchanan, George Wesley, 13, 24,
    33, 100

Caesar, 14
Cain, 107, 213–214
Calvin, John, 5, 7, 13, 23, 25, 52,
    104, 172
Canaan, 13, 24, 32, 41
charity, 52, 54, 137, 141, 164, 191–
    193
chastening, 124–125, 127
Christ
    as God's apostle, 24
    as High Priest, 21, 24, 33–34,
        35–37, 39–41, 43, 54–
        57, 60–61, 63–65, 67–
        68, 77, 91, 95, 97, 105,
        144
    as Intercessor, 21, 77, 84, 91
    as King, 12, 17, 36–37, 54, 61,
        101, 201

as Mediator, 15–17, 33, 44, 71
as priest, 201
as prophet, 201
as the Lamb of God, 68, 72, 91
as the Lord of glory, 159, 196
as the Prince of Peace, 195
doctrine of, 8
key to life & history, 8
Kingdom of, 9, 13–14, 25, 41,
    51, 85, 97
  triumph of, 1, 6, 8, 16–17,
      29, 73
  victory of, 13
lordship of, 144
offices of, 201
the atoner, 71–73
work of, 80
Christianity
  orthodox, 206
  vs. Judaism, 87
Christians
  as chosen people, 210
  persecution of, 14
church trials, 69
church, the, 80–81, 132, 144
  early, 20, 45, 51, 136, 179
  modern, 85, 88, 93, 96, 113
circumcision, 96
City of God, 13, 53, 112, 115, 132,
    137
City of Man, 210
Clement of Alexandria, 53
Clogg, Frank Bertram, 12, 17, 143–
    144
coming in clouds, 195
commandments governing speech,
    171
confession of sin, 40
conscience, 77, 81, 87–88, 137
consecration, 153
conspiracy thinking, 180
Conybeare, W. J., 6, 24
Core (Korah), 213–214

Couliano, Joan P., 211, 218
Council of Jerusalem, 5, 60, 143
Council of Trent, 165
covenant, 71–73, 83, 99, 100
  everlasting, 137
  first, 76, 80, 83
  law, 72, 83
  second, 92
  unity of, 72
  with Moses, 72
covetousness, 136
creation, 27, 104, 108, 121
credentials, 55
crown of life, 152

Darwin(ism), 104, 211
David, 31, 35, 67, 91, 127, 128, 180
Day of Atonement, 40, 79, 137
Day of the Lord, 9
deacons, 191
death penalty, 35, 60, 92, 95
dedication, 153
Delitzsch, Franz, 19, 40, 43, 56
Demas, 101
devil, 21, 119, 152, 183–184
diaconate, 93
dominion, 16–17, 29, 45
dominion mandate, 17, 19, 27
Donatists, 202
double-minded, 141, 151–153, 184
doulos, 145
duties
  religious, 136, 191
  social, 95, 136

easy-believism, 128, 164
Eddington, 104
Eden, 28, 195
Egypt, 196
elect, the, 28, 153, 205
Elijah, 117, 120, 181, 199–201
Elisha, 120, 200
Enemy, the, 205–207

Enoch, 108, 117, 213–214
environmentalism, 183
envy, 175
Ephraim, 115
Esau, 115
    non-faith of, 127–129
eschatology, 176
eternal security, 48
evil, 180, 184
exclusiveness, 89
Exodus, the, 24–25, 28–29, 209, 210
extreme unction, 200

faith, 25, 54, 96, 101, 103–105, 107,
    112–113, 119–121, 127, 129,
    147–149, 151, 189, 206
    (non) of Esau, 127–129
    and law, 29
    and obedience, 31–34, 44, 109,
        206
    and works, 101, 141, 149, 163–
        165, 184
    from Abel to Noah, 107–109
    man-centered, 25
    of Abraham, 111–113
    of Moses, 115–117
    of the saints, 119–121
    testing of, 147–148, 152
faithful, the, 152
fall, the, 28
false teachers, 217
Feuer, Avrohom Chaim, 43, 56
firstfruits, 153
Flood, 108, 195
fornication, 210
fraud, 192
freedom, 93, 157
    and remission of sin, 91–93
French, 148
Freud, Sigmund, 93
friendship, godly vs. worldly, 179

Gentiles, 44

glorification, 20
Gnostic(ism), 11, 15, 205–206, 209–
    211, 215, 218–219
God's law, 60, 188
    and charity, 191, 193
    and humility, 184
    and judgment, 188
    and moral relativsm, 192
    and sanctification, 21
    as a mirror, 156–157
    as the law of liberty, 156–157,
        160
    as the royal law, 116, 160
    need for, 40
    permanence of, 16, 60, 71
    prominence of, 72
    sacrificial, 87–88
    v. Caesar's, 14
    written on the heart, 72, 92,
        125
Godhead, the, 147
gold rings, 161
golden calf, 39, 131
Golden Rule, the, 161
gossip, 171–173, 187
grace, 180
Great Commission, 36, 60, 85
Greco-Roman thought, 161

Hannibal, 161
Harrison, Everett F., 5, 214
heart, 171, 172, 180
heaven, 27
heavenly sanctuary, 67–69, 76–77,
    84
Hebrews, 153
    as tied to the Epistle of James,
        144
    authorship, 5, 129
    pastoral group letter, 52
Hendriksen, William, 141, 143
heresy / heretics, 48, 209, 215, 218
Herodians, 128

high priest, 35–36, 43, 51, 56
history, 133
Hoffmann, E., 53–54
holiness, 25, 217
Holy of Holies, 53, 75–76, 84, 95
Holy Place, 53, 75–76
Holy Spirit, 16, 33, 48, 218
    indwelling of, 73, 180
    person of, 16
    speaking in the Law, 76, 92
Holy War, the, 183–185
homosexuality, 210
hope, 51–54, 96, 103
    and faith, 96
hospitality, 136
Howson, J. S., 6, 24
humanism, 11, 92, 156, 206
humility, 155–156, 175, 184, 187–188
Huther, J. E., 205, 215
hypocrisy, 184

incarnation, 8, 12–13, 16, 20–21, 36, 88
infiltration in Christianity, 205
inspiration, 8
irreverence, 213
Isaac, 112, 115, 128, 164
Israel, 144, 153, 209–210

Jacob, 72, 112, 115
James
    authorship of, 143
    brother of Jesus, 141, 143–145, 148
    brother of Jude, 205
    date of, 151
    epistle of, 85
        date, 143
    identity of, 143
    regarding speech, 213
Jeans, 104
Jephthae, 120

Jeremiah, 92, 196
Jericho, 119, 165
Jerusalem
    Council of, 143
    fall of, 123, 209
Jewish thought, 161
Jewish-Roman War, 66-70 A.D., 6, 51, 73
Job, 181, 199
John, 209
Johnstone, Robert, 183
Jonas, Hans, 211
Jonathan, 128
Joseph, 67, 115
Josephus, 179
Joshua, 31, 32
joy, 147
Judah, 115
Judaism, reversion to, 6
Judas, 128
Jude
    brother of James, 205
    brother of Jesus, 145, 205
    identity of, 145, 205
Judea, 179
judging, 48, 155, 187–188
judgment
    of God, 96, 100, 133, 195–197, 200
    on the rich, 191–193
    righteous, 213–215
justice, 12, 14, 17, 29, 41, 55, 57, 69, 100, 156, 176, 191, 195, 197
justification, 101, 108, 163, 165

kingship of Christ, 36–37, 63–65
knowledge, 175
Korah (Core), 213–214
kurios, 144

Lamentations, book of, 196
Lange, J.P., 184, 188
language, 213

language. *See* speech
last Adam, 16, 20, 29, 36, 41, 54, 95,
    96, 189
last days, 6, 195, 217
Last Judgment, 195, 210
Last Supper, 84
law, 60, 72, 83, 107, 184, 187–189
    of God, 160
        as a mirror, 156
    Roman, 14
    sacrificial, 87
lawlessness, 12
leadership, responsibility of, 167–
    169
Lenski, R.C.H., 24, 143, 155–156,
    175–176
leper, 200
Levi, 59, 61
Levitical priesthood, 34, 56, 59, 63,
    64, 67, 91, 96
    and the law, 68
    as typical, 68, 79, 84
    end of, 60–61, 64, 92
    law of, 64–65
    limitations of, 65
liberty, 156
lies, 173
liturgy, 75–76, 79
Lord of Sabaoth, 192
Lord's Supper, 137
lordship of Christ, 144, 151
Lot, 111
love feasts, 214
love thy neighbour, 160
lusts, 179
Luther, Martin, 184, 188

man
    -centered faith, 25
    dominion of, 16–17, 19–20
Marcion, 218
Mary, mother of Jesus, 143, 145
Mass, the, 65

maturity, 44, 47–49, 125
McAuliffe, Jospeh A., 5
mediator, 33, 35
    Christ as, 15–17
meekness, 155, 175, 180
Melchizedek, 43–44, 55–57, 63–64,
    67
    priesthood of, 59–61
mercy, 159, 161, 176
Methuselah, 108
Meyer, H.A.W., 183
Michael the Archangel, 213
Michael the archangel, 117, 187,
    213–215
millennium, 6
missions, 44
mockers, 217
Moffatt, James, 147–148, 155
moral purification, 184
moral relativism, 192
Morris, Leon, 9
Moses, 24–25, 28, 31, 40, 67–68, 71–
    72, 76, 83–84, 92, 129, 131–132,
    213
    faith of, 115–117
Moulton, James Hope, 141, 175
Moulton, W. F., 52

New Age thinking, 218
new covenant, 64, 71, 72, 80
new creation, 1, 13, 16–17, 31, 36,
    77, 84, 89, 92, 107–108, 173,
    197
new humanity, 20, 36, 54, 72–73,
    77, 84–85, 88, 92, 95, 109, 145,
    217
Nietszche, 173
Noah, 108–109, 113

oaths, 52–54, 65
    God's, 64
obedience, 44, 109, 156
    and faith, 31–34

old covenant
end of, 73
Old Testament, 144
original sin, 69, 107
orphans, 157

parable of the sower, 47, 49
parousia, 196
partiality, 159, 160
passover, 116
patience, 148, 176, 195–197, 199
Paul, 5, 73, 101, 103, 105, 127–128, 132, 161, 164, 169, 192, 209
peace, 176, 197
Peter, 101, 155
Pfeiffer, Charles F., 214
Pharisees, 184
Pink, Arthur W., 24
Plato, 76
Polycarp, 202
poor, the, 160, 163
poverty, 192
praise, 77, 137, 200, 218
prayer, 25, 148, 180–181, 200–201, 218
wrongful, 179
predestination, 16, 54, 80, 206
Presence of God, 79
preservation, 205
of the saints, 218
priesthood, 39, 60, 64
of Christ, 33–34, 37, 39–41, 60–61, 63–65, 67–68
of Melchizedek, 59–61
See also rite, 79
profanity, 184
Promised Land, 7, 25, 28, 41, 115
providence, 104
psychotherapy, 93
purification, 51, 84

Rahab, 119, 165
Ranken, F. S., 71

rapture, 6
regeneration, 14, 27, 36–37, 45, 54, 73, 89, 96, 125, 217
religion
non-biblical, 172
pure and undefiled, 155–157
Renaissance, 172
"respect of persons", 159–161
rest, 27–29, 31–32, 37
resurrection, 112, 120, 217
Reuben, 115
Revelation, Book of, 80
rich, the. *See* wealth
rings, 161
rite vs. reality, 79–80
rites, 75, 77, 92, 95–96
of atonement. *See also* atonement, rites of, 88–89
ritual, 75–76, 79, 88, 93
Robertson, A. T., 34, 144, 161, 209
Roman law, 14
Roman-Jewish War , 66 A. D., 180, 195
Ross, Alexander, 143, 148, 196
Ross, Robert W., 33
royal priesthood, 200
Ruthven, Malise, 14

sabbath (rest), 9, 13, 27–29, 31–32, 37
sacrament, 88, 200
sacrifice, 36, 39, 60, 65, 68, 71–72, 77, 85, 107, 112, 137
as typical, 84, 88
end of, 73
repetition of, 79, 84, 87–88, 91
typology, 35
voluntary, 88
saints, 218
salvation, 21, 23, 25, 27, 47, 149, 163–165, 218
theology of, 85

Samson, 120
Samuel, 120
sanctification, 20–21, 23, 45, 125,
    149, 163, 205
Sarah, 112
Satan, 88, 187, 189, 215
Saul, King, 128
Scofield, C. I., 92
Scott, E. F., 24, 105
second Adam. *See* last Adam
second coming, 85, 97
Second Commandment, 171
selfishness, 175, 176
separation of powers, 36
Sermon on the Mount, 1, 133, 141,
    143, 165, 172
servant, 143–145
sex, 136
shadow(s), 79, 84, 87, 89, 92–93
Shadrach, Meshach, and
    Abednego, 133
Shem, 56
Shepherd of Hermas, 184
sin, 12, 17, 21, 27, 31, 35–37, 40–41,
    73, 91–93, 100, 123, 152, 159,
    180–181, 187–189
    verbal. *See* speech
society, and atonement, 21
Sodom and Gomorrha, 209–210
speech, 141, 156–157, 175, 177, 184,
    187, 199, 201, 213
    commandments governing,
        171
    of leaders, 167–169
    revealing our nature, 171–173
sprinkling, 83–84, 96
status, 160
stoicism, 196
submission, 183
suffering, 123–125
synagogue, Christian, 144, 159–
    161, 164, 175, 179–180, 191,
    199, 202

Tabernacle, 69, 75
Tasker, R.V.G., 143, 167
Temple, the, 6, 24, 41, 51, 53, 60,
    65, 76–77, 80, 85, 91–92, 95, 96,
    100–101, 127–128, 144, 151
    system, 131
temptation, 147, 151–152
Ten Commandments, 83, 171
Tertullian, 49
testament, 71–72, 83–84
testing, 147, 152
The Assumption of Moses, 214
theosophy, 218
time, 188
time of reformation, 77
Timothy, 6, 137
tithes, 56, 59
Toner, P. J., 201
tongue, tongues. *See* speech
Tower of Babel, 108, 112–113, 195,
    210
Transfiguration, 117
Trent, Council of, 165
trust, 113, 119, 189
truth, 89, 100, 104
typology, 9, 39, 63, 76, 84
    Old Testament, 80

unction (anointing), 141, 199–202
Uzziah, 36

victory, 7, 27, 45, 47, 176, 185
Vincent, M. R., 8, 16, 20, 32, 44, 48,
    60, 64, 84, 96, 125, 145, 161,
    209

Wallace, David H., 214
war, 179
    origin of, 180, 183
    Roman-Jewish, 180
    within man, 184
wealth, 160, 191–192

wealthy, judgment on, 191–193
Weeks, Noel, 6
welfarism, 191–192
Wesley brothers, 117
Westcott, B. F., 12, 47, 53, 95–96, 100, 113, 136
widows, 157, 191
wisdom, 147–149, 161, 176
   humanistic, 176
   two kinds, 175–177

wisdom literature, 147, 176
Word of God, 32–33, 155
   summary, 33
works, 149, 167–168, 175, 184
   and faith, 163–165
world to come, 16–17, 48
Wyngarden, Martin J., 7

zeal, 176

The Author

Rousas John Rushdoony (1916-2001) was a well-known American scholar, writer, and author of over thirty books. He held B.A. and M.A. degrees from the University of California and received his theological training at the Pacific School of Religion. An ordained minister, he worked as a missionary among Paiute and Shoshone Indians as well as a pastor to two California churches. He founded the Chalcedon Foundation, an educational organization devoted to research, publishing, and cogent communication of a distinctively Christian scholarship to the world at large. His writing in the *Chalcedon Report* and his numerous books spawned a generation of believers active in reconstructing the world to the glory of Jesus Christ. He resided in Vallecito, California until his death, where he engaged in research, lecturing, and assisting others in developing programs to put the Christian Faith into action.

The Ministry of Chalcedon

CHALCEDON (kal•see•don) is a Christian educational organization devoted exclusively to research, publishing, and cogent communication of a distinctively Christian scholarship to the world at large. It makes available a variety of services and programs, all geared to the needs of interested ministers, scholars, and laymen who understand the propositions that Jesus Christ speaks to the mind as well as the heart, and that His claims extend beyond the narrow confines of the various institutional churches. We exist in order to support the efforts of all orthodox denominations and churches. Chalcedon derives its name from the great ecclesiastical Council of Chalcedon (A.D. 451), which produced the crucial Christological definition: "Therefore, following the holy Fathers, we all with one accord teach men to acknowledge one and the same Son, our Lord Jesus Christ, at once complete in Godhead and complete in manhood, truly God and truly man...." This formula directly challenges every false claim of divinity by any human institution: state, church, cult, school, or human assembly. Christ alone is both God and man, the unique link between heaven and earth. All human power is therefore derivative: Christ alone can announce that "All power is given unto me in heaven and in earth" (Matthew 28:18). Historically, the Chalcedonian creed is therefore the foundation of Western liberty, for it sets limits on all authoritarian human institutions by acknowledging the validity of the claims of the One who is the source of true human freedom (Galatians 5:1).

The *Chalcedon Report* is published monthly and is sent to all who request it. All gifts to Chalcedon are tax deductible.

Chalcedon
Box 158
Vallecito, CA 95251 U.S.A.

CPSIA information can be obtained at www.ICGtesting.com
Printed in the USA
BVOW07*1023111114

374520BV00001B/6/A